Mark-Oliver Reiser

Managing Complex Variability in Automotive Software Product Lines

Mark-Oliver Reiser

Managing Complex Variability in Automotive Software Product Lines

Subscoping and Configuration Links

Südwestdeutscher Verlag für Hochschulschriften

Impressum/Imprint (nur für Deutschland/ only for Germany)
Bibliografische Information der Deutschen Nationalbibliothek: Die Deutsche Nationalbibliothek verzeichnet diese Publikation in der Deutschen Nationalbibliografie; detaillierte bibliografische Daten sind im Internet über http://dnb.d-nb.de abrufbar.
Alle in diesem Buch genannten Marken und Produktnamen unterliegen warenzeichen-, marken- oder patentrechtlichem Schutz bzw. sind Warenzeichen oder eingetragene Warenzeichen der jeweiligen Inhaber. Die Wiedergabe von Marken, Produktnamen, Gebrauchsnamen, Handelsnamen, Warenbezeichnungen u.s.w. in diesem Werk berechtigt auch ohne besondere Kennzeichnung nicht zu der Annahme, dass solche Namen im Sinne der Warenzeichen- und Markenschutzgesetzgebung als frei zu betrachten wären und daher von jedermann benutzt werden dürften.

Verlag: Südwestdeutscher Verlag für Hochschulschriften Aktiengesellschaft & Co. KG
Dudweiler Landstr. 99, 66123 Saarbrücken, Deutschland
Telefon +49 681 37 20 271-1, Telefax +49 681 37 20 271-0, Email: info@svh-verlag.de
Zugl.: Berlin, Technische Universität, Dissertation, 2008

Herstellung in Deutschland:
Schaltungsdienst Lange o.H.G., Berlin
Books on Demand GmbH, Norderstedt
Reha GmbH, Saarbrücken
Amazon Distribution GmbH, Leipzig
ISBN: 978-3-8381-0525-3

Imprint (only for USA, GB)
Bibliographic information published by the Deutsche Nationalbibliothek: The Deutsche Nationalbibliothek lists this publication in the Deutsche Nationalbibliografie; detailed bibliographic data are available in the Internet at http://dnb.d-nb.de.
Any brand names and product names mentioned in this book are subject to trademark, brand or patent protection and are trademarks or registered trademarks of their respective holders. The use of brand names, product names, common names, trade names, product descriptions etc. even without a particular marking in this works is in no way to be construed to mean that such names may be regarded as unrestricted in respect of trademark and brand protection legislation and could thus be used by anyone.

Publisher:
Südwestdeutscher Verlag für Hochschulschriften Aktiengesellschaft & Co. KG
Dudweiler Landstr. 99, 66123 Saarbrücken, Germany
Phone +49 681 37 20 271-1, Fax +49 681 37 20 271-0, Email: info@svh-verlag.de

Copyright © 2009 by the author and Südwestdeutscher Verlag für Hochschulschriften Aktiengesellschaft & Co. KG and licensors
All rights reserved. Saarbrücken 2009

Printed in the U.S.A.
Printed in the U.K. by (see last page)
ISBN: 978-3-8381-0525-3

Acknowledgements

This thesis is a result of a cooperation between Technische Universität Berlin and Daimler AG, Berlin. The research was supported by Daimler AG through a research scholarship and partly financed by the European Commission through the European research project ATESST under the EU's 6th Framework Programme. At Technische Universität Berlin the research activities were conducted at the Software Engineering group of Prof. Dr. Stefan Jähnichen, and at Daimler AG they were affiliated to the "Methods and Tools" research department.

Now that the project has been concluded, I would like to thank my academic advisors: Prof. Dr. Stefan Jähnichen for his interest and support, and for providing a stimulating organizational environment for my research at TU Berlin; and Prof. Dr. Bernd Mahr for his support and advice towards the end of the work on this thesis. I would also like to thank my industrial advisor Prof. Dr. Matthias Weber from Daimler AG, now at Carmeq GmbH, for having initially identified the overall research challenge addressed here and for his great enthusiasm and inspiring feedback throughout my three years of work on the subject.

The countless discussions and research activities with colleagues from University, from Daimler AG, Carmeq GmbH and other companies as well as from the ATESST project are some of the reasons why the research leading up to this thesis was such a fascinating experience. They contributed in many ways to the findings presented in this work. I would also like to take this opportunity to thank my students who wrote their diploma theses on subjects related to my research for their motivation and their patience with my sometimes inchoate ideas.

Above all, I want to include a word of thanks which is long overdue. I'd like to say thank you to my parents, Christine and Herbert, for giving me a wonderful childhood and for providing me with a great start in life through all the love and caring encouragement anyone could ask for. By always putting my sister and myself first, they have shown us what it means to dearly love one's children.

Mark-Oliver Reiser
Berlin, December 2008

Contents

1 Introduction — **1**
  1.1 21st Century Automotive Development—the Transition to a New Technology . . 1
  1.2 Challenges in Automotive Product-Lines 3
  1.3 Proposed Solutions 5
  1.4 Research Background, Scope and Approach 6
  1.5 Related Literature and Work (Overview) 9
  1.6 Structure of the Thesis 10

I Automotive Software Product Lines — **11**

2 May I Introduce: Lines, Variants & Co. — **13**
  2.1 Software Product Lines 13
  2.2 Product Line vs. Family vs. Population 15
  2.3 Beyond Software 15
  2.4 Variability 16
  2.5 Binding of Variability and Binding Time 18
  2.6 Version vs. Variant 18

3 Modeling Software Product Lines — **21**
  3.1 What needs to be modeled ? 21
  3.2 The Purpose of Variability Modeling 23
  3.3 Modeling Artifact-Level Variability 24
  3.4 Modeling Product-Line-Level Variability 27
  3.5 Comparison and Discussion 31

4 Feature Modeling — **35**
  4.1 Purpose of Feature Modeling 35
  4.2 A Brief History of Feature Modeling 36
  4.3 What is a Feature anyway? 37
  4.4 Traditional Concepts in Feature Modeling 39
    4.4.1 Basic Concepts 39
    4.4.2 Cardinality Based Feature Modeling 40
    4.4.3 Features with Several Parents 42
    4.4.4 Parameterized Features 42
    4.4.5 Other Advanced Feature Modeling Concepts 43
  4.5 Formalization of Feature Modeling Concepts: The CVM Approach 43

		4.5.1 Formal Syntax of Basic Feature Models	44
		4.5.2 Formal Syntax of Advanced Feature Models	47
		4.5.3 Formal Semantics of Feature Models	49
	4.6	What is a Feature? (Revisited)	50
	4.7	Discussion	51

5 Applying Product-Line Engineering in the Automotive Domain — 53
	5.1	Characteristics of the Automotive Domain	53
	5.2	Global Coordination of Automotive Product-Line Variability	58
		5.2.1 Coordination of Small to Medium Sized Product Lines	59
		5.2.2 Coordination of Highly Complex Product Lines	60
	5.3	Unified Feature Modeling	62
	5.4	Summary and Outlook on Parts II and III	65

II Subscoping — 67

6 Subscoping — Motivation and Basic Idea — 69
	6.1	Product Sublines	69
	6.2	Limitations of Traditional Approaches	70
	6.3	Multi-Level Product Line Management as a Solution	71
	6.4	Subscoping	73
	6.5	Summary	74

7 Multi-Level Feature Models — 75
	7.1	Plain Feature Models	76
	7.2	Reference Feature Models	77
	7.3	Possible Forms of Deviation	79
	7.4	Restricting Deviations	84

8 Multi-Level Requirements Artifacts — 89
	8.1	Plain DOORS Modules	89
	8.2	Reference DOORS Modules	90
	8.3	Possible Forms of Deviation	90
	8.4	Restricting Deviations	91

9 Use Scenarios — 93
	9.1	Partial/Selective Coordination on Superline Level	93
	9.2	Full Coordination on Superline Level	94
	9.3	Adding Product Sublines	94
	9.4	Bottom-up Reuse	96
	9.5	Top-down Reuse	96
	9.6	Integration of Parallel Innovations	96
	9.7	Incremental Introduction of Feature Modeling	97
	9.8	Temporary Working Copy	97

10	**Advanced Considerations on Subscoping**	**99**
	10.1 Temporal Changes	99
	10.2 From Multi-Level Trees to Multi-Level Hierarchies	100
	10.3 Split and Merge	101
	10.4 Statistics on Multi-Level Artifacts	102
	10.5 Abstract Multi-Level Technique for Generic Artifacts	103
11	**Discussion and Related Work**	**105**

III Configuration Links 109

12	**Configuration Links — Motivation and Basic Idea**	**111**
	12.1 Traditional Techniques for Feature Configuration Definition	112
	12.2 Limitations of Traditional Configuration Definition	114
	12.3 Configuration Links as a Solution	115
13	**Formal Definition of Configuration Links**	**119**
	13.1 Plain Feature Models	119
	13.2 Configuration Links for Basic Feature Models	120
	13.2.1 Configurations	120
	13.2.2 Configuration Links	121
	13.3 Configuration Links for Advanced Feature Models	123
	13.3.1 Configurations	123
	13.3.2 Configuration Links	129
	13.4 Comparison of Basic and Advanced Forms	132
	13.5 Contradictory Configuration Specifications	134
	13.6 Required Refinements for Implementation	138
14	**Use Scenarios**	**143**
	14.1 Factoring Out Customer-Invisible Variability	143
	14.2 Prepackaging Customer Configuration	143
	14.3 Hierarchical Organization of Product Line Artifacts (Artifact Lines)	144
	14.4 Coupling Core Feature Models to Artifact Level Variability	144
	14.5 Variability in Component Hierarchies (Compositional Variability)	145
	14.6 Manufacturer/Supplier Interaction	145
15	**Advanced Considerations on Configuration Links**	**147**
	15.1 Equivalences	147
	15.2 Aggregating Configuration Decisions and Exclusive Folders	148
	15.3 Relating Configuration Decisions	149
	15.4 Prioritization of Configuration Decisions	150
	15.5 Configuration Decision Events	152
	15.6 Flexible Parameter Assignments	153
16	**Discussion and Related Work**	**155**

IV Evaluation — 159

17 Prototypical Implementation of a Variability Management Framework — 161
- 17.1 Yet another feature editor? — 161
- 17.2 Key Capabilities of the Framework — 162
- 17.3 Constituents and Architecture of the Demonstrator — 164
- 17.4 Details on Selected Capabilities — 165
  - 17.4.1 Feature Modeling — 165
  - 17.4.2 Creating and Editing Configurations — 165
  - 17.4.3 Editing Configuration Decisions — 166
  - 17.4.4 Textual Variability Specification with VSL — 169

18 Prototypical Implementation of Multi-Level Requirements Artifacts — 173

19 Case Studies — 175
- 19.1 The eSafety Case Study — 175
  - 19.1.1 Background, Content and Objectives — 175
  - 19.1.2 Lessons Learned — 178
- 19.2 The N-Lighten Case Study — 181
  - 19.2.1 Background, Content and Objectives — 181
  - 19.2.2 Lessons Learned — 183

V Conclusion — 187

20 Summary and Outlook — 189
- 20.1 Summary of Contributions — 189
- 20.2 Outlook — 190

VI Appendices — 193

A An Information Model for Automotive Variability Management — 195

B Constraints in Multi-Level Feature Models — 219

Bibliography — 223

Index of Terms — 233

Chapter 1
Introduction

Over the past two decades, several new paradigms of software development were introduced by the research community, for instance, component- or aspect-oriented development. Common to all these approaches is their focus on a certain idea or vision of the overall software engineering endeavor to which they tailor all development activities and techniques. This is also the case in product-line oriented software development. Here, the focus of development is shifted from individual software products to a software manufacturer's overall product line, which means the set of products he has on offer. Instead of developing the products in parallel and independently from one another, only a single, but variable product—called the product line infrastructure—is being built; the actual products offered to the customer are then derived from that infrastructure through configuration. A key objective of all product line approaches is to make the product line a genuine, tangible entity within the development and evolution process and to strategically manage the commonality and variability between the individual product instances within the line's scope. This basic idea of product-line orientation suits very well the situation in the automotive industry, with its huge product ranges and its extensive variability. However, when applying traditional product line methods and techniques to the automotive domain, practitioners are still faced with substantial difficulties that arise from several significant characteristics of this domain.

This thesis is aimed at clearly identifying the challenges of automotive product lines and offering two key solution concepts to several of these challenges. In the remainder of this introductory chapter, an overview of my work will be given and its position among related research activities will be explained. In the section to come, we will look at the latest trends in automotive system development that gave rise to this research question and justify its great practical relevance. The next two sections will then briefly introduce the most important challenges as well as my proposed solutions. Two sections on related literature and the research's scope and approach follow, before the chapter concludes with some remarks on the dissertation's overall structure.

1.1 21st Century Automotive Development—the Transition to a New Technology

For the last fifteen years and for at least another fifteen years to come, the automotive industry has been undergoing a radical change due to the advent of software in cars. While automotive systems have traditionally been defined by mechanical and electrical components, more and more functions are today implemented by software-controlled electronics [BvdBK98]. Figuratively speaking, the driver no longer directly steers the car's wheels, but instead merely provides input to a computer system, which is actually in control of the wheel's orientation while speeding at 90 mph over the freeway. The driver thus shares his fate with a writer who no longer directly accelerates the arms of his typewriter toward the paper, but instead provides his input to a computer over a keyboard and mouse until he eventually receives a printout. In the case of modern steer-by-wire systems, it is not even uncommon to see the driver's demand disregarded by the computer in order to ensure vehicle stability.

Such a transition from mechanics and electrics to software-controlled electronics is not a completely new event. The aerospace industry, for instance, underwent the same transformation ten to fifteen years earlier. It is interesting to see how this time lag results from the different needs and constraints in these domains—esp. the distinct significance of aspects such as cost reduction, weight reduction, system availability and compliance to statutory safety standards, mass production and after-sales services: as long as electronics were relatively expensive, only an airplane's high demand for weight reduction, for example, could justify their employment. Despite several similarities, the two domains are unfortunately quite different in how they react to this technological agitation. Most importantly, the automotive industry is a highly marketing driven, mass-production market with short innovation cycles, is less pertinent to state regulation and supervision[1] and shows differences in the relation between market participants, esp. the manufacturer-customer relationship and the relations between manufacturers and suppliers. Therefore, the aerospace industry will not be of too much use as a model for the automotive industry throughout the remainder of this work, but we will come back to it occasionally.

Automotive electronics have become the major source of innovation. As in other domains, more and more electronic control units (ECUs) find their way into the product and, even more importantly, their functionality is more and more implemented in software, not only in hardware [Gri05]. This emergent use of software has led to an enormous increase in the number and complexity of different vehicle functions, a modern luxury class passenger car may contain well over 70 networked ECUs and 500MB of code [RH04]. This increase is partly driven by growing customer expectations, competition and innovation pressure [Win07], and partly by the changed attitude of development engineers and management personnel: if additional features are desired or a problem in the design requires some stop-gap solution, adapting the software is often perceived as the fastest and cheapest solution, and since changing software seems to be a limited effort only, this is done readily and frequently. This impact of newly introduced software is also not at all a new event and is well known in software science. In 1986, Frederick P. Brooks called this the *conformity* of software and identified it as one of the essential difficulties in software engineering [Bro86].

The increasing number and complexity of vehicle functions goes hand in hand with an explosion in system variability, caused by the need for product differentiation within a manufacturer's product range and the demand for customization of products [BvdBK98, Win07]. This does not only concern variability directly visible to the customer, usually implemented in the form of optional equipment, but also all the little variations on lower, technical levels. In principle, every change in any part of the software of some sensor, actuator or ECU introduces a new function variant, usually with a different behavior at the interface. And it is not only the function that is changed but also any artifact related to it, e.g. for testing and diagnosis.

---

[1] In this respect, the automotive industry has been catching up in recent years, due to the increasing significance of environmental and safety requirements.

In addition to this increase in system complexity and variability with its profound impact on development, software is also driving fundamental changes in all other phases of the automotive life cycle [BvdBK98]. For example, it has become commonplace for repair workshops to simply exchange software on one or several ECUs in order to remove some potential problem, sometime even without the customer noticing the effect.

The downturn of this development were unprecedented intricacies in production and after-sales logistics as well as a substantial quality problem. Car breakdown statistics showed that a significant increase in vehicle failures that was observed during the late nineties of the last century and the first half of our decade were largely caused by malfunctions of vehicle electronics [KS04, ADA04]. By the middle of the present decade it was clear that something had to change, nicely summarized by Stephan Wolfsried for Daimler AG in the sentence: "We want to restore people's confidence in [automotive] electronics" [FAZ04]. Despite first improvements in this respect, the issue remains a vital challenge for the automotive industry because these early improvements were mainly achieved by reducing innovation speed and function differentiation [Aue04]. But this way it is not possible to tap the enormous potential of software for the automotive industry in the areas of cost reduction, product customization, product differentiation, inventive vehicle functions and innovative sales channels.

Assistance must come from several sources, especially growing standardization on the technical level, mainly of subcomponents (the AUTOSAR [Hei04, SHS$^+$05] initiative is a prominent example here), introduction of so-called "electronic platforms" providing a technological foundation for several vehicle models, and strict avoidance of unnecessary variations [FAZ04]. However, pivotal improvement must come from enhancing a company's processes, methods and tools to embrace the design, management and evolution of the company's overall product line. The approaches and techniques for product-line oriented software development proposed by the research community over the past decade are intended precisely for this purpose. However, as indicated above, their direct application in the automotive domain poses several substantial problems, which will be briefly presented in the coming section before the solutions proposed in this dissertation are briefly sketched in Section 1.3.

1.2 Challenges in Automotive Product-Lines

Product-line orientation leads to a rather holistic approach to software development. Organizing the individual products as instances of a global product line infrastructure and rigidly managing the products' commonalities and variabilities has great impact on all phases of software development and their relation to one another as well as to the company's organizational structures. In particular, the overall development process is divided into two fundamental phases: development and evolution of the infrastructure, referred to as domain engineering, and derivation and adaptation of product instances, called product engineering. In addition, variability is usually a cross-cutting aspect that influences such diverse areas as marketing and product conception, development on the technical level, production, sales, after-sales care, and management.

This broad scope of product line orientation is one of the most important reasons why the following characteristics of the automotive domain pose such a great challenge to product-line engineering approaches.

1. **System Complexity.** The sheer multitude of sophisticated electronic functions in modern cars, such as electronic stability control, navigation systems, parking assistance

or adaptive cruise control, has made automotive systems extremely complex. It has been shown above how the advent of software fosters this development. Another important reason for increasing system complexity is the diverging scope and life-cycle of individual subsystems and development artifacts. A subsystem like a wiper or a brake-by-wire system is usually not only built into several vehicle models produced in parallel (e.g. A-Class, C-Class, E-Class) but also into several consecutive generations of these models; each subsystem has its own such scope and life time. This may equally apply to individual development artifacts, such as the requirements specification of a certain wiper system.

2. **Product Line Complexity.** The product range of a global car manufacturer often comprises several brands (such as Mercedes-Benz, smart, Maybach, Freightliner, Mitsubishi Fuso and many more in the case of Daimler AG [DAG08]), each usually divided into passenger cars, commercial vehicles and special vehicles, such as taxis or ambulances, and each such division made up of several lines (e.g. A-Class, C-Class, E-Class) and models (e.g. C220, C240). In addition, each of these vehicle models is further customized to address such aspects as local legislation or different customer needs and expectations, resulting in a vast number of variation points within all kinds of development artifacts.

3. **End-Customer Variability vs. Technical Variability.** In many classic application domains of product-line engineering approaches—such as special-purpose operating systems—the implementation-level variability is directly visible to the customer. In the automotive domain, however, the end-customer should perceive only a subset of the actual system's variability. Ideally it should even be possible to present a completely orthogonal view of the internal variability to the customer, in order to be able to adapt and prepackage it according to marketing considerations.

4. **Manufacturer-Supplier Relationship.** Large-scale industrial systems usually integrate a multitude of subsystems and components supplied by third parties. Because each supplier needs to tailor its product line to the needs of several different manufacturers, this product line has to be developed completely orthogonally, leading to a technically intricate manufacturer-supplier interaction. Furthermore, a supplier will be reluctant to disclose all the details of his product line strategy to a manufacturer for strategic, economic and legal reasons. In particular, this would weaken his position in contract negotiations with the manufacturer. Feature models, which are used throughout this thesis, often contain much strategic information and are therefore especially sensitive in this respect.

5. **Heterogeneity.** The software and hardware components, the development artifacts and the development processes employed in an automotive company can be of a highly heterogeneous nature:

    - *Heterogeneity of Runtime Environments and Software Styles.*
      The on-board software of modern cars interacts with execution environments of very diverse natures. For example, processors, operating systems, and communication networks differ greatly between motor control and telematics. The software also comprises such diverse software styles as hard real-time embedded software

1.3. Proposed Solutions

(esp. in the case of motor control) and software relatively similar to desktop applications (esp. the entertainment and telematics system).

- *Heterogeneity of Development Artifacts.*
  Automotive development involves such diverse artifacts as requirements specifications, analysis and design models, test case descriptions, executable code, production databases (e.g. logistics), marketing and sales information systems, data for after-sales support (e.g. diagnosis, software update) and internal and external documentations (e.g. for service workshops or the end-customer).
- *Heterogeneity of Methods, Processes and Tools.*
  The means of development employed in automotive corporations are also highly heterogeneous: even within a single company, many different methods and tools are used, sometimes, for historical reasons, even for a single purpose, and when cooperation between manufacturers and suppliers is taken into account, heterogeneity increases further dramatically.

6. **Organizational Complexity.** For example, not only are today's global car manufacturers organized in groups of several large divisions, each comprising a multitude of units, departments, teams and projects, but automotive development is also highly distributed among the manufacturer and its suppliers. Since each supplier usually works for several different manufacturers, a complex network of relationships arises, in which virtually everyone is at least indirectly related to everyone else. In addition, the influence on processes, methods and tools is, for several reasons, very limited, which calls for concepts that can be flexibly adapted and incrementally introduced.

This is just a brief summary of the most important challenges of automotive product line engineering which were primary targets during the preparation of this thesis; a more detailed description and discussion will be given in Section 5.1.

1.3 Proposed Solutions

Initially, the obstacles presented in the previous section were investigated in parallel and independently from one another. The expectation was that each problem, or at least each group of problems, would require a dedicated technical concept. This is the reason why several concepts were devised during the preparation of this thesis and early publications were targeted specifically at one or two of the above challenges (e.g. [RW05]).

However, as the various concepts evolved, it turned out that they can be generalized and merged into two fundamental concepts that extend traditional variability modeling and product-line engineering. The various challenges described above thus represent use cases for these concepts. These two concepts are:

- **Subscoping.** Whenever the paradigm of product-line oriented development is to be applied to a highly complex product line, such as that of a global automotive manufacturer, the engineer is faced with a difficult decision: managing everything as a single, gargantuan product line is virtually impossible owing to its enormous complexity, but when dividing the range of available products into several smaller independent lines, systematic reuse and strategic variability management across these portions—one of the key benefits of the product-line approach—is lost. It is the purpose of subscoping to avoid these two alternatives by offering a compromise between a single global and several smaller, independent product lines. With this technique, it is possible to split up a huge product line into smaller, independent sublines but still strategically steer their commonalities and variabilities on a global level.

- **Configuration Links.** In this thesis, I argue that including configuration in the focus of variability modeling as a first-class citizen is a promising way to deal with several of the above challenges on the basis of variability management. This means that variability models are not only used to define the common and variable characteristics of the line's products but also to define under which circumstances each characteristic will be selected or deselected for a product. Thus, configuration is not seen as a manual, interactive process taking place when an actual product is derived and delivered; instead it is predefined during domain engineering and is thus turned into a core activity during definition of the product line infrastructure. Of course, a certain degree of manual configuration will always remain, but especially in industrial contexts there are many uses for predefined configuration as will be shown in Part III, esp. in Section 14.

  The technical concept for achieving this is a *configuration link*, which allows the configuration of one variability model (the target model) to be defined in terms of a given configuration of another variability model (the source model). Then, from any given configuration of the source model, a configuration of the target model can be derived. In particular, such a mechanism allows the separation of end-customer variability from technical variability, helps deal with heterogeneity of all sorts, aids in realizing the manufacturer-supplier relationship and provides a means of modularizing the product-line infrastructure while taking into account its variability.

Again, this is only intended to provide a brief overview and impression of the major contributions of this work. Details will be given below in Part II for subscoping and in Part III for configuration links. A more complete list of contributions can be found in the concluding chapter at the end.

1.4 Research Background, Scope and Approach

Background

The research presented in this thesis has been conducted in close cooperation with a research department at Daimler AG between mid 2004 and mid 2007. During that time, this department was in the process of extending its focus on requirements management, one of the department's main competencies, with an interest in variability management and product-line orientation. Another important source of inspiration and feedback was the ATESST project, a European-funded research project within the 6th framework program. The author was involved in the initial planning of this project and in the preparation of the project proposal; therefore it was possible to designate an entire work package to variability management and perfectly align it to the objectives of this thesis. Recently, close contacts to Carmeq GmbH, an electronics and software subsidiary of Volkswagen AG, became an important source of feedback.

1.4. Research Background, Scope and Approach

Scope

The overall research objective and scope was partly determined by practical questions and problems encountered at Daimler AG, and partly by the aim to come up with ideas and concepts that are general enough to represent interesting contributions from a theoretical, scientific point of view. Another important guideline was the aim of coming up with solutions which are actually applicable in practice. As indicated above, the product line orientation of automotive development is closely linked to most, or even all areas of a company's processes, methods and tools. It is therefore completely unrealistic to give an answer to all the open questions in this field or to provide a single, comprehensive methodology that solves all issues. But even if such a complete approach could be formulated, it would be of limited use in practice, because in order to implement it, a company would need to extensively change its organization and processes, which is not at all a viable option in large corporations (cf. remarks on "limited influence on processes and methods" above and in Section 5.1). Therefore, one complete, monolithic process or method will not be presented in this thesis, but instead several fundamental technical concepts will be provided that can be employed in a variety of ways and can be flexibly adapted to the specific needs of a certain use case in a company, department or project. The combination of these technical concepts may form a framework or methodology for complex variability management, but they are still not intended to provide a complete, rigid process for product-line oriented development.

In addition to this choice for targeting a "tool box" of flexible technical concepts, several other initial presumptions and decisions regarding the research scope have to be noted:

- **Focus: Automotive Domain.** The most important focusing of this thesis was, of course, to target the automotive domain. The reason for doing so was not only the aforementioned cooperation with Daimler AG, but also the fact that the automotive domain makes for an intriguing and challenging application domain of software product lines. However, since this research lead to rather basic concepts, these concepts and many associated observations are arguably applicable to most other industrial domains in which software-intensive systems are developed.

- **Focus: Manufacturer Perspective.** This research is based on the perspective of an automotive manufacturer, rather than that of a supplier. This means that the focus lies on the development of the complete system rather than on the development of individual subsystems; consequently activities on higher abstraction levels, such as analysis, specification, integration, and testing, were the primary source for motivating the use cases, rather than low-level design and implementation activities[2]. The reason for this bias is two-fold: firstly, as indicated above, the more interesting research questions arise from the complexity of the manufacturer's perspective and, secondly, this thesis was prepared in close cooperation with Daimler AG, which naturally creates a manufacturer perspective.

- **Assumption: Insufficiency of Variability Avoidance.** While the previous presupposition decides among several alternative approaches discussed within the research community, alternative considerations on how to fundamentally attack the above obstacles also exist in practice. Most importantly, many practitioners favor the idea of

---

[2]Of course, no sharp distinction can be made here. Sometimes the manufacturer carries out more phases of development, sometimes less. Innovative subsystems are often even completely developed by the manufacturer.

variability avoidance. Instead of providing sophisticated concepts and methodologies for managing enormously complex variability within an automotive product line, variability should simply be avoided and reduced as far as possible; the remaining variability can then be managed pragmatically with existing techniques. It is an ongoing discussion in the automotive domain if this is actually a feasible option for some manufacturers or even the industry as a whole, or if variability should rather be embraced and used aggressively as an opportunity to foster innovation and product differentiation to achieve competitive advantage [Mau02]. A definite decision between these two extreme standpoints cannot and need not be made here. It is sufficient to say that the research presented below was based on the assumption that *an automotive product line always comprises at least a certain minimum amount of variability, which cannot be avoided or simplified any further and is still sufficiently complex to call for a dedicated variability management* (empirical evidence for this assumption is given in [Mau02]).

- **Focus: Variability Management.** The following discussion is primarily focused on variability management, which constitutes one core activity of product-line engineering. The other core areas of product-line research, such as process issues, appropriate company organization, or scoping [Sch02], are not specifically investigated, but, of course, incidentally considered. Within variability management the focus lies on variability modeling. The reason for this concentration of scope was that suggestions related to process and organization are far more difficult to put into practice in a company than more technical concepts such as novel modeling means, which can usually be adapted to a concrete use context quite well. Also, advanced variability modeling and management means can be a highly valuable tool in dealing with the above challenges, as will be substantiated throughout the remainder of this thesis.

- **Assumption: Feasibility of Feature Modeling.** As an important presupposition, feature modeling was deemed an appropriate variability management tool for tackling the obstacles in automotive product lines and was thus chosen as the basis for all the techniques proposed below. Feature modeling is a well-established, fairly consolidated conception; it provides a good compromise between completely informal, pragmatic approaches and strictly formal, rigid ones; it is positioned on an appropriate abstraction level for the rather broad reach of the challenges in scope; and it is accessible to a broad audience in industry. However, there are no truly compelling factual reasons to choose feature modeling. Some researchers prefer other variability management means (e.g. decision tables [MJA+04]) or question the feasibility of structurally modeling a complex industrial system's commonalities and variabilities altogether [BLPW04]. Such a differing stance could have been followed too and good progress could also arguably have been made in the above challenges. But the details of the proposed solutions would look very different. Therefore, it was an indispensable prerequisite for achieving feasible results to clearly position this research effort in this respect as early as possible.

Approach

The findings of this thesis were obtained in the following way. At first, the author's involvement in a number of projects at Daimler AG—all concerned with variability issues to some extent—lead to several research questions as outlined by the challenges described above. The most important of these projects are the EAST-EEA project, a European project which was one of the predecessors of the AUTOSAR initiative, the FOX project, an internal Daimler project aimed at providing a methodology for function orientation applicable across the automotive sub domains, and the DEEP-C project, an internal effort to establish an integrated and continuous documentation and change management of all information relevant to a car's electronic and electric system. Even though this involvement was in some cases only passive or relatively short, it was an excellent opportunity to learn how variability issues show up in relatively diverse application contexts. These concrete variability issues in their specific contexts could then be generalized into the aforementioned challenges of automotive product lines.

Based on these challenges, the solutions proposed in this thesis were then devised relatively independently from a concrete project or application context. To be certain that they keep in touch with the demands in practice, they were regularly presented to and discussed with engineers and researchers at Daimler AG and Carmeq GmbH as well as in the ATESST project and with colleagues at TU-Berlin. Discussions during conferences and workshops also proved a valuable source of inspiration and feedback during this phase.

In a third and final step, the concepts were thoroughly evaluated in several case studies and extended examples. This will be discussed in detail in Part IV. Of course the last two steps were not strictly sequential but it was an iterative process of evaluating and enhancing the concepts.

In summary, this means that the actual work started in a concrete context with a very practical viewpoint, then shifted to a broader, more theoretical research perspective and, finally, returned to its practical background for evaluation. This approach proved to be highly feasible. It enabled the research work to be well-anchored within practical issues and at the same time open enough to draw scientific conclusions and devise scientific concepts that are not only applicable to a very specific practical context. It was also extremely rewarding and stimulating to experience both worlds, the industrial and the academic environment. Trying to find a compromise that makes the best of both these backgrounds was a great, fascinating challenge.

1.5 Related Literature and Work (Overview)

This section provides an overview of other research efforts related to the objectives of this dissertation. Detailed comparisons, especially an account of precise differences and similarities, will be given below throughout the text, wherever terms and concepts are introduced.

The basic idea of taking into consideration an entire family of software products—that show a fair degree of similarity—dates back to the seventies of the last century [Par76]. However, the precise realization of this idea and the interpretation of the terms software product family and line changed substantially around 1990, as will be shown in detail in Section 2.1. Recent research in the field of software product line engineering can be roughly divided into two areas: on the one hand variability management and modeling and on the other issues related to process and organization. This distinction is also reflected in the structure of the two most important textbooks and overviews for the field of software product lines [CN02, PBvdL05]. These also provide a multitude of further references. As was indicated above, questions related to process and organization, for example whether domain and product engineering should be performed by a single or two distinct teams of engineers [BKPS04], lie outside our scope and we therefore concentrate on variability management and modeling.

Variability management is dedicated to providing a sound terminological framework for determining what "variability" actually means and what related conceptions have to be considered in this context. And, based on this, variability management provides techniques for specifying and managing over time the variable aspects of a given system. In recent years, many authors emphasize that it is crucial to investigate a system's commonalities together with its variabilities, leading to commonality and variability management. For the sake of brevity, this term will not be used in the following, even though the significance of considering commonalities is also recognized by the author and is, in fact, of particular value to the automotive domain. The actual techniques for variability management can be of very diverse natures, for example, [GS04] provides an unconventional terminology. If they take the form of a modeling language, then the term variability modeling is used. A good example of a variability management technique that does *not* make use of modeling is decision tables (as proposed in [MJA+04], for example). However, as mentioned above, the focus in this thesis was put on feature modeling as a certain form of variability modeling.

Feature modeling has become a popular instrument for variability management. Initially, research in this field focused on extending the original notion of feature modeling as introduced by Kang et al. in 1990 [KCH+90], by adding new concepts and enhancing the expressiveness of the models. Over the past one or two years, the focus has shifted toward consolidating the feature-modeling concepts proposed so far and integrating them into what could be called a unified feature-modeling technique. One such consolidation effort is the attempt, in several recent publications, to put feature modeling on a sound formal basis, [Bat05a, CHE05a, SHTB06]. Others seek to overcome the diversity of the various feature techniques that currently exist side by side by using a unified approach for feature modeling, e.g. [AMS06]. These efforts will be further investigated in Part I, especially at the end in Section 5.3. However, no single, generally accepted approach has evolved yet, so this unification effort must still be considered as work in progress.

Another important body of literature is concerned with making variability management techniques applicable to use cases of extremely high complexity. Often, these publications also have a focus on complex industrial settings, usually indicated by terms such as "embedded systems" or "software-intensive systems". Important publications in this respect are those on product populations by Rob van Ommering et al. [vO00, vOvdLKM00, vO04], several from Thomson and Heimdahl [TH03], several of Klaus Pohl et al. [BLPW04, BLP05], and a number of publications from within the automotive industry, e.g. [RT04].

1.6 Structure of the Thesis

The following presentation is structured in four major parts. Part I introduces the concepts of software product lines, variability and feature modeling. In addition to the state-of-the-art, the author's own take on these conceptions is presented and detailed considerations on applying them in the automotive domain are provided, including an overall organizational scheme for automotive product line engineering (Chapter 5). Parts II and III then motivate and define in detail the novel concepts of subscoping and configuration links, respectively. An account of the evaluation of the proposed solutions is given in Part IV. Finally, the text concludes with a summary and outlook.

Part I
Automotive Software Product Lines

Chapter 2

May I Introduce: Lines, Variants & Co.

The decision to organize software development according to the product-line paradigm has many implications and a profound impact on the overall development activity. Therefore it is important to achieve a clear understanding of the basic terms and concepts, in particular of product line and variability. Unfortunately, the scientific community has not yet come up with a single, generally-accepted opinion on this matter. Many publications only define some of the basic terms and concepts, leaving the relation to the others unstudied; others miss out on important aspects of individual concepts.

Due to this relatively unconsolidated state of definitions in literature, this chapter tries to serve two purposes: firstly, a summary of the most important definitions is given and secondly, the author's own interpretation of the terms is provided which is aimed at forming a consistent terminological framework for the concepts proposed below in Part II and III.

2.1 Software Product Lines

The fundamental term of product-line oriented software development is, of course, that of a *software product line*. Hereby, an interesting shift in focus of research can be observed compared to an earlier understanding of the term. To illustrate this briefly, we introduce the two most influential definitions here.

In 1976, David L. Parnas first coined the term software product line and defined it as follows:

> "A set of programs constitutes a [software] product line whenever it is worthwhile to study programs from the set by first studying the common properties of the set and then determining the special properties of the individual members." [Par76]

Notably, only such software products form a software product-line, that have a certain degree of commonality while at the same time showing substantial differences. This combination of commonality and variability is one of the key characteristics of a software product-line. And the question of what degree of commonality is necessary in order to be able to apply product-line oriented development methods is one of the most important—and difficult—questions of the field. In case the products differ too much from one another, the overhead of describing them as members of a single product line is too high in order to gain substantial benefit from this approach.

Parnas proposed to manage a product-line by composing its individual products from reusable modules or components with clearly defined interfaces, thus setting the direction of

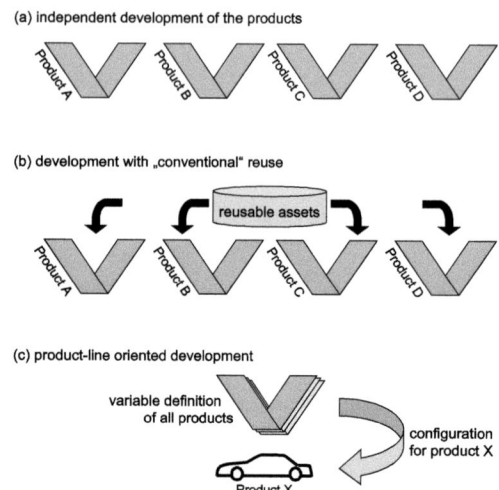

Figure 2.1: Product-line oriented development in comparison.

research for the coming decades. From today's point of view, this early approach to product-line development could be called a "classical" or "conventional" reuse approach.

The aforementioned shift in focus then occurred in the early 1990's, which is reflected in the following definition of Clements and Northrop:

> "A software product line is a set of software products ... that are developed from a common set of core assets in a prescribed way." [CN02]

Now, the individual products are no longer each developed in parallel by composing reusable parts. Instead, the products are derived from a single, common product definition—the *product-line infrastructure*—in a prescribed way. Instead of describing each product separately, there is only a single description of the product line together with a definition how individual products differ from this prototype. To achieve this, all development artifacts that are part of the product-line infrastructure (e.g. requirements documents, component diagrams, Matlab/Simulink models, test case descriptions) are defined in a variable form if their content varies from product to product. The individual products derived from the product-line infrastructure are then referred to as *product instances* or simply *products* of the product line.

The difference between a product-line approach and conventional reuse is illustrated in Figure 2.1. In the case of conventional reuse there is still a complete system description for each product, even if these descriptions are made-up of reusable parts (cf. Figure 2.1.b). How the reused assets are combined is defined for each product separately. This is not the case with product-line oriented development: There, only one, variable system description is defined (Figure 2.1.c).

In summary, we can thus define a software product-line as follows.

2.2. Product Line vs. Family vs. Population

> **Definition 1.** A *software product line* is a set of software products that share a certain degree of commonality while also showing substantial differences and that are derived from a single, variable product definition—the *product-line infrastructure*—in a well-defined, prescribed way. □

For completeness, we go on with:

> **Definition 2.** A *product instance* or simply *product* of a software product line is a particular, fully configured software product that was derived from the line's infrastructure. □

As a consequence, development is now divided into two separate phases: the development and evolution of the product line infrastructure (called *domain engineering*), and the definition of individual product instances to be derived from that infrastructure (called *product engineering*).

With product-line engineering, the products can now be viewed as members of an embracing product line, thus shifting the focus of development and evolution from the individual products to the entire product line: the product line becomes a first-order entity of development. The benefit of this approach is that the relations between the individual products—in particular their commonalities and variabilities—become tangible entities of development and evolution, which is a prerequisite for strategic product line scoping, product tailoring to market needs and rigid reuse of all kinds of development artifacts within the product line.

2.2 Product Line vs. Family vs. Population

Sometimes the term *software family* is used as a synonym for software product line. Another possibility, however, is to think of a software family as a very complex software product line, possibly made-up of several smaller software product lines. For example, the Mercedes Benz C-Class C320 would be a typical product line while all Mercedes Benz vehicles, passenger cars as well as commercial vehicles, together form a product family. Since such a "composition" of product lines is of high relevance to the automotive domain—as will be shown below in Chapter 5—the second understanding is preferable for the purpose of this thesis.

In some publications the term *product population* is used to refer to complex, aggregated product lines, e.g. [vO00]. The term is rather uncommon in German-speaking countries.

2.3 Beyond Software

Up to this point, only software product lines were considered, in order to adhere closely to conventional product-line terminology as applied in the software engineering community. In the automotive domain however, we usually do not encounter pure software products but instead deal with software / hardware systems in which software is embedded within a hardware context, which is also subject to the overall development activity. To reflect this, we simply replace the term "software" in the above definitions by "software-intensive system" or simply "system" and thus speak of product lines / families of software-intensive systems or *system product lines / system families* for short.

On the level of a basic understanding of the term product line this widening of focus does not make a significant difference and the discussion in the previous sections remains equally

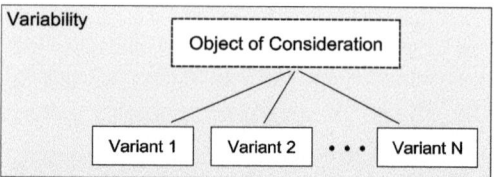

Figure 2.2: Terms and concepts associated to the basic notion of variability.

applicable. For example, the necessity of a certain degree of commonality and diversity between the products (cf. Section 2.1) also pertains to the hardware-part of a system line. On a more detailed, methodological level however it makes a huge difference: additional development artifacts are usually applied when hardware design becomes part of the development activity.

2.4 Variability

The notion of variability is one of those not clearly defined in many publications, arguably because it is deemed obvious or self-explanatory. However, many discussions with engineers from Daimler AG and Carmeq GmbH have shown that often there is a great uncertainty and hesitation regarding the precise meaning of expressions like variant, variation point or feature, which are not the subject of this section but rely on a clear understanding of variability as a fundamental concept. Furthermore, the precise interpretation of the notion of variability has a major impact on the overall organizational scheme of product-line oriented development (as explained in Chapter 5). Therefore, the basic notion of variability deserves a closer look here.

Generally speaking, *variability* means that a certain entity exists in several, different forms. We can define:

> **Definition 3.** Variability denotes the diverseness of a certain entity of consideration, thus called a variable entity. □

Correspondingly, a *variant* can be defined as follows:

> **Definition 4.** A variant of a variable entity is a certain form of this entity, which differs from all other possible forms in at least one characteristic. □

In other words, the variants are the varieties in which the variable entity may occur.

Apart from the basic notion of variability and the variants these definitions introduce another important conception: the "entity of consideration" or "variable entity". This is the embracing concept—the "umbrella"—under which all variants can be subsumed. It is usually abstract in the sense that it does not have a correspondence in the real world. The relation between variability, variable entity and its variants is illustrated in Figure 2.2. An important observation from this terminology is that it does not make sense to speak of variants without making clear what the variable entity is.

In principle, the above definitions are completely independent from product-line engineering and software development. Why this is so important becomes obvious when the definitions are applied to software product lines: there is not only a single way to apply them but instead

2.4. Variability

Table 2.1: Meaning of common cardinalities.

Variability of ...	Variable Object	Variants
the entire product line	product line	products
development artifacts	artifact	configurations of artifact
variable artifact section	variation point	variation point variants

there are several different levels in a product-line setting on which the notion of variable entity / variant can be applied. First, we may look at the variability of the entire product line, which means the product line is seen as the variable entity while the individual products make up the corresponding variants. Second, each development artifact can be seen as a variable entity of its own, with the artifact's configurations as its variants (variability of the artifacts). Finally, each individual location within such a variable artifact at which the artifact's content differs from one configuration to another can be seen as a variable entity; in this case the different forms that the artifact may take at this very point then represent the variants. These locations within an artifact at which variability actually occurs are usually referred to as *variation points*. Altogether, this gives us three different levels of variability within a single product line, summarized in Table 2.1. Note that when looking at a single product line, we only have a single possible variable entity (i.e. the product line itself), whereas on the level of the artifacts we have several (i.e. each artifact) and on the level of variation points we have in turn several for each variable artifact.

Since variability therefore occurs in many different contexts even within a single product line, it is of great importance to clearly keep apart these different cases. In literature, this is not always the case: for example, the different forms of content that an artifact may show at a variation point are usually simply called "variants", not clearly distinguishing them from artifact configurations and products of the product line.

Above, the term variability was defined to denote the fact that a certain entity is variable and exists in several different forms. An additional use of the term variability refers to what is actually different, i.e. the differences between the various forms of the variable entity. In other words, whenever the variable entity's variants differ from one another in a certain aspect, this is called a(!) variability, whereas those aspects that are identical for all variants are viewed as commonality.

Example 1. Manufacturer MF offers a product line of mobile phones consisting of three models, S (for Simple), M (for Medium) and A (for Advanced). S has a black and white display, while the others have color displays. Only A has support for T9 (an advanced text input mode). All models have the same 1 mega pixel camera supplied by supplier X. All three models are tri-band devices, i.e. they can establish a communication over GSM bands 900, 1800 and 1900 Mhz. □

First of all, on the product line level, we have the variability of the abstract entity "phone offered by manufacturer MF". The two forms of displays and the T9 support only provided by model A evidently constitute variability within this product line. The camera on the other hand and its resolution is clearly an example of commonality. In addition to the variability of the entire product line, the differences in functionality will certainly have an impact on the development artifacts that capture the requirements for the phone devices, their software or hardware design or that provide test cases for evaluation, leading to variability of these artifacts as well as variability on the level of individual variation points within these artifacts.

2.5 Binding of Variability and Binding Time

Another important notion related to variability is *binding time*. Variability may be resolved or *bound* at various points in time during development, production and post-production. For instance, the display variability in Example 1 above will be bound before production, because it must be clear whether a black-and-white or color display must be built in. The variability of T9 support may be bound immediately after production, by parameterization of the phones software. This way, the same software can be used for phones with and without T9 support; the differentiation is achieved by post-production configuration. The binding time can be different for each variation within the product line.

As a special case, variability may also be bound at runtime. Such variability is then called *runtime variability*. The tri-band functionality in Example 1 is such a case: all three models are shipped with this functionality, which means they are all equipped with hardware capable of using the three GSM bands mentioned above and with software that can select the appropriate band or switch from one to another if necessary. Therefore, according to the above definition of variability, we ought to view this as commonality, because the hardware and software realizing tri-band functionality is identical in all three models. However, there actually is some form of variability, because the GSM band used for communication changes. Runtime variability does not result in a difference in the product instance's hardware or software, but instead constitutes a functionality of the products, a common functionality in fact. Product-line engineering approaches differ in whether they view runtime variability as a variability of the product-line or not. The rational for treating runtime variability just like ordinary variability is that the only difference is the binding time. During the early phases of commonality / variability analysis it may not be clear whether some variability will be bound prior to runtime or at runtime. Also, what may be runtime variability for some models can be ordinary variability for other models. To put it simple, the binding time determines whether some variability is realized through a variation of the product instances' hardware or software (binding prior to runtime) or if it has to be realized through a special, common functionality of the product instances (runtime binding).

2.6 Version vs. Variant

When introducing the concepts of variability and product lines in industrial projects, practitioners often complain about the relation between variability and versioning not being clear. In particular, the differentiation between a variant and a *version* often seems obscure. Both have in common that they introduce a change to some entity thus defining a new form of that entity. But what is the difference?

In principle, a distinction between the two concepts can be drawn quite clearly by taking into consideration the objective of the change introduced. A variant introduces an optional change which is only intended for certain situations (in the other cases the original form of the entity being changed remains in effect); a version, in contrast, introduces a change which is intended to completely replace the old form of the changed entity in the future, making it obsolete. We can thus define

2.6. Version vs. Variant

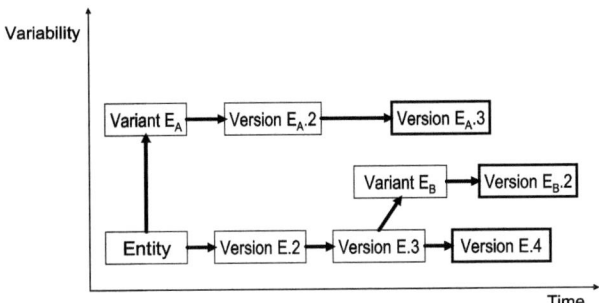

Figure 2.3: Relation of variants and versions.

Definition 5. A version is a new, different form of an entity which is intended to replace the original form of that entity. □

For the sake of consistency we need to amend the earlier definition of the term variant in Definition 4 as follows[1]:

Definition 6. A variant of a variable entity is a certain form of this entity, which differs from all other possible forms in at least one characteristic and which does not make any of these other forms obsolete but is instead intended to be employed as an additional variety in parallel with them. □

In summary, variants introduce differing forms of an entity which are valid in parallel, whereas versions introduce differing forms in a consecutive way, where each new version replaces all prior versions. This is illustrated in Figure 2.3.

In practice however, this distinction is usually not as clear. First of all, versions often do not actually replace older versions in a strict sense (in that case there would not be any need to keep the prior version and the entity could simply be changed directly). Old versions are instead often still needed and valid in future to a certain extend. If they are needed only for reference or as a fall-back solution in case of critical problems with a new version, then this would not really be in conflict with our definition; but if the old version is used in parallel with the new one because, for example, the new version is not backward compatible—which is also often the case—then, according to the above differentiation, we would need to speak of a variant, in contrast to ordinary usage of these terms. Furthermore, the role of *branches* as commonly employed in version management is ambiguous with respect to the above differentiation. If the branch introduces an additional form of the entity that will be used and delivered in parallel with the entity's original form, then it would be considered a variant. Yet, branches often only intend to support collaborative development, i.e. parallel modifications on the same entity which will be merged later on. Such a branch could neither be classified as a variant nor a version.

Despite this certain vagueness of the proposed differentiation, it proved useful in education and practice in order to explain the basic idea behind variability management and its relation to traditional version management.

---

[1] In fact, this definition represents a new version (or variant?) of Definition 4.

It is important to note that these intricacies in differentiation appear primarily on the level of pure variability terminology. As soon as the concept of variability is augmented with the idea of product-line engineering, the difference to version management becomes apparent, because version management does not have such a consequential stance on the overall organization of the software development as the notion of product lines.

Chapter 3
Modeling Software Product Lines

This chapter gives an overview of product-line modeling. Precisely speaking, it is examined what *additional* modeling activities are necessary when traditional software development is enhanced by the idea of product-line orientation (Section 3.1) and what modeling techniques are available to support them (Sections 3.3 and 3.4). This survey of available modeling techniques will show what basic groups of techniques are proposed in literature, but is not intended to present each of them in every detail. Instead, a single technique—namely feature modeling—will be highlighted and presented in detail in the following Chapter 4, because it is the basis for the ensuing discussion later in this thesis.

3.1 What needs to be modeled ?

A good starting point for the investigation of product-line modeling is traditional software development, where a single, non-variable software product is delivered. In this situation, the software product is being built by iteratively manipulating a number of *development artifacts*, which each capture information on a certain aspect of the final product to be delivered. According to their purpose and level of abstraction these artifacts can be grouped into analysis, design, implementation and test artifacts. Correspondingly, the overall development activity can be separated into an analysis, design, implementation and verification & validation phase. This is illustrated in Figure 3.1, where the development process is depicted as a large 'V', in allusion to the V-process model of software development [Fed97, HH05]. It should be noted that the V-model of software development has drawn substantial criticism (for an overview with further references see [Som04]); here and throughout this thesis it is only used symbolically for depicting any development process without suggesting a certain style of software process organization.

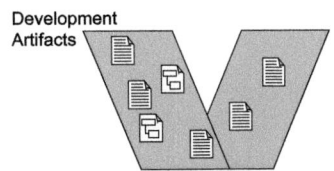

Figure 3.1: Artifacts in traditional software development.

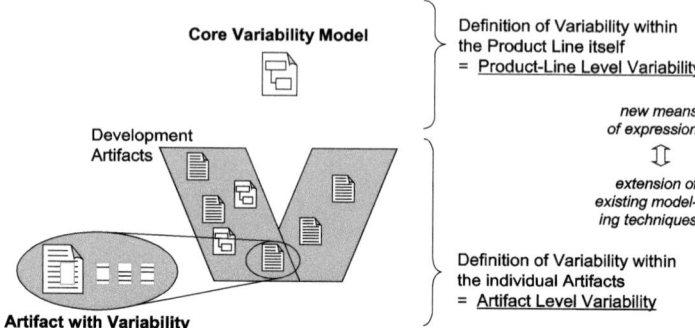

Figure 3.2: Artifacts in product-line oriented software development.

When making the transition to product-line oriented development, several changes have to be applied to this picture. In this case, not only a single product is being developed but several more or less distinct ones. It is the characteristic trait of product-line engineering that these products are not developed independently from one another but together within a comprehensive development pursuit (cf. Chapter 2). In particular, the information captured in the development artifacts is not documented separately for each product but together for all products within the product-line's scope. This means that now variability may occur within each development artifact: Whenever some content of an artifact is applicable only to some of the line's products, then this content becomes variable, thus introducing a variation point in this artifact. In Figure 3.2 this is depicted for the enlarged artifact only, but may of course occur in the other artifacts as well.

As explained in Section 2.1 an important objective of a product-line oriented development approach is that the product line itself becomes a first-order entity of development. To actually achieve this, an additional artifact[1] is needed to capture the relevant properties of the product line itself. It will then provide the basis for scoping, evolution and strategic management of the entire product line. In Figure 3.2 this is represented by an artifact symbol located above the other artifacts. Another, rather pragmatic reason for having this additional artifact is that even in relatively simple cases the overall variability defined in the other, lower-level artifacts can become very complex while each of these artifacts only describes a certain fraction of it. Therefore, a useful overview on the overall variability from a global perspective is required.

In summary, we have identified two areas of product-line modeling:

1. Modeling of the variability of the development artifact's contents
   (artifact-level variability),

2. Modeling of the variability of the product line itself in an additional artifact
   (product-line variability).

These two cases of modeling the variability of a product line will be investigated below in two

---

[1]For simplicity we will here assume that this is a single artifact. As will be shown later in Section 5.2.2, several artifacts are needed in complex cases.

3.2 The Purpose of Variability Modeling

separate sections (Sections 3.3 and 3.4). But before doing so, we will have a closer look on what "modeling variability" means precisely.

3.2 The Purpose of Variability Modeling

Generally speaking, *variability modeling* is aimed at presenting an overview of a product line's commonality and variability. Depending on the form of variability modeling, commonality may either be addressed only indirectly, i.e. everything which is not explicitly defined to be variable is implicitly defined to be common, or directly, i.e. certain aspects are explicitly defined to be common in order to highlight them and to document the decision to make them common. In order to stress the fact that variability modeling at least indirectly addresses also commonality, sometimes the term *commonality / variability modeling* is preferred.

As is the case for all modeling activity, variability modeling tries to achieve its goals by way of abstraction. This means that some aspects of the entire information related to a product line's variability are deliberately left out of consideration in order to reduce the amount of information to a level that is manageable and to put emphasis on the important aspects while hiding unnecessary detail.

The information captured in a variability model then serves as a basis for defining variability within the artifacts that make up the product-line infrastructure as well as for configuring individual product instances and deriving them from the infrastructure. Let us investigate a brief example.

Example 2. A Matlab/Simulink model contains a certain block B1 which has to be replaced by some other block B2 depending on the selected product instance. □

In such a situation it is the responsibility of the product line's variability model to allow for configuration of individual product instances (i.e. to select and define them) and to define when B1 is to be used without replacement and under what circumstances B1 needs to be replaced by B2. How this is done in detail highly depends on the variability modeling technique being applied. This will be described in detail in Section 3.3.

According to the paradigm of orthogonal variability modeling [BGdPL+03], the variability between the products in a product line is documented and managed as a separate, orthogonal aspect of development, called *variability dimension*. This dimension is thus clearly set apart from the *artifact dimension*, i.e. the definition of the development artifacts, such as requirements, component diagrams, state charts and test cases. However, variability is usually not only addressed in the variability dimension alone. As pointed out in the previous section, the variability's precise impact on the development artifacts is usually described within these artifacts themselves. The fact that in these cases some aspects of variability are also defined in the artifact dimension need not necessarily be seen as a violation of the orthogonal variability modeling paradigm, because the definition of variability aspects in the artifact dimension only relates to where and how the artifact is affected by variability. The primary focus of variability management—i.e. the presentation of an overview of the entire product line's variability, definition of dependencies between variations and the global coordination of variability across several artifacts—is still clearly the responsibility of the variability dimension.

Table 3.1: Diversity of means to express artifact-level variability.

Type of Artifact	Example of Possible Means of Expression
Requirement Specification	all requirements are defined to be optional and they each get a logical expression that defines validity
Component Diagram	variable composition of components from a library
Class Diagram	classes with dotted lines to express optionality
C Program Code	preprocessor macros (e.g. `#ifdef`)
Aspect Oriented Language	aspects which are optionally woven-in

3.3 Modeling Artifact-Level Variability

As indicated above, it is the responsibility of artifact-level variability modeling to define *where* a certain artifact's content differs and *how* it differs at that point. For example, in a UML2 class diagram the return type of a certain method may be different from one product to another; then it has to be defined that this method's signature is variable and what the possible return types are, e.g. `void` and `int`. Or in a user documentation a certain sentence may have to be adapted depending on the product the documentation is intended for; here it must be defined which sentence is variable and which alternative formulations are applicable. These examples already show two of the most important properties of artifact-level variability modeling:

1. The nature of the applied modeling means heavily depends on the type of artifact for which the variability of content is to be defined,

2. These modeling means form an extension to the modeling technique used for the artifact.

Table 3.1 gives an overview of the manifoldness of techniques to express variability within development artifacts. In a requirements document a possible solution is to state that all requirements are optional by default and a logical expression—added to each requirement—then states the context in which the corresponding requirement is actually valid. An expression of `True` means that the requirement is always valid, i.e. it is mandatory. In a component diagram the situation is a bit more complex. Here many different structural properties can be variable, such as interfaces, communication links or sub-components. One solution is to build a repository of reusable components in which also alternative variants of components for similar purposes are provided. The final complete system is then built by composing a selection of these components. The freedom which components to chose and how to interconnect them then introduces the variability into the overall system. In program code there already exist several traditional means to express variability. In the C language for example, pre-processor macros (such as `#ifdef`, `#else` and `#endif`) can be used to introduce variability which will be bound prior to compile time. The interesting special case of conditional statements was already discussed in Section 2.5. A newer, very interesting option for expressing variability in a development artifact is provided by aspect-oriented software development (AOSD). Here, an *aspect* defines that some additional content (called an *advice*) is added at various places in an artifact; the places where advices can possibly be inserted are called *join points* and the definition at what points a certain advice is actually to be inserted is a so-called *point cut*. The process of actually changing the artifact by adding the advices at the locations defined

3.3. Modeling Artifact-Level Variability

by the point cuts is called *aspect weaving*. When aspects are defined to be optional—possibly by tagging them with a logical expression similar as indicated above for requirements—then they are in fact defining variability. Aspect-orientation was initially devised for programming code, but in recent years much effort has been undertaken to apply these concepts to other artifacts, in particular software design models, e.g. [LR04, MO04]. A detailed discussion of the potential as well as the difficulties of applying AOSD concepts in the automotive domain is given in [MRW06].

Further details of individual approaches for expressing variability in development artifacts are beyond the scope of this chapter and thesis. Let us instead examine the fundamental differences between such approaches and if basic groups of them can be identified. When looking at the above examples, it shows that they can be categorized along two criteria:

1. Internal vs. external definition:

   (a) *Internal*: artifact variability is explicitly expressed within the artifact meaning that the possible optional or alternative design decisions are explicitly defined as part of the artifact description. Here, the decisive criterion is not the location where the variability information is placed but the fact that the methodology used as the basis of the artifact's definition is *amended* by means to express variability. Above, this is clearly the case in the C pre-processor macro example.

   (b) *External*: artifact variability is described outside the artifact, meaning that the possible design decisions are captured elsewhere than within the artifact specification. Again, the question where the artifact's methodology is extended or not is more important than the location of the additional information. The best example for an external variability definition is obviously one that makes use of aspects.

2. Alterative vs. generative/constructive configuration:

   (a) *Alterative artifact configuration*: artifact configuration is realized by modifying a default artifact model. This kind of configuration is used in the C code pre-processor example above and when using aspects.

   (b) *Generative/constructive artifact configuration*: artifact configuration is realized by generating the final, configured artifact and/or by composing it out of basic elements from an overall pool of (variable) artifact elements. The component composition example above follows this scheme.

Here, 2.b could be further differentiated into approaches that are truly generative and such approaches which simply compose the final, configured artifact by only putting together reusable parts without further changes or additions. But since this distinction has no significant impact on the characteristics of the technique from a methodological standpoint, we can simply treat it as a single group, called "generative" in the following.

These two distinctions (1. and 2. above) then define basic groups of artifact-level variability techniques and essential concepts for the modeling of artifact-level variability. This is summarized in the category matrix shown in Table 3.2. However, the concepts that correspond to these groups are not mutually exclusive and can therefore be combined in many ways. For example, it is possible to have an approach that is generative in principle, but the constituents out of which the complete system is composed are themselves defined in a variable form which may fall in the category of artifact-internal techniques (e.g. subcomponents,

Table 3.2: Category matrix of artifact-level variability management approaches.

	Internal	External
Generative / constructive	—	e.g. variable composition of components from a library
Alterative	e.g. explicit variation points and variants	e.g. aspect-oriented model transformation

which are defined by component diagrams with explicit variation points). Another example would be an approach which combines external/alterative and external/generative techniques by providing a mechanism for defining both modifications to artifacts as well as rules for the composition of artifacts out of reusable parts.

Several noteworthy considerations regarding these groups of artifact-level variability modeling techniques should be highlighted. First of all the example of aspect orientation for the external / alterative approaches may suggest that the mechanism used to define the modifications always needs to be some formal transformation specification which allows for automated configuration of the artifact. This is not true. In fact, it can also be perfectly feasible to define the modifications to the artifact very informally in natural language. The disadvantage of losing the automated configuration may well be compensated by the advantages of simplicity of the technique and an enormous flexibility, depending on the project context. For example, projects that do not frequently produce configurations of their artifacts or projects that closely interact with non-technical personnel (e.g. marketing, management) are usually appropriate for such an informal technique. The same applies to external / generative approaches where the details of composition may be defined informally. An example of an approach using natural language to define alterations and/or composition is PuLSE from Fraunhofer IESE, Germany [MJA+04].

Second, internal approaches—such as extensions to explicitly express variation points and their variants in a model—have certain advantages but also important limitations. They are usually relatively easy to understand and can be used intuitively. Because they have to be defined separately for each modeling technique anyway (being an extension to such a technique as described above), they usually integrate well into that technique and can be tailored to support its specific characteristics. Finally, because they document the variability-induced alternative content (e.g. alternative design decisions) together with the overall artifact and in the same modeling technique, they ensure that all these related aspects are documented in a single place and in a consistent form. On the other hand, an artifact-internal variability specification often leads to significant difficulties: often a single conceptual variability (e.g. the wiper has a rain sensor) affects an artifact at many different locations and this variability's definition is therefore split across many variation points and, conversely, at a single location many different conceptual variabilities can have an impact and are thus mingled into a single variation point, often leading to a combinatoric explosion of the number of alternatives. As a consequence, in complex cases it is usually difficult if not impossible to obtain an overview of an artifact's variability from a conceptual point of view only on the basis of its artifact-internal variability specification. In these cases a separate definition of such a conceptual view on variability—as provided by the variability dimension—is indispensable.

Alternatively, artifact external approaches can be used to cope with the described shortcomings of internal approaches. Beyond that, they also provide more flexibility with respect to an artifacts structure: in contrast to the internal variability modeling approach, which is bound to the principal structure of the default model, an external variability modeling mechanism can change entire parts of a design and rearrange or exchange completely independent design fragments. However, a difficulty with this approach is that things become extremely complex when several transformations affect the same location in an artifact.

An interesting trait of artifact-external techniques is that the external variability definitions can be added to the variability dimension specification, i.e. the variability model on the product-line level. In an extreme case, the definition of artifact-level variability is merely an annotation to the product-line level variability model. Since the details of this are closely related to what form of product-line level variability model is used (i.e. decision tables, decision trees/graphs, feature models), further information is given in the next section where product-line level variability is described. At this point it should only be mentioned that decision tables are best suited for incorporating artifact-level variability information and feature models are not well suited for that.

Interestingly, no techniques are published at present in the product-line community that fall in the category of internal / generative approaches. At first sight this seems to be a contradiction in principle: if the final, configured artifact is not explicitly defined beforehand but only generated/composed during configuration, then there is no artifact in which variability information could be defined internally. However, it is not necessary that "internal" refers to an artifact that exists before and after configuration. It may well refer to the constituents from which the final, configured artifact is generated from. In that sense, an internal / generative approach would put the information necessary to variably generate the final artifact into—or onto—the constituents. For example, when having a library of reusable components out of which the final complete system will be composed during configuration, then these components could be tagged with information how they are to be put together under certain circumstances. A project at Daimler AG, aimed at function-oriented reuse of requirements, developed a library for requirements (called "Funktionsbibliothek") which clearly followed this approach [DFHH06].

It is very difficult to provide general guidelines for when to apply which group of artifact-level variability techniques, especially because also many combinations of them are conceivable. Nevertheless, experience from various projects at Daimler AG seems to indicate that if the differences and commonalities are rather clearly defined and the artifact variability is mainly local and technically motivated, then an artifact-internal variability description is advantageous. Especially in cases where variability results in a rearrangement of the design or when it is suitable to treat variability as an orthogonal special case to a mostly applicable standard case, an external approach is favorable. Because of its complexity however it should probably only be used in cases where this flexibility is needed. In all other cases an internal approach should be favored. At this point it should also be noted, that for many types of artifacts the details of external approaches are research in progress, in particular aspect-oriented modeling and model transformation techniques.

3.4 Modeling Product-Line-Level Variability

Roughly, three forms of variability modeling can be distinguished: *feature modeling*, *decision tables* and *decision trees/graphs*. Figure 3.3 shows an excerpt of a decision table as presented in [MJA$^+$04], a case-study of the PuLSE approach devised at Fraunhofer IESE, Kaiserslautern,

ID	Description	Subject	Constraints	Resolution	Effect
	...				
T9	Does the phone have T9 support ?	SMS		yes	step 6 of use case 'send message' is obligatory; extension 6a of use case 'send message' is obligatory
				no	step 6 of use case 'send message' is removed
	...				
Cam	Does the phone have a camera ?	CAM		yes	...
				no	...
Res	What is the camera's resolution ?	CAM	Cam==yes	1MegPix 2MegPix	-
	...				

Figure 3.3: Excerpt of a sample decision table (taken from [MJA$^+$04]).

Germany. A decision table usually refers to one or more variable development artifacts, in the example this is a use case diagram for the use case 'send message' (not shown). Each line in a decision table represents a decision to be taken in order to configure the corresponding variable artifact(s) of the table. Each such decision has an ...

- ID, i.e. a unique identifier for the decision,

- Question which formulates the decision to be taken in natural language,

- Subject used to group several semantically related decisions,

- Constraint that limits the decision's validity which allows a filtering of decisions not valid in a certain context,

- List of possible resolutions, i.e. possible answers to the question and

- Single effect per resolution that describes how the corresponding variable artifacts have to be changed in order to configure them in alignment to the decision taken.

The number and precise meaning of each column in a decision table varies from one approach to another, but the example shown here illustrates the basic idea of decision tables and their most common concepts. Two columns deserve further explanation: the constraint and the effect. With constraints it is possible to define interdependencies between decisions to hide decisions when they are no longer valid because of some other decision taken earlier or to restrict the available resolutions. For example, if the decision 'Does the phone have a camera ?' was answered with 'no', the decision 'What is the camera's resolution ?' is no longer valid and can be hidden during configuration. Likewise, decisions in decision tables can sometimes be organized hierarchically.

The effects on the other hand describe the impact of a certain resolution on the development artifacts. As a natural language specification of variability-induced modifications to an artifact they represent an example of an artifact-external variability technique with informal definitions which are incorporated into the specification of product-line level variability (as discussed in the previous section).

Similarly, also decision trees define decisions to be taken in order to configure one or more variable artifacts. However, the decisions are represented and arranged graphically. Figure 3.4 shows a small example of such a decision tree. The advantage is that some selected

3.4. Modeling Product-Line-Level Variability

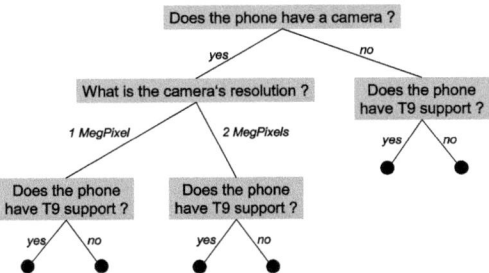

Figure 3.4: Example of a decision tree.

dependencies between the decisions can easily be defined in that way. For example, the fact that decision 'What is the camera's resolution ?' is invalid in case the camera is dismissed altogether is clearly visible in the tree. Also the number of possible product configurations is easily ascertainable, because each leaf in the decision tree corresponds to exactly one product configuration. However, this also points at an important problem of decision trees. They tend to become extremely large in complex cases. This can be avoided by using directed acyclic graphs instead of trees (i.e. a "tree" in which a node may have more than one parent). Decision tree approaches (e.g. [TGTG05]) differ from one another in many details, but these are not required for the following discussion.

Feature models are the third form of variability modeling in the variability dimension. A feature is a characteristic or trait that an individual product instance of a product line may or may not have [PBvdL05]. A feature model therefore provides an overview of both the common and variable characteristics of the product instances and the dependencies between them. Figure 3.5 shows an example. Each node in the tree depicts a feature (e.g. CruiseControl, Wiper). During configuration, features are selected or deselected. Child features may only be selected if their parent is. Each child feature has a cardinality stating whether it is mandatory, i.e. it needs to be selected if the parent is, optional, i.e. it may or may not be selected if the parent is, or if it can be selected more than once (so called cloned features ; e.g. Wiper). When a feature is selected more than once, all its descendants can be configured separately each time the feature is selected. For example, if two wipers are selected during configuration of the feature model presented in Figure 3.5, then the RainSensor can be configured independently for each of the two. In addition, several children of a single feature can be grouped to express a certain dependency between them, e.g. the alternativity between Simple and Adaptive in Figure 3.5. More general dependencies between features of different subtrees can be expressed through feature links which usually are depicted as an arrow (e.g. between RainSensor and Radar). Furthermore, features may be parameterized meaning that if the feature is selected during configuration, a value of a certain type has to be provided, for example when Radar is selected, the minimum distance to the next car has to be supplied as an integer value (cf. Figure 3.5). Again, the details of feature modeling approaches (for an overview refer to [SHTB06]) differ greatly. Further details will be presented in Chapter 4.

Since all three forms of modeling product-line level variability basically have the same purpose—presenting an overview of the product line's variability and providing a basis for configuration—it makes sense to ask whether they are basically equivalent and are merely

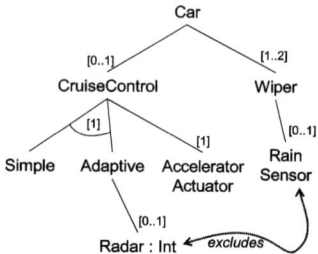

Figure 3.5: Example of a feature model.

different ways of presentation for the same information. In order to tackle this question more systematically, we examine whether the different forms of variability modeling can be translated into one another without loss of information.

Translating a decision table into a feature model is quite straightforward. For yes/no decisions, a simple feature is created; for value decisions, a parameterized feature is added; and for decisions with a finite set of enumerated resolutions, a parent feature is created together with a child for each of the allowed resolutions. Decisions' constraints are turned into feature links. The problems with this translation are:

(1) The natural-language description expressing the decision to be taken cannot be expressed in the feature model. The features' textual descriptions are not normally formulated in such a way. However, the description of a feature could still be used for this purpose, or an additional attribute could easily be introduced, if desired.

(2) Decision constraints can refer to several other decisions in a complex way. Since feature links are often defined as links from one single source feature to a single destination feature, this technique is less expressive. Again, this is not a fundamental problem for the translation because a more flexible feature linking concept could be provided.

(3) In addition, the feature model created from a decision tree in this way will be very flat. Since we only require that all the information from the decision table can be expressed and is therefore present in the feature model, this is not really an obstacle to such translation. However, it already points to an important problem that we will encounter below when examining translation in the opposite direction.

Despite these limitations, the translation from a decision table to a feature model works relatively well. Unfortunately, this is not true for the opposite direction. Basically, we can create a decision for each feature that is not mandatory as follows: for simple features a yes/no decision is created, and for parameterized features a value decision is provided; alternative features are merged into one decision with one resolution per feature. Parent-child relations are mimicked with decision constraints. While this mapping works well in principle, several critical mismatches and problems can be identified:

(4) Feature links can easily be formulated as decision constraints. However, in that case the dependency needs to be added to either the source or target decision, while a feature link represents a dedicated entity between the two. Also, one feature link can easily be kept apart from other feature links affecting the same feature and from dependencies that are expressed as parent-child relations, feature groups, etc. In decision constraints, all these dependencies

3.5. Comparison and Discussion

get mingled within a single constraint.

(5) The hierarchical structuring defined through the parent-child relationships gets lost. Although the dependency expressed in a parent-child relation (i.e. the child may only be selected if the parent is selected) can be preserved in the corresponding decision constraint, it is not possible to document the fact that this dependency came from a parent-child relation. In other words, when looking at the decision table, it is no longer possible to distinguish between the dependencies that are to be interpreted as parent-child relations or hierarchy and those that are to be interpreted as feature links. This problem could be solved by introducing hierarchy in decision tables. However, it would then no longer be possible to edit them with standard office applications, which is one of the most important advantages of decision tables.

(6) Typed edges, i.e. types of parent-child relations, cannot be expressed in a decision table.

(7) Cloned features cannot be translated into standard decision tables. Of course, a similar concept could be incorporated in decision tables—i.e. several lines of the table would be replicated during configuration and then configured separately for each copy—but such a mechanism is not available in any of the common decision table approaches.

(8) Mandatory features cannot be translated into decision tables. This results in the most important difference between the forms of variability dimension modeling: in contrast to decision tables and decision trees/graphs, feature modeling does not primarily focus on the decisions to be taken during configuration and the resulting effects on the variable artifacts. Instead, feature modeling focuses directly on the differences and similarities between the product line's individual products. More specifically, feature models list all important characteristics of the individual products and state whether these characteristics are common to all products or vary from one product to another.

To this extent, decision diagrams/trees are very similar to decision tables. There is only one additional difference that arises when comparing them to the other two forms of variability dimension modeling:

(9) Decision diagrams/trees bring all configuration decisions into a certain order. For example, if feature f1 and f2 exclude each other (defined by a feature link), then neither has priority over the other. By contrast, in a decision tree with decisions d1 and d2—corresponding to f1 and f2, respectively—either d1 is asked before d2 (and consequently d2 won't be asked at all if d1 is answered with yes) or d2 before d1 (and d1 is therefore skipped in the case of a positive answer to d2). In the first case, d1 has "priority" and in the second d2. Even though this does not make a difference on a technical level, it is of great importance from a methodical point of view.

In summary, we can say that there are fundamental differences between the three forms of variability dimension modeling.

3.5 Comparison and Discussion

As indicated in the previous two sections, a multitude of different techniques have been proposed for modeling variability both on the artifact level and the product line level. Most of these techniques come in a variety of flavors; an attempt to unify some of them has already been undertaken or is currently in progress, e.g. for feature modeling [SHTB06, RTW07b]. A few basic groups of techniques and thus a few fundamental approaches towards variability modeling have been identified above, for example feature modeling and decision tables. Unfortunately, how these main approaches relate to each other is not examined in detail and is not well understood. Are they merely different forms of presenting the same information or are there fundamental differences in how they address variability modeling? Since all these techniques are aimed at modeling variability, this situation is unsatisfactory from a theoretical, conceptual point of view: when proposing different ways to treat variability, it should be clear how they differ and why the distinction is necessary. Moreover, there is also a practical problem with this splitting up of basic approaches: When two or more independent product lines need to be related to each other or integrated into a single higher-level product line, different variability modeling approaches are usually applied in the individual product lines. In this case, it must be clear how these approaches relate to each other. Such product line integration is of particular importance in industrial settings; for example, in the automotive industry car manufacturers usually need to integrate the products, i.e. sub-systems, from numerous suppliers' product lines.

First of all, a single technique for variability modeling both on the artifact and product-line level is not realistic. These two cases of variability modeling are of very different nature actually: In the variability dimension (i.e. product-line level), an overview of variations across many artifacts is to be provided on an abstract, conceptual level while in the artifact dimension (i.e. artifact level), the variations of an individual artifact, the impact of variability, need to be defined precisely. Thus, the technique for the artifact dimension introduces variability in an existing artifact while the technique for the variability dimension constitutes an additional artifact of its own.

Consequently, the highest degree of integration that is conceivable would be to have a single technique for managing variability in the artifact dimension and another for the variability dimension. In the artifact dimension, however, the fundamental approaches towards variability modeling illustrated in Table 3.2 differ greatly and are aligned with very diverse methodological requirements and project contexts (as described in Section 3.3). Therefore an integration would not make sense at this point. The next lower level of integration would be to provide a single, integrated technique for each of the four cells of Table 3.2. But also this is not feasible in practice, because of the great diversity of the development artifacts that need to be covered by these techniques. For example a requirements specification may call for very different means to express variability than a test case description; similarly, the concept of aspect-orientation proved feasible for weaving variability into program code but its application to design models is still a challenging research issue. This diversity can be seen as being orthogonal to the two dimensions of Table 3.2. In order to ensure usability it is necessary to tailor the variability technique to the specific characteristics and needs of the artifact in question. Hence, the artifact dimension does not have great potential for a further integration of techniques.

For the variability dimension, on the other hand, this is much different. The variability dimension represents an artifact of its own and has a global perspective spanning all other development artifacts. It therefore needs to be independent of the artifacts' specificities anyhow. In addition, it was stated above that the different basic approaches towards variability modeling in the variability dimension all share the same major objective: establishing a global perspective on variations within the product line and defining dependencies between them. Practical considerations also suggest an integration of approaches: While the definition of the precise impact of variability inside an artifact (i.e. the purpose of variability modeling in the artifact dimension) usually is the responsibility of a single team working on the corresponding artifact, the global variability dimension is frequently subject to coordination between teams,

3.5. Comparison and Discussion

departments and even companies. Therefore, an integration in this area would be of high practical value.

However, substantial disparities between the basic approaches for variability dimension modeling, esp. the lack of commonality and hierarchy in decision tables, were identified in Section 3.4. An integration will therefore be a challenging task and requires significant further research. In this thesis, no effort is made to integrate feature modeling with decision tables and trees/graphs, because the Daimler lab REI/SM did not use decision tables or trees. A further unification of feature modeling approaches however was investigated closely. Section 5.3 provides a detailed report of this effort.

Chapter 4

Feature Modeling

In the previous chapter, an overview of modeling software product lines was given. Two areas of modeling were identified to be specific to product line settings—modeling variability of the entire product line and modeling variability of the development artifacts' content—and a survey of modeling techniques that support these areas was presented. This chapter now focuses on a single modeling technique for product-line level variability modeling, namely feature modeling. This will then form the basis for defining the advanced concepts proposed below in Parts II and III.

4.1 Purpose of Feature Modeling

First of all, the key purpose of feature modeling deserves a brief mention. To achieve the objectives of variability modeling (cf. Section 3.2), a feature model lists all variable characteristics of a variable entity (e.g. a product line) which differentiate the entity's variants (e.g. the products of the product line), i.e. which are present in some but not in all variants. In addition, dependencies between these characteristics are defined in order to limit the configuration space. This information then serves as the basis for configuring individual variants: by selecting and deselecting the (non-mandatory) features of a feature model, each variant can be uniquely identified.

However, for this purpose alone no dedicated modeling technique would be required. It could be achieved by a simple set of boolean configuration parameters. This is shown in Figure 4.1, where the configuration space defined by a simple feature model is also represented as a set of five parameters. Of course, the dependencies defined by the parent-child relationships and the arcs which denote alternative child features are not expressed by the set of configuration parameters alone and would need to be added in some form. Already this simple example shows that a flat list of configuration parameters would be difficult to manage in complex cases, especially when considering dependencies. A feature model on the other hand allows to group

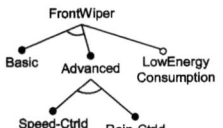

BASIC	Bool
ADVANCED	Bool
SPEED_CTRLD	Bool
RAIN_CTRLD	Bool
LOW_ENERGY	Bool

Figure 4.1: A sample feature model and its replacement as configuration parameters.

and organize features hierarchically and provides means to straightforwardly highlight the most common cases of dependencies with dedicated graphical symbols, i.e. the parent/child-relations. Therefore it can be stated that another important aim of feature modeling is to present a clear and manageable view on complex variability.

The increased manageability of feature modeling opens up a range of additional areas of application: it can assist in scoping the product line, i.e. in deciding what different products should be on offer and which characteristics they should have, it can be used as a means of communication between various actors of development, such as management, marketing, development, sales or even clients and it can support domain analysis in general. In the last case, features play a significantly different role than in the other cases: they are used as "coarse-grained requirements" here.

In summary the main objectives of feature modeling in the context of product line engineering are:

- Define the variability of the product line, i.e. list the characteristics in which the products differ from one another,

- Provide a basis for configuration of individual products,

- Make complex variability manageable by providing a clear, orderly view on the variability,

- Provide a means of communication between diverse actors, including non-technical personnel (e.g. management, marketing, development, sales, OEM vs. suppliers, clients) and

- Support for product line scoping and domain analysis in general (features as "coarse-grained requirements").

The advanced areas of application listed in the last two items rely on additional information in the feature model. Instead of only documenting the variable characteristics, the feature model also needs to capture important common characteristics of the product line, i.e. such characteristics present in all products. These areas of application are the reason for incorporating commonality in feature modeling, thus leading to variability/commonality modeling (as announced in Section 3.2).

Interestingly, these two advanced applications of feature modeling do not even rely on variability. Even if a completely invariable software is to be built, feature modeling can be a valuable tool for domain analysis: the feature model is only used to define implementation alternatives considered temporarily during the analysis phase and therefore only a single configuration of the feature model will actually be built and delivered in the course of the development project.

4.2 A Brief History of Feature Modeling

The basic idea of characterizing configurable entities with a set of so-called "features", which may or may not be present in the entity's individual configurations, is so elementary that it has countless precursors in many domains of computer science. For example, AND-OR graphs used in artificial intelligence to represent problem decompositions [Hal73] show significant similarities to feature models [CHE05a]. The same applies to functional unification grammars

4.3. What is a Feature anyway?

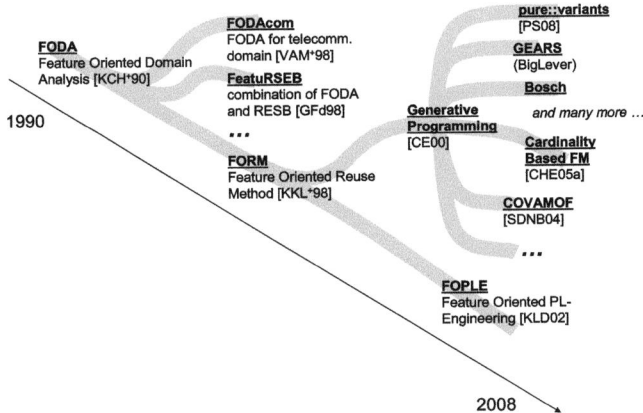

Figure 4.2: A selection of feature modeling approaches proposed in literature.

[Kay79, KB82], which were introduced in the late seventies of the last century by the computer linguistics community. The term "feature" was established in this context by Smolka with *feature logics* [Smo88], a variation and refinement of unification grammars.

However, the actual idea of feature *modeling*, based on feature diagrams with a graphical, tree-like notation, was introduced by Kang et al. in 1990 [KCH+90]. Their FODA methodology extended the focus from merely defining a configuration space to aspects such as visualization, organization, or assisting the communication between stakeholders. It was extremely influential and forms the major root of today's research on feature modeling in the product line engineering community [Bat05a, SHTB06].

Figure 4.2 gives and impression of the numerous refinements and extensions to the initial FODA technique and how they relate to each other. Of course, this picture is strongly simplified but shows nicely the line of research on which this thesis was mainly based: the initial FODA technique, the notational refinements in [CE00] and, most importantly, the integration in cardinality based feature modeling by Czarnecki et al. [CHE05a].

The individual modeling means provided by the feature modeling techniques proposed in literature—such alternative features or parameterized features—will be presented and discussed in detail below in Section 4.4. An in depth survey of the techniques themselves, their differences and how they evolved is not required here; it can be found in [SHTB07].

4.3 What is a Feature anyway?

But before presenting feature modeling concepts in detail, we first give a short discussion of the term *feature*, being the basis of all feature modeling. When speaking to engineers and practitioners during the early phases of adopting feature modeling and product line techniques, a considerable uncertainty and discontent with the notion of features and feature modeling can be recognized. The main criticism is that the term feature has a very fuzzy, unclear meaning or that there are many different forms of understanding the term feature within the automotive industry or even within a single company. This often leads to attempts to provide the term feature with a more concrete, specific meaning, for example "a component", "a function", "a customer-visible functional requirement", etc. While such specializations or clarifications can be of value in certain circumstances, the author believes that they are very problematic on a general, company-wide level and lead to a misuse of feature modeling, because the broad meaning of the term feature is closely related to the strength of the approach.

Just as variability modeling in general, also feature modeling is aimed at presenting an overview of the commonality and variability between the products of a product line and at supporting product configuration (Section 3.2, 4.1). But in contrast to decision tables and decision trees/graphs, feature modeling does not focus on the decisions to be taken during configuration and the resulting effects on the variable artifacts (Section 3.4). Instead, the focus of feature modeling directly lies on the differences and similarities of the product line's individual products. More concretely, feature models list all important characteristics of the individual products and state whether these characteristics are common to all products—i.e. each and every product shows the given characteristic—or are variable from one product to another—i.e. some products show this characteristic while others do not. Since the characteristics in which the products may differ from one another can be of very diverse nature (as will be exemplified in detail below in Section 4.6), we need a highly abstract term to refer to these characteristics, namely the term feature. And this is the reason why it is a good thing that it has such a broad meaning.

Therefore, the term feature should be defined with a broad meaning:

> **Definition 7.** A feature is a characteristic or trait in the broadest sense that an individual product instance of a product line may or may not possess. □

Several conclusions from this definition are to be stated:

- A feature is either present in a product instance or is not ; this means during product configuration it can be selected or deselected,

- A feature does not necessarily correspond to a sub-system or to a hardware or software component (features *may* correspond to a sub-system, e.g. "climate control" or "anti-blocking system", but this need not be the case, e.g. for a feature such as "low energy consumption"),

- A feature need not represent a certain functionality of the system, i.e. it is not necessarily a functional requirement, and

- A feature need not be customer visible.

The second last item, a feature need not represent a certain functionality, is of particular importance because it is in sharp conflict with common language use of this term, as for example in: "The iPhone has several novel features not seen before in mobile phones.".

Another important conclusion from the term's high level of abstraction is that a feature only denotes the fact that something is variable or common, it does not describe how it varies. A feature is merely a place-holder or a tag for some variability which needs to be defined elsewhere. Following the classic definition of a requirement as a definition of what is needed and not how it is realized [Dav89, WDT76], it can be stated that ...

4.4. Traditional Concepts in Feature Modeling

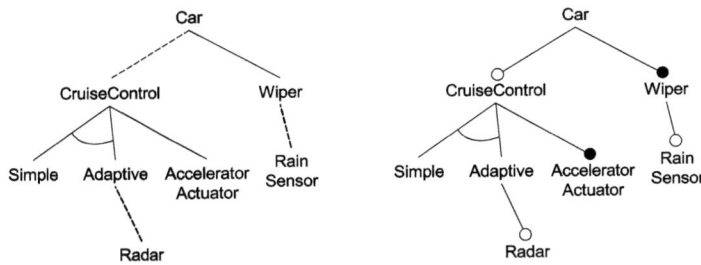

Figure 4.3: Example of a basic feature model in two alternative notations.

Definition 8. A feature only describes *what* is variable, not *how* this variability is realized. □

This observation corresponds to the distinction between variability dimension and artifact dimension and, accordingly, to the distinction of product-line level variability and artifact level variability.

In summary, the extreme broadness of the term feature is due to the high level of abstraction at which feature modeling takes place. This is the strength of feature modeling and otherwise—if the term feature would have a more precise meaning—feature modeling would not be able to serve its purpose as identified above in Section 4.1.

4.4 Traditional Concepts in Feature Modeling

We now have a clear idea of the purpose of feature modeling and its role in product line engineering and have a precise, albeit highly abstract definition of the term feature. We can now turn to a brief survey of the various concepts for feature modeling as they are traditionally proposed in literature.

4.4.1 Basic Concepts

The purpose of feature models is to show the common and variable features of the product line's product instances in a graphical presentation. Basic feature models in the form of feature trees were introduced by Kang et al. in 1990 [KCH+90]. Figure 4.3 shows an example of the same small feature tree in two common notations. The features are represented as the tree's nodes, e.g. CruiseControl or Wiper. Sometimes, the root node is seen as a special entity and referred to as the *concept*. But recently this became unpopular because it introduces a special case without true need.

Features are hierarchically structured: a *parent feature* may have one or more *child features*, which are connected with lines from parent to child. On a semantic level, this means that a child feature may only be present if the parent feature is. Therefore, the parent-child-relations and the feature tree's hierarchy induced by them can be seen as a special notation for some—not all—dependencies between features.

Child features that need to be present in all product instances that contain their parent are called *mandatory features* and are denoted with a solid line to their parent or a filled circle (e.g.

Wiper). It is very important to notice that mandatory features are not in all cases obligatory in the sense that they are present in all product instances of the product line. For example, Wiper is present in all product instances while AcceleratorActuator is only present in such products that have a CruiseControl (but in all of these). As a general rule, a mandatory feature represents a commonality, i.e. it is present in all product instances, if and only if all its ancestors are mandatory. Conversely, *optional features* are features that are present only in some product instances that contain their parent and thus need to be directly selected or deselected during configuration. They are denoted with a dashed line to their parent or an empty circle (e.g. CruiseControl, Radar, RainSensor). Optional features never represent commonality. In addition, two or more children of the same parent that mutually exclude each other are called *alternative features*. Their parent-child-relations are connected with an arc (e.g. Simple and Adaptive as two alternative forms of the Wiper). Precisely speaking, of two or more alternative features exactly one must be present in a product instance if and only if their parent is present. Therefore, during configuration, when the parent is selected, one of the alternative children must be chosen.

Consequently, the two semantically identical feature models shown in Figure 4.3 are to be interpreted in the following way: A car always has a wiper and may optionally have a cruise control. The wiper may come with a rain sensor. The cruise control always needs an electrical actuator in order to be able to influence acceleration. There are two alternative forms of cruise control: a simple one that simply keeps acceleration on a constant level and an adaptive one that keeps vehicle speed at a constant level (e.g. by increasing acceleration when the car drives up a slope). In addition, the car may be equipped with a radar. In that case, vehicle speed will be reduced when the distance to the car in advance falls below a certain threshold. Note that not all information given here is captured in the feature model. For example the meaning of the advanced cruise control is not obvious. Such information will be provided in a feature's textual description (not shown in the figure).

Finally, additional dependencies between features may be defined in a feature tree in the form of *feature links*. These usually serve to further constrain the set of valid configurations. For example, if the radar and the rain sensor used the same installation space in the vehicle's body, this could be defined with a feature link denoted by a bi-directional arrow between RainSensor and Radar labeled with "excludes". Feature modeling techniques differ a lot in what types of dependency links they provide and some simply leave this open. Typical types of dependencies are "excludes" (bidirectional) and "needs" (unidirectional). If feature A excludes B then A may not be present if B is and vice versa. If feature A needs feature B then A may not be present if B is missing but B may be present without A. Other feature links may give an advice to the user during configuration, e.g. if feature A "suggests" B this means you can select A without B, but you should have a good reason to do so.

In the remainder of this section, several advanced feature modeling concepts will be described. These can be seen as an optional add-on to basic feature modeling.

4.4.2 Cardinality Based Feature Modeling

An important extension to basic feature modeling is *cardinality based feature modeling*. Cardinalities for features were proposed by Czarnecki et al. in [CUE02] and feature groups with a cardinality were introduced by Riebisch et al. in [RBSP02]. According to this approach, each feature is assigned a cardinality similar to the cardinalities in UML class diagrams (e.g. [0..1], [1], [0..*], [0..4,8..12]). A cardinality of [0..1] means the corresponding

4.4. Traditional Concepts in Feature Modeling

Table 4.1: Meaning of common cardinalities.

Cardinality	Meaning for	
	Feature f	Feature Group g
$[0..1]$	f is optional	optional XOR
$[1]$	f is mandatory	exclusive or (XOR)
$[1..*]$		inclusive or (OR)
$[i..j]$	f can be built into the product n times with $i \leq n \leq j$	n features out of the list of grouped features can be built into the product with $i \leq n \leq j$
$[*]$	like above but with $n \in \mathcal{N}$	

feature is optional (e.g. CruiseControl and Radar in Figure 4.4), [1] means the feature is mandatory and a maximum cardinality greater than 1 means the feature may appear more than once in a single product instance. Several child features of the same parent may be grouped in a *feature group*. These feature groups also have a cardinality, stating how many features of the corresponding group must/can be selected for a single product instance. For example, a group cardinality of [1] means that exactly one of the group's features needs to be selected whenever their parent is selected (e.g. Simple and Adaptive in Figure 4.4). This corresponds to alternative features in basic feature models. Consequently, the traditional concepts of optional, mandatory, and alternative features can be all expressed with the single common concept of cardinality, which is summarized in Table 4.1.

Apart from this conciseness in its means of expression, the main contribution of cardinality-based feature modeling is to be seen in features with a maximum cardinality greater than 1, which are called *cloned features*. During configuration, such features may be selected more than once. In that case, the cloned feature's descendants may be configured separately for each selection of the cloned feature. For example, feature Wiper in Figure 4.4 must be selected at least once (the front wiper) but may also be selected twice (a front and a rear wiper). In the latter case, the decision whether to equip the wiper with a rain sensor can be taken separately for the front and rear wiper. In the box on the right side of Figure 4.4 this is illustrated with the means of basic feature modeling. However, notice the subtle differences between the two presentations: the cardinality based notation does not include the information that the two Wiper features represent the front and the rear wiper and that the mandatory one is the front wiper. In addition, dependencies between the two wiper configurations—for example the rear wiper may only be equipped with a rain sensor if the front wiper also has one, as defined by the "needs" link in the figure—cannot be expressed easily with cardinality based feature modeling.

For maximum cardinalities of 2 or 3 and sometimes maybe 4, the concept of cloned features can easily be exchanged with basic feature modeling concepts. For greater top cardinalities this is also possible in principle, but the feature models grow very large and highly redundant in these cases. For a top cardinality of * (infinite, i.e. the feature may be selected any number of times) this is no longer possible, of course. Therefore, cloned features are primarily intended for other things than a front and a rear wiper. A typical example where cloned features become particularly useful is the configuration of several electrical control units (ECUs) in a CAN network together with their operating systems, installed drivers and software tasks on application layer.

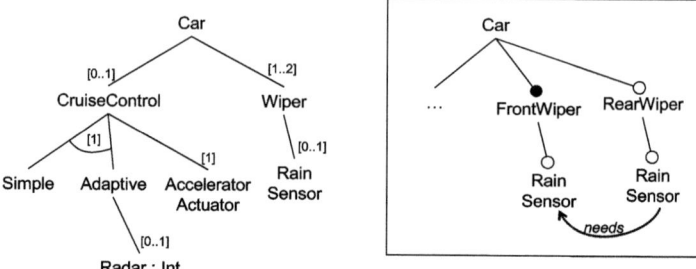

Figure 4.4: Example of a feature model with advanced concepts.

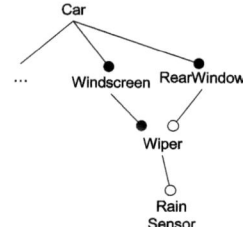

Figure 4.5: Example of a feature with more than one parent.

4.4.3 Features with Several Parents

An advanced feature modeling concept with similar objectives and consequences as cloned features are *features with more than one parent*. With this concept, feature trees are turned into directed acyclic graphs. The child feature can be optional with respect to one parent while at the same time being mandatory with respect to another parent. A feature f with n parents that is mandatory with respect to n_{man} of these parents ($n_{man} \leq n$) can be interpreted as a feature with a cardinality of $[n_{man} \ldots n]$. For example, Wiper in Figure 4.5 is a child of both Windscreen and RearWindow. The wind screen always has a wiper, whereas the wiper for the rear window is optional. Just as is the case with cloned features, the feature Wiper, when selected more than once, will be configured separately each time it is selected. This means that in the example the wiper of the wind screen may have a rain sensor while the one of the rear window has not and vice versa.

Most problems of cloned features described above also apply to features with multiple parents. An important difference is that multi-parent features are provided with more semantic meaning, because they are anchored below different parents, as can be seen in Figure 4.5.

4.4.4 Parameterized Features

Furthermore, a feature may have a single *attribute* of a certain type and is then called an *attributed feature* (initially proposed in [Bed02, CUE02]). This attribute is of an entirely different nature than a feature's basic attributes like name and description: while the values of the latter are specified during the definition of the feature tree, the value of an attributed feature is specified during the process of feature selection and is thus becoming a constituent of the product configuration, not the feature model definition. Consequently, an attributed feature not only has the states "selected" or "not selected" during product configuration—meaning that it will be built into the product or not—but also a value which is set if and only if the feature is selected and may be a string, integer or float. Other types are also conceivable and frequently proposed.

Unfortunately, this common terminology makes it easy to confuse the different kinds of attributes, namely basic attributes (such as name and description) and non-basic feature attributes. Therefore the non-basic attributes should rather be referred to as *parameters* and to features having such parameters as *parameterized features*.

An example of a parameterized feature is given in Figure 4.4. Feature `Radar` is supplied with a type declaration of `Int` (for integer). When during configuration the radar feature is selected, an integer value has to be provided to specify the minimum distance allowed. The fact that the integer value represents the minimum distance in meters is captured in the feature's documentation, similar as above for cloned features.

Usually, feature parameterization is defined such that a single feature may only have a single parameter (not several), which frequently is a source of criticism of automotive engineers. The rational for this restriction is that when a feature needs more than one parameter, it is preferable to add a child feature for each parameter instead of directly attaching the parameters to a single feature. Otherwise, information captured in the separation of the individual parameters would be "hidden" in the list of parameters even though this is usually information suitable to be captured in the feature model itself. According to the experience from the cooperation with Daimler AG, on which this thesis is based, this is true in most cases; but there are situations where the additional child features seem very artificial. Therefore it can be concluded that there are good reasons for both solutions and thus it is mainly a matter of taste and preference.

4.4.5 Other Advanced Feature Modeling Concepts

Many other concepts for feature modeling have been proposed in literature. For example, the feature tree's edges—i.e. the parent-child-relations—may be typed in order to specify whether the child is a specialization (`Simple` and `Advanced` in the above examples) or a part of the parent (`CruiseControl` and `Wiper`). Also, features may be organized in several layers of refinement. Further details of advanced feature modeling concepts are beyond this overview.

4.5 Formalization of Feature Modeling Concepts: The CVM Approach

A textual description of basic and advanced feature modeling concepts, as provided in the previous section, will always remain inexact, leaving important details unspecified. Unfortunately, many feature modeling approaches proposed in literature are only defined in this form and therefore suffer from such an imprecision (as pointed out and substantiated with several examples in [SHTB06]). In the context of this thesis, in which the novel concepts of subscoping and configuration links shall be introduced and precisely defined, such vagueness is unbearable; a sound formalization of a concrete feature modeling approach is required as a basis for the discussions in Parts II and III.

A range of different formalizations for features and feature models have already been proposed in literature. They differ in what mathematical theory is used as a basis (e.g. plain set theory, formal languages), which feature modeling concepts are covered, and in the precise syntax and semantics of these individual concepts. In addition, the purpose of such formalizations can differ greatly, for example a formalization may be used only to precisely define the details of a feature modeling approach or it may be intended to provide input for some tool framework, such as constraint checkers, in order to perform various analyses on the models. An early overview of various feature modeling formalizations was given in [Bat05b] (accompanied by the technical report [Bat05a]). A more up-to-date overview of existing formalizations including a comprehensive survey of differences in the approaches' syntax and semantics can be found in [SHTB07].

Unfortunately, all of the available feature modeling formalizations proved insufficient for the purpose of this thesis. Most importantly, no comprehensive and sound formalization of cardinality-based feature modeling, esp. cloned features, was available at the time of preparation of this thesis, as shown by Schobbens et al. [SHTB07]. In addition, most existing feature modeling approaches tend to specialize the syntax and semantics to fit a specific application area or a certain vision of how feature modeling is to be employed. In contrast, an important design goal of the formalization presented in this section was to make the approach as flexible and generic as possible, such that most feature modeling approaches proposed in literature can be seen as a special case of it. This way, it will be straightforward to apply the concepts of subscoping and configuration links, which will be defined as an extension of that flexible approach, to most preexisting feature modeling approaches from literature. For all these reasons a new formalization of feature modeling is given here, which, of course, constitutes a new feature modeling approach in its own right, called **CVM**.

In summary, this section serves two purposes: it (1) shows exemplarily how to precisely formalize the feature modeling concepts described narratively in the previous section and, at the same time, (2) presents a novel feature modeling approach called **CVM**, that served as the basis of the definition of subscoping and configuration links and was implemented as part of the prototypical variability management framework presented later in Chapter 17.

4.5.1 Formal Syntax of Basic Feature Models

Let $\mathcal{F}$ be the set of all features. Then, to define a feature model FM out of the set of all feature models $\mathcal{FM}$, we start with an ordered 4-tuple $FM = (F, Parent, Man, Alt)$ with

$$\begin{aligned} F &\subseteq \mathcal{F} \\ Parent &\subseteq F \times F \\ Man &\subseteq F \\ Alt &\subseteq F \times F \end{aligned} \quad (4.1)$$

F is the set of features in feature model FM, the relation $Parent$ relates parent features to their children, Man is the set of mandatory features in FM, and Alt relates alternative siblings to each other. To denote the feature model in cases where this is not obvious we write F_{FM}, $Parent_{FM}$, and so on. For a feature $f \in \mathcal{F}$ we define

$$f \in FM \iff f \in F_{FM} \quad (4.2)$$

4.5. Formalization of Feature Modeling Concepts: The CVM Approach

and f is called a feature of the feature model FM. Note that we do not require F to be non-empty; a feature model with an empty set of features is called an empty feature model (non-empty respectively).

For each $(p, c) \in Parent$ the feature p is called the parent of feature c and c is called a child of p. $Parent$ is required to be irreflexive and asymmetric:

$$\forall f \in F : (f, f) \notin Parent \tag{4.3}$$
$$\forall f_1, f_2 \in F : (f_1, f_2) \in Parent \Rightarrow (f_2, f_1) \notin Parent \tag{4.4}$$

Also a feature may not have more than one parent, so it is required that

$$\forall p_a, p_b, c \in F : (p_a, c) \in Parent \land (p_b, c) \in Parent \Rightarrow p_a = p_b \tag{4.5}$$

which means that $Parent$ must be injective. A feature $f \in FM$ with

$$\nexists\, p \in F : (p, f) \in Parent \tag{4.6}$$

is called a root feature, one with

$$\nexists\, c \in F : (f, c) \in Parent \tag{4.7}$$

a leaf feature. This also means that $Parent$ will usually neither be left-total nor surjective. For convenience, we define the properties $isRoot \subseteq F$ and $isLeaf \subseteq F$ as

$$isRoot(f) \iff \nexists\, p \in F : (p, f) \in Parent \tag{4.8}$$
$$isLeaf(f) \iff \nexists\, c \in F : (f, c) \in Parent \tag{4.9}$$

Based on $Parent$ we can define a relation $Predecessor \subseteq F \times F$ as

$$(p, s) \in Predecessor \iff \begin{array}{l}(p, s) \in Parent \lor \\ \exists c \in F : (p, c) \in Parent \land (c, s) \in Predecessor\end{array} \tag{4.10}$$

Obviously $Predecessor$ is not injective. We can now postulate our final requirement on $Parent$ by stating that it has to be defined such that $Predecessor$ is asymmetric.

The above restrictions on $Parent$ can be elegantly expressed by lending terminology from graph theory [GY05, Ste07]. To do so, we consider the directed graph G defined by $G = (F_{FM}, Parent_{FM})$, called G_{FM} in the following. This graph will not be connected in all cases, because we want allow to have more than one root feature, as stated above. Consequently, we cannot say that G_{FM} is a tree. However, the connected components of G_{FM} are trees or, more precisely, directed out-trees. Formally, we state that for each connected component $C = (V_C, E_C)$ of G_{FM} it is

$$|V_C| - 1 = |E_C| \tag{4.11}$$

In summary, by applying another term from graph theory, it all comes down to requiring that $Parent$ is defined such that G_{FM} is a (directed) forest.

The subset Man of F is the set of mandatory features in FM. It suggests itself to call a feature mandatory if and only if it is contained in Man, and optional otherwise. Some feature modeling techniques require

$$isRoot(f) \implies f \in Man \tag{4.12}$$

but technically this is not necessary and from a methodological point of view it makes sense to allow root features and thus complete feature trees that are optional, especially if several root features in a single feature model are allowed (as in the above definition).

The binary relation *Alt* defines alternative siblings. By using the term "sibling" here we imply that the following must be required:

$$(f_1, f_2) \in Alt \land f_1 \neq f_2 \implies \exists p \in F : (p, f_1) \in Parent \land (p, f_2) \in Parent \quad (4.13)$$

This means that alternative features must have a parent, i.e. must not be root features, and must be children of the same parent. In addition, we require:

$$\forall f_1, f_2, f_3 \in F_{FM} : (f_1, f_2) \in Alt \land (f_1, f_3) \in Alt \implies (f_2, f_3) \in Alt \quad (4.14)$$

i.e. *Alt* must be euclidean and therefore will always be symmetric and transitive. Note that *Alt* being euclidean does not follow from proposition (4.13), because this does not model the "is sibling of" relation but only requires alternative features to be siblings.

In principle these requirements on *Alt* would suffice. In particular we do not necessarily have to require *Alt* to be reflexive. However, when formalizing feature groups below, we will find it extremely helpful to apply terminology associated with equivalence relations, and therefore—for the sake of consistency—we choose to demand reflexivity also here. This means we not only require *Alt* to be euclidean but to be an equivalence relation.

In summary, we obtain the following definition.

Definition 9. A *basic feature model* is an ordered 4-tuple

$$FM = (F, Parent, Man, Alt)$$

which meets the following requirements. F is a finite set, called the set of features in FM. *Parent* is a binary relation over F such that the graph $G_{FM} = (F, Parent)$ is a forest of directed out-trees. *Man* is a subset of F, the set of mandatory features in FM, and *Alt* is an equivalence relation over F with

$$(f_1, f_2) \in Alt \land f_1 \neq f_2 \implies \exists p \in F : (p, f_1) \in Parent \land (p, f_2) \in Parent$$

For F, *Parent*, *Man*, and *Alt* we also write F_{FM}, $Parent_{FM}$, Man_{FM}, and Alt_{FM} respectively. □

The main purpose of this definition is to provide a basis for the formalization of the concepts proposed later in Parts II and III. To further facilitate these discussions two additional partial convenience functions are introduced here:

$$\begin{aligned} parentOf \quad &: \quad F \to F \\ p = parentOf(c) \quad &\iff \quad (p, c) \in Parent \end{aligned} \quad (4.15)$$

and

$$\begin{aligned} childrenOf \quad &: \quad F \to \Pi(F) \\ c \in childrenOf(p) \quad &\iff \quad (p, c) \in Parent \end{aligned} \quad (4.16)$$

with $\Pi(M)$ being the power set of an arbitrary set M, as will be defined in a moment below in equation (4.18). Together, these two functions provide a concise means to denote a feature's parent and children.

4.5. Formalization of Feature Modeling Concepts: The CVM Approach

4.5.2 Formal Syntax of Advanced Feature Models

In order to reach a formal explanation of advanced feature models, let us start with parameterization. Given a basic feature model FM, the partial function $Type_{FM}$ is defined as

$$Type_{FM} \ : \ F_{FM} \rightarrow \Pi(\mathcal{V}) \setminus \phi \quad (4.17)$$

$$\Pi(M) \ = \ \{U \mid U \subseteq M\} \quad (4.18)$$

with $\mathcal{V}$ being the set of all possible values of parameterized features. At this point we do not really need to know anything about the contents of $\mathcal{V}$, but usually we will have something like

$$\mathcal{V} = \mathbb{R} \cup \Sigma^* \quad (4.19)$$

with Σ^* being the set of finite sequences of elements from the alphabet Σ including the empty word ϵ. A feature $f \in FM$ is called a *parameterized feature* if and only if

$$\exists \, (f, T) \in Type_{FM} \quad (4.20)$$

and then T is called the type of f, written as $Type_{FM}(f)$. As a shorthand we define

$$isParameterized(f) \Longleftrightarrow \exists \, (f, T) \in Type_{FM} \quad (4.21)$$

Similarly, cardinalities of features in a feature model FM can be defined with a function $Card_{FM}$:

$$Card_{FM} : F_{FM} \rightarrow \mathcal{C} \quad (4.22)$$

Note that $Card_{FM}$ is required to be left-total. $\mathcal{C}$ denotes the set of all legal cardinalities. The simplest definition for $\mathcal{C}$ is

$$\mathcal{C} = \Pi(\mathbb{N}_0) \setminus \phi \quad (4.23)$$

i.e. a cardinality is simply a non-empty set of natural numbers. A more constructive formalization, closer to a possible implementation of feature modeling concepts, is defined by the following grammar given here in an extended Backus-Naur-form (EBNF):

$$Cardinality \longrightarrow \text{"} [\text{"} \ Interval \ (\text{"} , \text{"} \ Interval \ )* \ \text{"}] \text{"} \quad (4.24a)$$

$$Interval \longrightarrow [\ Number \ \text{"}..\text{"} \ ] \ (\ Number \ | \ \text{"} * \text{"} \ ) \quad (4.24b)$$

$$Number \longrightarrow (\ \text{"0"} \ | \ \text{"1"} \ | \ ... \ | \ \text{"9"} \ )\!\!+ \quad (4.24c)$$

Of course, not all words defined by this grammar are legal cardinalities. For example, the numbers in the intervals must appear in ascending order and the Kleene star should only appear in the last interval.

To easily distinguish several special cases with respect to a feature's cardinality we define

$$isOptional(f) \Longleftrightarrow Card_{FM}(f) = [0..1] \quad (4.25)$$

$$isMandatory(f) \Longleftrightarrow Card_{FM}(f) = [1] \quad (4.26)$$

$$\begin{aligned} isCloned(f) \Longleftrightarrow \ &\neg isOptional(f) \ \wedge \ \neg isMandatory(f) \ \wedge \\ &\neg \ Card_{FM}(f) = [0] \end{aligned} \quad (4.27)$$

with feature $f \in FM$. Note that $isCloned(f)$ is true exactly in those cases where the maximum cardinality is greater than 1.

To allow for feature inheritance, i.e. one feature inheriting the child features of another feature (which in literature is often called feature reference as mentioned above), we provide a relation

$$Inherit_{FM} \subseteq F_{FM} \times F_{FM} \tag{4.28}$$

and say for $(f_i, f) \in Inherit_{FM}$ that feature f_i inherits from feature f. Apparently we allow for multiple inheritance since we do not require $Inherit$ to be right-definite. But $Inherit$ has to meet several other requirements, in particular no cycles may appear in the inheritance tree of a feature. Inheritance is known to define a directed acyclic graph when multiple inheritance is allowed, because a single feature may then inherit from several other features and, as always, several features may inherit from a single, common feature which means that a tree structure is out of the question. Bearing in mind the above discussion on the *parent* relation, we can concisely express this by stating that the graph defined by

$$G_{FM}^{Inh} = (F_{FM}, Inherit_{FM}) \tag{4.29}$$

must be a directed acyclic graph, often also called an acyclic digraph or a DAG. We could in addition demand that G_{FM}^{Inh} satisfies

$$G_{FM}^{Inh} = R(G_{FM}^{Inh}) \tag{4.30}$$

with $R(G)$ being the transitive reduction of a graph G (see [PS03]). That way "shortcuts" in the inheritance relations of a feature would be forbidden. However, such shortcuts do no harm given the semantic of inheritance we described above informally (i.e. the inheriting feature inherits the children of the features it is directly or indirectly inheriting from) because if a feature is inherited twice it will nevertheless be added only once to the set of children[1]. Also, such shortcuts are usually allowed in programming languages that provide (multiple) inheritance and allowing them helps keep the definition of advanced feature models minimal. Therefore this additional requirement is dismissed here.

The last advanced feature modeling concept we want to provide a formalization for is that of feature groups. In fact, we already defined groups of features through *Alt*. The only difference is that we now have to also provide a cardinality for each group. So, similarly as for *Alt* above, we define for a feature model *FM* a relation *Group* with

$$Group_{FM} \subseteq F_{FM} \times F_{FM} \tag{4.31}$$

and require it to be an equivalence relation. In order to provide a cardinality for each feature group, we enlarge the domain of *Card* by the quotient set of F_{FM} by *Group*. We then get

$$Card_{FM} : F_{FM} \cup F_{FM}/Group \setminus \{M \mid |M| = 1\} \to \mathcal{C} \tag{4.32}$$

Now it becomes obvious why it is a good idea to require *Group* (and for consistency also *Alt* above) to be reflexive and, consequently, an equivalence relation. For a feature $f \in FM$ we can call its equivalence class of F_{FM} by *Group* the *feature group* of f in *FM* and, by applying standard notation for equivalence classes, we can write $[f]_{Group}$ for it. Similarly, the quotient set of F_{FM} by *Group* represents the set of all such feature groups in *FM* and can be denoted by $F_{FM}/Group$. A feature $f \in FM$ is called a *grouped feature* if and only if

$$|[f]_{Group}| > 1 \tag{4.33}$$

---

[1] Of course, when providing a formal semantic we would need to make sure that this is actually the case. Later in Chapter 13 this will be taken care of in proposition (13.25).

4.5. Formalization of Feature Modeling Concepts: The CVM Approach

i.e. if it is grouped with other features.

In an overall definition of advanced feature models, *Group* and *Card* then replace *Alt* and *Man* respectively while *Inherit* and *Type* need to be added. We thus obtain

Definition 10. An *advanced feature model* is an ordered 6-tuple

$$FM = (F, Parent, Inherit, Group, Card, Type)$$

with the following properties. F is a finite set, called the set of features in FM. *Parent* is a binary relation over F such that the graph $G_{FM} = (F, Parent)$ is a forest of directed out-trees. The binary relation *Inherit* over F defines inheritance relationships such that the graph $G_{FM}^{Inh} = (F, Inherit)$ is an acyclic digraph. *Group* is an equivalence relation over F with

$$(f_1, f_2) \in Group \land f_1 \neq f_2 \implies \exists p \in F : (p, f_1) \in Parent \land (p, f_2) \in Parent$$

and $[f]_{Group}$ is called the feature group or simply group of f. Given $\mathcal{C}$ as the set of all valid cardinalities, the (left-total) function $Card_{FM} : F \cup F/Group \setminus \{M \mid |M| = 1\} \to \mathcal{C}$ defines cardinalities for features and groups. With $\mathcal{V}$ as the set of all legal values, the partial function $Type_{FM} : F \to \Pi(\mathcal{V}) \setminus \phi$ defines types of parameterized features: for each $(f, T) \in Type$, f is called a parameterized feature and T is called the type of f. □

Again, it is a good idea to provide some additional constructs for convenience. Since all features within a single feature group have the same parent, it makes sense to perceive this parent feature as the group's parent and define a function to obtain such a group's parent:

$$\begin{aligned} parentOf \quad &: \quad F_{FM}/Group \to F_{FM} \\ f = parentOf(g) &\iff \exists f' \in g : (f, f') \in Parent \end{aligned} \quad (4.34)$$

For $(g, f) \in parentOf$ we call f the(!) *parent* of group g and g a(!) *child group* of f. It was possible to reuse the function name from equation (4.15) due to different domains in both cases; we thus have two versions of *parentOf*, one for features and another for groups. We can now define a function to obtain the set of all child groups of a given feature as

$$\begin{aligned} childGroupsOf \quad &: \quad F_{FM} \to \Pi(F_{FM}/Group) \\ g \in childGroupsOf(f) &\iff f = parentOf(g) \end{aligned} \quad (4.35)$$

Obviously leaf features do not have any child groups.

4.5.3 Formal Semantics of Feature Models

The great relevance of a solid formal definition of feature modeling semantics was pointed out in [SHTB06]. However, the formalization of feature models presented here is only intended to provide a basis for the definition of the new concepts proposed later in this thesis, not as a general discussion of alternative feature modeling formalizations proposed in literature. And since an important characteristic of multi-level feature models (as introduced in Part II) is that they can be defined on a purely syntactical level, the formalization of feature modeling semantics can be postponed until Chapter 13 in Part III, where configuration links will be defined and formal semantics will be needed for the first time.

50   Chapter 4. Feature Modeling

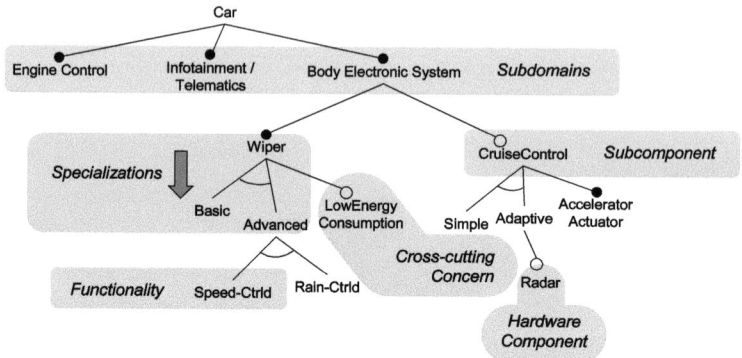

Figure 4.6: Examples showing the broadness of the term "feature".

4.6 What is a Feature? (Revisited)

In Section 4.3 above, the high level of abstraction of the term "feature" was emphasized and it was stated that this broadness is a prerequisite to raising the full potential of feature modeling. Now, after having discussed the concepts of feature modeling techniques, we are in a position to revisit this issue and provide examples.

Figure 4.6 shows a sample feature model in which the various uses of a feature are indicated. One of these is of particular interest, because it shows best the importance of being aware of the broadness of the term feature: the use as a cross-cutting concern. If a modeler has in mind a more restricted idea of a feature, for example a feature being something like a component or "function", he will usually model the variability of Wiper with respect to energy consumption by introducing two variants of each Basic, Speed-Ctrld and Rain-Ctrld, leading to a highly redundant model. With the high abstractness in mind, one can factor out this cross-cutting variability by introducing a single feature LowEnergyConsumption directly below Wiper. It is exactly at this point where feature modeling's high level of abstraction shows its significance.

Another important issue of feature modeling is its great degree of freedom in expressing variability. The above CruiseControl for example could also be modeled in several alternative ways without significantly changing the model's meaning. One possibility might be to not have two alternative features Simple and Adaptive but a single, optional feature called SpeedAdaptation together with a dependency link from Radar to SpeedAdaptation, as shown in Figure 4.7. This great degree of freedom in feature modeling is closely related to the broadness of the notion of a feature. It is often a source of discontent among practitioners. However, such a freedom of expression is also found in most other areas of modeling, even if it is in many cases probably not as extensive. And it is relatively easy to cope with this peculiarity as long as the modeler is aware of it and keeps in mind that he should not look out for a single correct solution among many wrong ones but instead simply aim for a solution that best reflects his vision of the variability at hand.

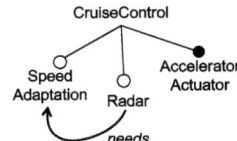

Figure 4.7: Alternative feature model with mainly the same meaning.

4.7 Discussion

The various feature modeling concepts described above are of very different usefulness in the automotive domain. Benefits and weaknesses of individual modeling concepts from the perspective of the automotive domain have been discussed above. As a rough guidance in general, it can be recommended to confine oneself to basic feature modeling whenever possible. The only exception is feature parameterization, which is probably indispensable and useful in most use cases of automotive feature modeling and does not introduce too much additional modeling complexity. Cloned features are very useful in some situations (e.g. ECU network configuration, as described above), but should be used sparingly and only at those points in a feature model, where they are truly necessary, due to the intricacies associated with this concept.

Chapter 5

Applying Product-Line Engineering in the Automotive Domain

After having examined an individual variability modeling technique in the previous chapter, we can now return to the overall organization of product-line oriented development. We will thus take up the discussion from Chapter 3, but in contrast to the general viewpoint there will now focus on the specific characteristics and needs of software-intensive automotive systems and adapt the big picture presented in that chapter accordingly.

5.1 Characteristics of the Automotive Domain

Naturally, before doing so, the first step must be a thorough investigation of the characteristics and needs of the automotive domain with respect to variability and product line engineering, which will be presented in this section. Other characterizations of the automotive domain can be found in [WW02] and [Gri03], but they are not focused on variability. A slightly modified version of the following analysis will appear in [RW08].

Most of the following observations are arguably each applicable to various other domains of industrial, software intensive systems, such as medical technology [Wij00] or mobile devices [Bos05]. They are therefore not characteristics of the automotive domain in a strict sense. However, their combination and precise manifestation are quite unique to this domain.

The following characteristics fall into the four categories of system complexity, product line complexity, heterogeneity, and organizational context (summarized in Table 5.1). The following discussion is structured according to these categories.

System Complexity

Multitude of Vehicle Functions. Modern cars comprise a vast number of electronic functions, such as electronic stability control, navigation systems, parking assistance or adaptive cruise control. And the number of these functions is ever increasing, due to an increasing pressure to develop innovative products and an increasing need for product differentiation. For example intelligent engine control systems might use high-precision road maps in the future to predict the optimal parameters for motor management, thus reducing fuel consumption while increasing performance. In addition to the sheer number of vehicle functions, these functions are increasingly interrelated. Fifteen years ago the wiper system, for example, was a more or less isolated subsystem within the car; today, wiping often depends on whether the reverse gear is engaged, whether doors or windows are open or on the vehicle speed.

Table 5.1: Characteristics of automotive software product lines.

System Complexity	Multitude of Vehicle Functions
	Long Product Life-Cycles
	Diverging Scopes and Life-Cycles
Product Line Complexity	Complex Model Ranges
	Enormous Complexity of Artifact-Level Variability
	Complex Resolution of Variability Over Time
	Complex Dependencies Throughout the Process
	Multitude of Orthogonal Views on Variability
Heterogeneity	Heterogeneity of Runtime Environments and Software Styles
	Heterogeneity of Development Artifacts
	Heterogeneity of Methods, Processes and Tools
Organizational Context	Complexity of Organizational Structures
	Manufacturer-Supplier Relationship
	Limited Influence on Processes and Methods
	Incremental Introduction

Long Product Life-Cycles. The life-cycle of a certain generation of an upper-class model usually comprises 3 years of development, 6 years of production and sales and 15 years of operation, maintenance and customer service. This results in an overall product life time of at least 20 to 25 years.

Diverging Scopes and Life-Cycles. The subsystems and subcomponents have diverging scopes and life-cycles. For example, one subsystem like the wiper may be used in A-Class and C-Class models, while another like the climate control may be used in C-Class, E-Class and in some commercial vehicle models (diverging scope). Similarly, subsystems such as a wiper or a brake-by-wire system are usually not only built into several vehicle models produced in parallel but also into several consecutive generations of these models; and often, during the production of one generation of a vehicle model, such a subsystem may even be replaced by another, i.e. the introduction of a new subsystem does not necessarily coincide with the introduction of a new vehicle model. These life-cycles usually differ from one subsystem to another (diverging life-cycles).

The same may apply for individual artifacts. For example the specification of a certain wiper system may be used for A-Class and C-Class models, even if the implementation of the A-Class and C-Class wiper are developed independently from one another, possibly because they are contributed by different suppliers.

Product Line Complexity

Complex Model Ranges. The overall structure of automotive product lines, i.e. the range of vehicle models on offer, is of remarkable complexity, at least for the large global car manufacturers. For example, the product range of such a manufacturer often comprises several brands (e.g. Mercedes-Benz, smart, Maybach, Freightliner, Mitsubishi Fuso and many more in the case of Daimler AG), each possibly divided into divisions such as passenger cars, com-

5.1. Characteristics of the Automotive Domain

mercial vehicles and special vehicles such as taxis or ambulances, and each such division made up of several lines (e.g. A-Class, C-Class, E-Class) and models (e.g. C220, C240). In addition, these models usually have to be delivered in different configurations to the various global markets, such as North-America, Europe, Middle-East and Asia, and they are usually offered in a number of distinct styles (e.g. Classic, Elegance, Sport).

Enormous Complexity of Artifact-Level Variability. In addition to the multitude of vehicle models, each of these models is further customized to address local legislation or different customer needs and expectations, often realized as optional equipment. Other sources of variability include

- Functional differences between and functional constraints of body variants (e.g. limousine, station wagon, etc.) and drive-train variants.
- New technical standards originating from industrial areas which are at best partially controlled by the automotive industry. The main area here is telematics and entertainment, for example with their interface to a wide range of mobile phones.
- Different realization variants on the level of detailed specifications, design models, implementations and testing artifacts, e.g. due to sensor and actuator variants.

For these reasons, a development project of a luxury vehicle today is based on a function kit that includes several thousand technical functions. Based on the above criteria, each of these functions needs to be selected or deselected, which leads to a vast number of variation points within all kinds of development artifacts.

Complex Resolution of Variability Over Time. In the domain of automotive software development, variabilities are bound at different times of the product life cycle, e.g. basic features are selected during development time, country codes are bound during production, and additional pre-installed SW-features may be activated by the after-sales process.

Complex Dependencies Throughout the Process. In the automotive domain, it is very important to support dependencies between variable properties of the system. There are various sources for these dependencies. They can originate form management decisions, they can be based on apparent logical facts (e.g. a delivery vehicle without a rear window has no need for a rear wiper), or they may result from dependencies on the design and implementation level (e.g. different display variants have far-reaching consequences on the functionality offered and the human machine interface of operating the functionality). Some dependencies need to be defined explicitly, e.g. in a feature model, while others can be derived from more detailed specifications or design models. The most important aspects to note about this dependency complexity are:

- Enormous amount of dependencies,
- Dependencies arise and have to be managed on different abstraction levels (e.g. management or marketing decisions vs. technically motivated dependencies on implementation level),
- Derived dependencies need to be distinguished from explicitly defined dependencies,
- Automatic analyses are indispensable due to the overall complexity (esp. consistency checks).

Multitude of Orthogonal Views on Variability. Variability aspects are relevant not only for engineering, but also for management, marketing, production, acquisition and sales, and also the end-customer. However, the different actors and activities involved lead to different needs and expectations. Development engineers, for example, need to work with a much more fine-grained feature model than, say, management. Furthermore, changes in variability on the level of realization decisions should normally not be made visible to marketing and salespeople nor to the end-customer. Another example is the packaging of variability in order to reduce the amount of decisions during the customer-configuration, or to emphasize to the customer certain combinations of functionality. All these circumstances lead to many orthogonal views on the complete system's variability.

Heterogeneity

Heterogeneity of Runtime Environments and Software Styles. The runtime environment of automotive software systems is of a very diverse nature. This applies to both the hardware environment, i.e. the execution unit and communication facilities, as well as the software environment, i.e. the operating system and service layers. In the traditional subdomains of automotive development—namely motor control, power train, body electronics (wiper, climate control, lights, etc.) and entertainment—very different runtime environments are applied. This also profoundly changes the nature of the application software met in the respective fields. Consequently, very diverse styles of software are interacting within a single complete system: motor control software, for example, is a classic case of hard real-time embedded software, whereas telematics software is quite similar in its nature to desktop application software.

Heterogeneity of Development Artifacts. In the automotive area, variation needs to be controlled during the entire life cycle:

- In the development artifacts (esp. analysis, design, and test artifacts),
- In executable code,
- In the production databases,
- In the marketing and sales systems,
- In after-sales systems such as diagnosis and software update systems,
- In all sorts of internal and external documentations (e.g. for service workshops or the end-customer).

There exist now well established tools for specific process aspects, e.g. requirements management, function modeling and change management. Such tools sometimes offer pragmatically grown mechanisms to support variability. This means that a comprehensive approach needs to support projects in which different variability mechanisms are used in different process steps.

Heterogeneity of Methods, Processes and Tools. Owing to the organizational complexity within automotive manufacturers and the distribution of development among a manufacturer and many external suppliers, a multitude of different development methods, processes and—consequently—different tools are involved and need to be integrated within the global

5.1. Characteristics of the Automotive Domain

product line. Sometimes even for a single purpose different methods and tools may be employed within the same company, often for historical reasons. Consequently, an approach for product-line oriented automotive development must be capable of embracing constituents of a highly diverse nature. Future standardization efforts will help to reduce this problem to some extent, but it will remain an important issue, as will be explained below.

Organizational Context

Complexity of Organizational Structures. The organizational context in which automotive development takes place is extremely complex. Industrial groups are usually made up of several subgroups with many divisions, departments and units. Owing to the increasing flexibility of the global economy with its mergers and outsourcing, different departments within the same company may well have diverse backgrounds and traditions. It is therefore a great challenge to introduce product line concepts with their profound impact on overall development organization in such a context.

Manufacturer-Supplier Relationship. Large-scale automotive systems usually integrate a multitude of subsystems and components supplied by third parties. Because each supplier needs to tailor its product line to the needs of several different manufacturers, this product line has to be developed completely orthogonally, leading to a technically intricate manufacturer-supplier interaction. An automotive manufacturer is therefore faced with the necessity to integrate the orthogonal product line strategies of a multitude of suppliers into his own product line strategy.

In addition to these technical intricacies, this interaction is also very sensitive from a strategic and legal point of view: a supplier S will be careful not to reveal all the details of its product line planning to a manufacturer M_1, because this will disclose his strategy as well as parts of the strategies of the other manufacturers M_n the supplier deals with, which are the competitors of M_1. Feature models in particular are an especially sensitive artifact in this context.

Limited Influence on Processes and Methods. The accentuation of heterogeneity above might give the impression that heterogeneity is rather a deficiency of today's industry to be overcome by new, comprehensive development means, instead of being specifically supported by them. Should we not aim to find methodologies that overcome heterogeneity instead of encouraging it? Of course, to some extent this is true, and there are several joint efforts of the automotive industry and research institutions to reduce heterogeneity by means of standardization, for example the AUTOSAR partnership [AUT08] or the European project ATESST [ATE08]. However, heterogeneity will ever remain an issue in industrial contexts, because the control on a corporation's processes and tools is quite limited [RTW07b]. While being surprising or even disturbing for the outsider at first, this hesitation in adopting novel concepts has several good reasons:

1. Adopting of new methods takes time and is thus expensive,

2. Introducing new concepts is always involved with risks,

3. Tool suites already integrated within the company's process represent substantial investments (not only w.r.t. software licensing but also training of personnel, etc.),

4. Among the tens of thousands of employees of large corporations, not everyone will be able or willing to employ the same methods and tools, due to diverse backgrounds and mentalities,

5. Computer science is an evolving discipline and, whenever progress is made, there exist—at least for a while—several alternatives and in most cases it is impossible to say in advance which is the best way to proceed,

6. Normally there is no one single solution that serves everybody's needs, especially when considering the diverse needs that differing development processes impose on methods and tools.

For all these reasons, the influence on a company's processes, methods and tools is quite restricted.

Incremental Introduction. One of the consequences of this limited influence on processes and methodologies is that novel procedures and concepts always have to be introduced incrementally. A step-by-step introduction of product line methods, processes, and tools is necessary in many domains. But this is particularly true for the automotive domain and the prerequisites for a step-wise introduction are especially intricate here. Already the longevity of automotive systems, as described above, gives cause to this problem, because compatibility with legacy artifacts, subcomponents, and information systems needs to be assured at all times. But also the complex organizational structures within an automotive manufacturer, the distribution of work between the manufacturer and its suppliers, and the enormous economic consequences of an organizational failure or delay during development and production are of significance here.

These factors make it virtually impossible to introduce new processes or methods at once on a global scale or even only for a subdomain like telematics, body electronics or motor control. Instead, only a bottom-up approach is usually realistic: at first, new methods and tools are introduced for selected subsystems only (e.g. the wiper or climate control) or even only for individual development artifacts (e.g. certain requirement modules or a set of test cases). Then, these will be further integrated into a comprehensive product line for a complete vehicle model.

5.2 Global Coordination of Automotive Product-Line Variability

Since a product line's infrastructure usually consists of a multitude of variable artifacts, there is the need for a centralized coordination of variability across all these artifacts on a global level. This is particularly true for the automotive domain with its highly complex product lines and families. There are two schemes that can be applied for such a global variability coordination: a traditional one described in literature in several variations and an advanced one which is newly introduced and proposed here for managing complex cases. Both will be described in this section.

As a basis for the following discussion, reconsider the situation in product-line oriented software development as described in Section 3.1 and depicted in Figure 3.2: All information of relevance during the development process is captured in a multitude of development artifacts (e.g. requirements documents, component diagrams, Matlab/Simulink models, test case descriptions). These artifacts were depicted with document symbols on the gray V, which

5.2. Global Coordination of Automotive Product-Line Variability

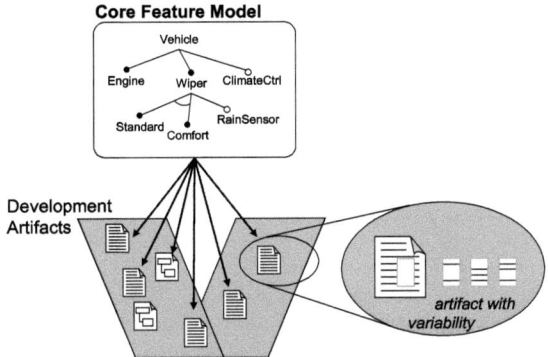

Figure 5.1: Product-line coordination with a core feature model.

symbolized the development process. Each of these artifacts can be defined in a variable form if its content varies from one product instance to another, which was exemplarily shown in Figure 3.2 for the enlarged artifact on the left. Two different levels of variability management in a product line context were identified: variability on the artifact level and variability on the product line level. How precisely variability is defined within an artifact was identified to be highly dependent on the type of artifact and the approach being used (cf. Section 3.3).

In the following, we concentrate on how to organize and manage the complex variability across the numerous artifacts of the product line. To achieve this, we will add more detail to the basic scheme from Figure 3.2.

5.2.1 Coordination of Small to Medium Sized Product Lines

One way of achieving the global perspective is to introduce a single *core variability model* for all artifacts (cf. Figure 5.1). Feature models are especially suited for this purpose due to their high level of abstraction. This core variability model is then used as a basis to define the binding of variability in all artifacts, which is shown in Figure 5.1 in form of the arrows from the core feature model to the variable artifacts. This means that for each variation point within an artifact, the specification of when to use which variant is formulated in terms of configurations of the core feature model. For example, consider the fictitious Matlab/Simulink model from Example 2 on page 23, in which a block B1 needs to be replaced by a variant B2 for some product instances. In such a case, it would be defined that B2 is used if—for example—the feature RainSensor is selected and that otherwise B1 remains unchanged. This way, the entire variability within the product line's artifacts is related to a single configuration space represented by the core feature model. And when a complete configuration of the core model is given, i.e. a certain product instance is chosen, the configuration of all artifacts can be derived from that.

Another example could be the simple mechanism for defining variability within a requirements specification, which was outlined in Section 3.3: each requirement is thought of as being optional and is tagged with a logical constraint that evaluates to true in and only in those cases, in which the corresponding requirement is applicable. When we first discussed this mechanism, we did not state how the configuration context is defined, i.e. what variables are available for use in these constraints and when and how values will be assigned to them. Now we have a possible answer: following the scheme described at the beginning of this section, the selection status of the core variability model's features would be used, i.e. a boolean variable for each feature would be defined which is true if and only if the feature was selected during configuration.

This organizational pattern is well suited for small to medium sized system product lines, that are developed by only a relatively small number of teams or departments within a single company and that comprise only a moderate number of artifacts of low or medium complexity. Product lines of automotive suppliers offering clearly delimited subsystems often fall into this category. For example, a supplier offering a product line of rain sensors or of climate controls can probably employ this scheme of product line coordination.

5.2.2 Coordination of Highly Complex Product Lines

The organizational pattern described in the previous section cannot be used for highly complex product lines, such as an automotive manufacturer's product range. When considering the characteristics of the automotive domain as identified in Section 5.1 this becomes fairly obvious:

1. Due to the complexity of the overall organizational context a multitude of different organizational units are involved in the development of a single automobile, including departments and divisions within the manufacturer as well as external suppliers. If all these organizational units were required to directly relate their artifacts to a single core feature model, interdependencies of an enormous, unmanageable complexity would be created. In addition, these interrelations would nullify the benefits expected from an organizational partitioning and a division of labor.

2. The diverging scopes and life-cycles of subsystems as well as individual development artifacts would further add to the complexity of these interrelations: at the same time the single core feature model would have to comply to legacy variability specifications in soon-to-be-abolished artifacts as well as to novel variabilities in innovative vehicle functions. This way, former decisions on how to organize and structure the complete system's variability would have to be carried on for ever.

3. Finally, the heterogeneity of all development means, and especially the resulting manifoldness of the artifact-level variability specification mechanisms, would permeate the core feature model, if development artifacts were directly related to it.

Especially in such intricate development contexts, feature modeling has great potential: for example, features may serve as a link between management, marketing and development in a single company and as a link between companies to facilitate communication, thus becoming the core of all variability and evolution management.

For the above reasons it is not possible to directly relate all variable artifacts to a single, global feature model. Instead, it is here proposed to organize each development artifact as its own small product line. Similarly, several artifacts may be combined and may be managed together as a single small-sized product line. Of course, the instances of these subordinate product lines are different in nature from the instances of the overall product line: in the first

5.2. Global Coordination of Automotive Product-Line Variability

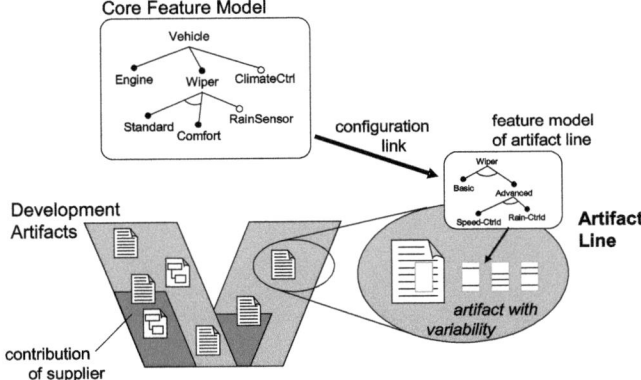

Figure 5.2: Product-line coordination with a core feature model and artifact lines.

case we have an initialized, non-variable development artifact, such as a test-case description or a requirements specification, while in the latter case we actually have a product, e.g. an automobile. To emphasize this fact these small-sized "product lines" of development artifacts are referred to as artifact lines.

Definition 11. An *artifact line* is a subordinate product line which comprises only a single or a few selected artifacts within the infrastructure of a superordinate, large-scale product line; its product instances are the fully resolved configurations of this or these artifacts. □

The main property distinguishing an artifact line from a simple variable artifact is that the artifact line is provided with its own local feature model (cf. Figure 5.2). This feature model is used to publish an appropriate view of the artifact's variability to the actors interested in instances of this artifact. This makes the one or more artifacts in the artifact line independent from the global core feature model of the overall product line.

The link between the artifact line and the overall product line is achieved by defining the configuration of the artifact line's feature model as a function of the configuration of the core feature model of the overall product line, as illustrated by the solid arrow in Figure 5.2. Then, whenever a configuration of the core feature model is given, the configuration of all artifact lines can be deduced from it. In most cases, these links are directed in the sense that configuration can be propagated from the core feature model to those of the artifact lines, and not the other way round.

Artifact lines may, in turn, be composed of other, lower-level artifact lines. To achieve this, the feature models of the lower-level lines are linked to the top-level line's feature model in exactly the same way as described before for an artifact line's feature model and that of the overall product line. In this way, variability exposed by the lower-level artifact lines may be partly hidden, diversely packaged or presented in a different form.

Consequently, two sorts of variability information are hidden by the artifact line's feature model: first, the details of how variability is technically defined within the specific artifact (e.g. with explicitly defined variation points together with variants for them or with aspects that may optionally be woven into the artifact), and second, in the case of composite artifact lines, the details of how variability is exposed by the lower-level artifact lines. Both cases of concealment are referred to as *configuration hiding*. This configuration hiding is key to supporting the diverging life-cycle of individual development artifacts as well as the complex network of manufacturer-supplier relationships described above. In addition, such a hierarchical management of variability is an effective instrument to reduce the combinatoric complexity of product-line engineering, because the artifact local feature models can reduce the complexity of variability within the artifact to a level which is appropriate for its use within the overall product line.

Instead of having a single core feature model, it is also conceivable to hierarchically decompose this core model into several feature models linked by way of the concept used to link the artifact lines' feature models to the core. For example, two core feature models could be used to distinguish a customer viewpoint and an engineering viewpoint on variability, as explained in [RW05].

5.3 Unified Feature Modeling

How, then, does this framework tackle organizational complexity, diverging life-cycles, and heterogeneity ? To illustrate this, we first examine the traditional situation without artifact lines. We have, in this case, (a) the overall product line's core feature model, (b) the artifacts with their variability definition mechanisms and (c) some link between the two (cf. Figure 5.1). Items (b) and (c) are highly artifact-specific, i.e. the variability definition mechanism must be tailored to the specific nature of the artifact and its corresponding method and tool. In addition, they must be adapted to the feature-modeling technique used for the core feature model because they are directly related through the link between the two. Consequently, it is impossible to devise and formulate the many individual mechanisms for variability definition without being aware of the modeling technique for the core feature model, and vice versa. Given the fact that many tool vendors are currently enhancing their tools, together with the underlying methods, by proprietary concepts for expressing variability, this is a show-stopper for managing a system family through a central global feature model.

By contrast, when inserting an additional feature model between the core model and the variable artifact (as illustrated in Figure 5.2) the situation is different: At first sight, not much has changed because everything is still related to everything else. However, if we assume that the feature modeling technique used for the core feature model and the artifact line's model was extremely flexible, such that virtually any variability specification mechanism could be perceived as being a special case of our flexible feature modeling language, the artifact's feature model could be a highly artifact-, method- and/or tool-specific variability specification and, at the same time, be used as a feature model. The advantage would be that the link between the feature models would no longer span diverse methods but could be defined within a single methodology and tool.

Example 3. Let us consider three development artifacts: a piece of C source code, a state-machine model in some modeling tool T and a set of test case specifications (whether the source code is intended to be an implementation of the behavioral model or not is irrelevant here). Assume that variability for the source code is expressed by means of preprocessor macros and that tool T provides a

5.3. Unified Feature Modeling

variation point- / variant-based technique for introducing variability in state machines, where each variant is supplied with a propositional formula specifying when it is valid; the formulas of a single variation point's variants must be disjoint. Finally, the test team decided to use a feature tree managed in the commercial tool pure::variants [PS08] to systematize variability. In the case of the source code, the variability specification simply consists of the set of preprocessor variables and their allowed values, i.e. the values that are used within the code in preprocessor commands, such as `#ifdef` and `#ifndef`. In the case of the state machine, the Boolean variables used in the logical expressions form the variability specification. □

The goal is now to come up with a feature-modeling technique that is flexible enough to treat the variability specifications in the C source code and the models of tool T as normal—if degenerate—feature models. Similarly, the feature tree of pure::variants should be incorporated. Then, the link between the global product line's core feature model and certain configurations of these three artifacts could be formulated in a single methodology and tool, thus eliminating the heterogeneity of the artifact-level variability specifications.

Therefore, the feature modeling technique used for automotive product line engineering according to the framework proposed in Section 5.2.2 must be as flexible as possible. It is referred to in the following as a *unified feature modeling* technique. In the remainder of this section, we examine in detail what "flexible" means in this context.

To achieve this, we will now deduce several requirements for a feature modeling technique in order to be successfully employed in such a manner.

(1) First of all, since the feature-modeling technique we are seeking must—according to the above framework—be able to express feature models of many other existing feature techniques and tools, it is required to comprise all important feature-modeling concepts proposed in the literature in recent years. The only exception here are concepts that can straightforwardly be mimicked by other concepts. The principal concepts that need to be supported include:

- Parent/child relationship,

- Mandatory and optional features,

- Features with a cardinality above 1, i.e. cloned features [CKK06],

- Typed edges, i.e. typed parent/child relationships,

- Feature groups (i.e. the ability to group several children of a feature and impose a constraint on them, e.g. that they are alternative, without affecting the other children; having several of these groups below the same parent),

- Feature references (i.e. features that are reused and appear more than once within the same feature model, thus turning the feature tree into a directed acyclic graph),

- Parameterized features (i.e. features that are not merely selected or deselected during configuration of the feature model but, if selected, are—during configuration—also assigned a value of a certain type; often this is also referred to as a feature attribute),

- Links between features of various types (such as f_1 "requires" f_2 or f_1 "excludes" f_2).

Nevertheless, some concepts may also be completely ruled out, in case they are deemed to lie outside the scope of feature modeling. For example, Czarnecki et al. have suggested this for reference attributes in [CKK06]. But this should only be done, if the concept in question is not used by any important, well-established feature modeling techniques.

In addition, many classifications and additional characterizations for features have been proposed, e.g. an assignment of features to different layers [KKL+98], binding times [Bos00, vGBS01] and a distinction between primitive and compound features [SHTB06]. Directly adding all these different notions to the modeling technique would make it very complex; this problem can be solved with the next required concept.

(2) As described in the previous section, the technique is supposed to be used as a means of communication between many different departments, projects and even companies. In these situations, there will often be a need to supplement the information in the feature models with some additional meta-information (e.g. customer visibility for features). The approach must therefore provide means to define custom attributes, their types and allowed values. It should be possible to attach these custom attributes to features, edges (parent/child relationships) and links between features. Naming conventions should be part of the feature-modeling technique to avoid conflicts between attribute and type identifiers when feature models of different organizational units are incorporated into a single system family. For example, a naming scheme similar to that of Java classes and packages (e.g. org.xml.sax and org.w3c.dom for XML parsers) could be used.

This concept could also be used to cover the numerous classifications and characterizations of features mentioned above. For these, certain "custom" attributes together with possible values and their semantics could be standardized in the feature method so that they would not contribute to the structural concepts but would be available when needed. The various link types and types of edges proposed in the literature could also be supported this way.

(3) In addition, it should be possible to deliberately determine the order of features. This is true of both the order of root features in the model and the order of child features within their parent's list of children. While order does not have a semantical meaning in feature modeling, it is often used to structure and organize features. This is especially true of very flat but wide feature "trees", which often arise early on when adopting the notion of feature modeling.

(4) Furthermore, the feature-modeling technique should be careful to avoid—both on the syntactical as well as the semantical level—any unnecessary special cases or restrictions, that are aimed at imposing a certain style of feature modeling. For example, root features should simply be treated as features not having a parent; grouped features should simply be features that have a feature group as their parent instead of a feature; feature models with more than one root feature should be allowed. This is because such restrictions always increase the risk that some special forms of feature modeling or variability specification introduced by proprietary tools will not be supported. This applies in particular to "degenerate" feature models that are not normally perceived as feature models but should be covered by the variability modeling technique for the reasons given in the previous section: e.g. sets of booleans or sets of enumerates.

(5) The entire technique, both syntax and semantics, must be based on a solid formal foundation. As Schobbens et al. have shown in [SHTB06], this is necessary to prevent ambiguities within the approach. But it is also necessary to prevent misinterpretations when applying it or when defining syntactical and semantical mappings from proprietary techniques to it.

5.4. Summary and Outlook on Parts II and III   65

(6) Finally, the technique should comprise an open, reusable reference implementation as well as a mapping to XML, in order to facilitate providing support for it.

However, a feature-modeling technique that met all the above requirements would be enormously flexible. And great flexibility of modeling means always entails additional difficulties for the modeler. Thus, an important motivation for many of the feature-modeling techniques proposed in the literature was to avoid just that by carefully selecting the most appropriate concepts and ruling out the inappropriate or not really necessary ones. We do not question this objective, but we feel that the question as to which feature modeling concepts are appropriate cannot be answered for all application domains and contexts in the same way. We therefore propose to devise a highly flexible and comprehensive modeling technique but restricting its use depending on the needs of the concrete application context. The question as to which feature-modeling concepts are appropriate then turns into the question: In which situations should each concept be used and in which not? This leads us to an additional requirement for the modeling technique.

(7) The technique should provide ways of restricting its use for certain feature models. For example, features with a cardinality greater than 1 are very useful in some contexts, while the additional complexity they introduce is unnecessary in other contexts; it should therefore be possible to restrict the upper bound of cardinalities to 1 where this is deemed appropriate.

Furthermore, it should be possible to restrict use of the technique to a subset of concepts, corresponding to the concepts provided by a certain established feature-modeling technique from literature (e.g. FODA [KCH+90] or FORM [KKL+98]) or an established feature-modeling tool, such as pure::variants.

Such restrictions could be imposed by way of a general constraint mechanism. Constraints that realize such restrictions could then be called *compliance constraints*[1], to highlight that fact that they enforce compliance with a certain modeling technique or tool.

5.4 Summary and Outlook on Parts II and III

To set up a product line organization according to the scheme envisioned in Section 5.2.2 above, we require two core concepts. Firstly, a flexible feature modeling approach which can be used as a parenthesis around most existing variability specification techniques. A detailed discussion of this, including a list of requirements, was presented in Section 5.3 of this chapter. The CVM approach formalized in Section 4.5 would be a good starting point for such a unified feature modeling technique, but further work in this direction should be performed as a collaborative undertaking of the research community, not as part of a thesis. Secondly, we require a concept that provides us with the link from the core feature model to the artifact lines' feature models. And the link from an artifact line's feature model to that of a contained, lower-level artifact line. And the link from the customer-oriented feature model to the core technical feature model. For all these cases and more, we will use configuration links as introduced in Part III. But before, another technique for coping with the complexity of a large-scale industrial product line is presented: subscoping. This is not contained in the big picture of Section 5.2.2, instead it is to be seen as orthogonal to the breakdown into artifact lines. In the end, we will have two means of partitioning a gargantuan product line:

---
[1]Not to be mistaken with conformance constraints as defined in [RW06].

subscoping, i.e. segmenting the line's scope, and introducing artifact lines, i.e. segmenting the line's infrastructure along development artifacts and structural units.

Part II

Subscoping

Chapter 6

Subscoping — Motivation and Basic Idea

This chapter motivates the conception of subscoping and provides a brief overview of its basic idea. As a stating point for this discussion we will briefly come back to the challenge of product line complexity, which was identified as one of the characteristics of the automotive domain in Section 5.1.

6.1 Product Sublines

As explained above, a global car manufacturer's overall product range is usually made up of vehicle lines (e.g. A-Class, C-Class, E-Class), which are in turn further subdivided into vehicle models (e.g. E240, E320, E320 CDI with diesel engine). Also, there often is a breakdown into passenger cars, freight vehicles, other commercial vehicles and possibly further categories. Moreover, today's large corporate groups usually consist of large subgroups or brands (e.g. Mercedes-Benz, smart, Maybach, Mitsubishi Fuso). This situation is illustrated in Figure 6.1. All these models, lines, series etc. are hierarchically related to each other: for example, all models of a particular vehicle line share certain characteristics, just as all vehicle lines of a vehicle series do. Sometimes vehicle models are even further subdivided, leading to additional levels. Another common source of additional hierarchical levels is related to cases where, for example, some vehicle lines (e.g. C- and E-Class) share characteristics that other sibling vehicle lines (in this example the A-Class) do not. Then, another box would have to be added to Figure 6.1 above these overlapping vehicle lines to represent their common characteristics resulting in an additional, intermediate hierarchical level.

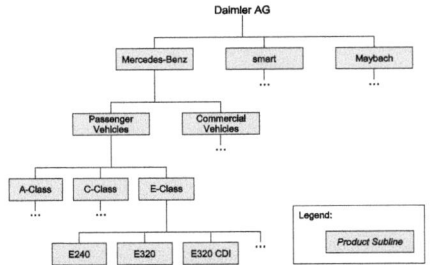

Figure 6.1: Example of a complex product/project structure.

In summary, this means there are several, hierarchically structured "contexts" in which development takes place. For these contexts, the term *product subline* will be used in the following, or simply *subline* for short. More formally,

> **Definition 12.** Given two product lines PL_1 and PL_2, the product line PL_2 is called a *product subline* of PL_1 if and only if
> $$p \in Scope(PL_2) \implies p \in Scope(PL_1)$$
> i.e. the scope of PL_2 must be subset of the scope of PL_1. In that case PL_1 is called a *product superline* of PL_2. □

Each shaded box in Figure 6.1 can thus be seen as such a product subline. Following traditional terminology from set theory, we define:

> **Definition 13.** A product subline is called a *proper product subline* if and only if its scope is a proper subset of its superline's scope. □

Correspondingly, several other characterizations of sets can be applied to sublines. For example, two sublines PL_a and PL_b of product line PL are called *disjoint*, if and only if their scopes are disjoint.

In many cases, sublines are reflected in a car manufacturer's organizational structure as divisions, departments or other organizational units or as temporary projects, which have an organizational impact for at least some time. This gives product sublines a significance that goes beyond methodological considerations. Effectively organizing the entire development, production, sales and after-sales process with these sublines in mind is of paramount importance in large-scale industrial settings.

6.2 Limitations of Traditional Approaches

When applying existing product line concepts—especially feature modeling—to this situation, one would have to choose between two basic approaches:

1. Organizing each *leaf* product subline as a separate product line of its own; these sublines would then be defined by one product line infrastructure each.

2. Organizing all product sublines in one global product line/family; the sublines would then become partial configurations of a single global product line infrastructure.

For automotive development, neither possibility is truly satisfactory. In the case of the first approach, this is immediately obvious: if the product sublines are treated as separate, independent product lines, there is no way to document and manage the commonalities and differences between them, which means that all the benefits of product-line-oriented software development are not available on the level above the individual (leaf) sublines.

The shortcomings of the second approach are not as obvious. Theoretically, it would be possible to have one global product line infrastructure because all the company's brands, lines and models are merely additional variations on an imaginary company-global variable car (e.g. the "Daimler automobile"). But such a monolithic product line organization would be enormously complex due to the immense system and product line complexity in the automotive domain (cf. Section 5.1): first of all, even for a single car model, well above a thousand technical features are necessary to distinguish which functionality is mandatory and which is optional in principle—regardless of final marketing decisions. Secondly, one must consider the product range complexity, i.e. the large number of models offered by today's automotive manufacturers such as General Motors, Renault or Daimler. And finally, the number of different models is only the tip of the iceberg, because each model is offered in many different markets with differing legislation, in many different styles (e.g. Classic, Elegance, Sport), and so on. Thus, a monolithic product line infrastructure would be unmanageable, especially when it comes to complex evolution activities, such as

- Adding new product sublines,
- Implementing and managing changes in the system's structure over a long period of time,
- Making *local amendments*, i.e. amendments that are valid for only a single or only a few product sublines.

The last item is of particular relevance here. When heading for a single, global product line, each local amendment unnecessarily complicates the global product line infrastructure. This becomes unbearable in domains where local amendments are very common. Unfortunately, the automotive domain falls into this category, mainly for the following reasons:

- Sometimes a product subline requires amendments that are so far-reaching and so special that they would unnecessarily complicate the development artifacts of other sublines a great deal, e.g. if the structure of the climate control's embedding in the overall system differed fundamentally from A- to S-Class,
- Amendments may be needed to solve urgent problems that do not exist in other product sublines or to solve problems that will be treated differently in future models (*stop-gap solutions*),
- Innovations devised in the context of a single product subline may need to be introduced locally at first, in case a discussion and coordination with the departments responsible for the other product sublines takes too long or is not immediately necessary and can therefore be postponed (*local innovations*).

Another problem with the global approach is that it has to be introduced in a company at once—which is extremely difficult, if not impossible in the automotive domain (cf. issue "Incremental Introduction" at the end of Section 5.1). It would be preferable to start developing local product line infrastructures for each subline and be able to later harmonize them over a longer period of time, step by step, and move only those functions and subcomponents to a higher-level product subline that are already sufficiently harmonized and consolidated.

For these reasons, a different procedure for organizing a product line infrastructure in complex organizational contexts is proposed in this thesis. It can be seen as a compromise between one gargantuan global product line and many small independent product lines.

6.3 Multi-Level Product Line Management as a Solution

In order to feasibly manage a superline together with its sublines, the *multi-level approach*, or *multi-level product line management*, focuses on individual development artifacts of the

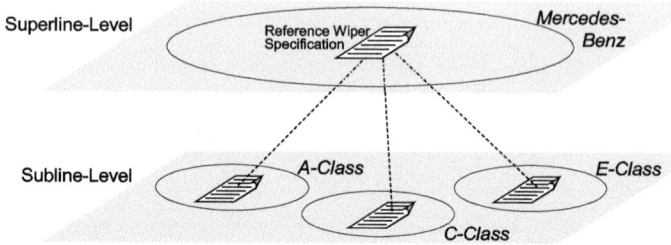

Figure 6.2: Relating subline artifacts to a reference artifact on the superline level.

sublines and turns them into an anchor point for the organization and management of the superline. This is achieved in two steps:

1. At first the artifacts of each subline are left completely unrelated to those from the other sublines and they can be developed and evolved independently. This means we start with organizing each subline with its own, independent product line infrastructure (solution no.1 in the enumeration at the beginning of Section 6.2).

2. Then, for a group of semantically related artifacts from two or more sublines—in the standard case one artifact per subline—a *reference artifact* is defined on the superline level. This reference artifact serves as a template for the local, subline-specific artifacts and provides a means to strategically steer commonality and diverseness of these lower-level artifacts.

This is illustrated in Figure 6.2, where the multi-level management of an imaginary wiper specification artifact is shown. Three sublines use a wiper specification: A-Class, C-Class and E-Class. Each subline can adapt and amend its own specification artifact independently from the others. However, by relating them to the reference wiper specification on the superline level, the deviations from this template can be tracked and managed. In particular, certain forms of deviation can be forbidden, which eventually leads to a unification of the subline specific interpretations of the reference specification. In practice, the three subline specifications and the reference specification could be realized, for example, as four DOORS modules, which are interrelated with the multi-level concept presented below in Chapter 8.

It is the responsibility of the multi-level approach to provide means (a) of precisely denoting certain individual changes in a subline artifact with respect to the superline artifact and (b) of specifying which of these are allowed or disallowed.

Obviously, such a technique has to be geared to the specific structure and character of an artifact's content; the possible forms of deviations in a feature model will be different to those in a Microsoft Word text document. Consequently, there exists in principle a specific *multi-level technique* for each type of artifact. In this thesis, two such artifact-specific multi-level techniques will be presented: multi-level feature trees and multi-level requirements artifacts

6.4. Subscoping

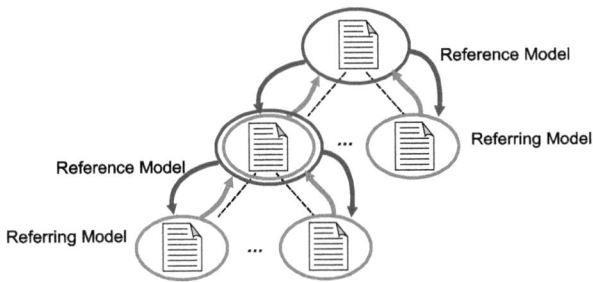

Figure 6.3: A multi-level artifact hierarchy.

(Sections 7 and 8). In addition, it will be discussed whether these specific techniques can be generalized into a single abstract multi-level technique applicable to all kinds of artifacts, leveraging common meta-modeling techniques (Section 10.5).

The concept of a reference artifact now allows for a hierarchically structured tree of artifacts that reflects the fragmentation into sublines described above. Each node in the tree of sublines shown in Figure 6.1 would then be represented by an artifact that is both a reference artifact (for the lower-level artifacts) and a referring artifact (with respect to the higher levels), except for the root which is only a reference artifact, and the leaves which are referring artifacts only. This is illustrated in Figure 6.3. Such a tree of reference/referring artifacts is called a *multi-level artifact tree* or a *multi-level artifact hierarchy*[1] (or *multi-level tree/hierarchy* for short).

At this point, it has to be emphasized that when following the multi-level approach, not all development artifacts involved in subline development have to be managed on the superline level. It is well feasible, for example, to limit the global management on the superline level to the core feature models of the sublines: only for the sublines' feature models is a reference model provided on the superline level, while all other artifacts of the sublines do not have a reference artifact. This way, global management of the superline is limited to the system's core characteristics as captured in a feature model, ignoring specification, design and implementation details. Similarly, feature models and requirement specification artifacts could be centrally managed, while ignoring design and implementation details. Such different application scenarios will be categorized and described in detail in Section 9.

6.4 Subscoping

With such a pragmatic global coordination of the superline that does not unnecessarily hinder the autonomous development of the sublines, we have achieved our primary goal of finding a compromise between the two extremes of having either one large, global product line or many small, completely unrelated ones. However, the multi-level management of artifacts has another important benefit. Due to the reduced scope of a subline, the complexity of variability within a subline's artifact may be reduced substantially: such variabilities that

---
[1]The term "hierarchy" is also applicable if more than one reference artifact is allowed per referring artifact, which will be discussed as an advanced concept in Section 10.2.

only exist *between* sublines, but not within a certain subline, will disappear completely in the context of this subline; consequently no variation points will have to be introduced in this subline's artifacts for these variabilities, which may greatly reduce their complexity. More concretely, if a wiper specification can be formulated for A-, C- and E-Class separately in three DOORS modules, each of these modules will be far less complex than a single specification for all models, because options and variations that only occur in the other models need not be documented at all.

The separation of a product line into several sublines is therefore not only a necessity in the automotive domain but even provides additional benefits. We can thus consider such a product line separation to be a general technique for reducing the complexity of variability in a large-scale product line. Precisely this is expressed by the term *subscoping*:

> **Definition 14.** The activity of reducing the complexity of a large product line PL by dividing it into several disjoint sublines $PL_{1...n}$ with
>
> $$\text{Scope}(PL_1) \cup \text{Scope}(PL_2) \cup ... \cup \text{Scope}(PL_n) = \text{Scope}(PL)$$
>
> is called *subscoping*. □

It is important to note that the above definition does not make any assumptions on how the superline and its sublines, are organized and managed. In principle, we would also speak of subscoping if the sublines were developed completely independently from one another by applying traditional product line approaches. However, it was shown in the previous section that such a course of action is infeasible within an automotive context. The multi-level approach can therefore be seen as a prerequisite for subscoping in the above sense.

6.5 Summary

Subscoping is the practice of reducing a large product line's complexity by dividing it into several smaller sublines. In order not to lose the benefits of product-line orientation above the individual sublines, the multi-level approach provides techniques permitting to develop these sublines relatively independently from one another while still strategically planning and managing the superline on a global scale. Consequently, the multi-level approach can be seen as a technique which renders subscoping possible.

At the beginning of this chapter, the fragmentation of an automotive manufacturer's product line into a multitude of sublines had to be perceived as a problem and a challenge. Now, with the multi-level approach at hand, it is possible to effectively deal with these sublines. We can thus make a virtue of the automotive domain's need for subscoping and actively encourage subscoping as a means to reduce complexity.

Chapter 7

Multi-Level Feature Models

In this chapter, the concept of multi-level feature models is described in detail. The main goal is to find modeling means to reflect the hierarchical organization of product sublines from Figure 6.1. This is achieved by introducing the notion of *reference feature models*: traditional feature models are enhanced with the option of having such a reference feature model (described in detail in Section 7.2). The reference model then serves as a template and guideline for the *referring feature model* by defining default features together with their default properties and by defining which deviations from these defaults are allowed. Thus, the reference model becomes a means to strategically drive the content of the referring model without inhibiting deviations where this is deemed unobjectionable. It is important to note that reference feature models are no longer used to directly define legal feature selections and thus possible product configurations (the traditional purpose of feature models). Instead, they affect product configuration only indirectly by influencing the content of the referring model, which is the actual basis for product configuration.

To formulate a feasible framework for allowing or disallowing certain deviations from a reference feature model, we first examine which forms of deviation are possible in principle (Section 7.3). We then decide which of these deviations can be restricted in the reference model and how such restrictions can be defined (Section 7.4).

To keep the following description concise, it is a good idea to separate two viewpoints: a static one and a dynamic one. First, we consider only static feature trees at a certain point in time, without taking into account how their evolution over a long period of time can be managed. Then, in a separate step, we examine such long-term temporal changes and how they affect the concept as an advanced consideration in Section 10.1.

The fictitious example in Figure 7.1 is used throughout this chapter to illustrate these concepts. It shows a CruiseControl (CC) system that comes either in a Standard or Adaptive version. In the latter case, vehicle speed is reduced when the distance to the car in front falls below a certain threshold. In an advanced version, this is controlled by a Radar. In "Series A", a low-end model, the radar is never used and has therefore been removed to simplify the local feature model. Moreover, a stopgap solution was needed: for some vehicle configurations, a version of the CC with less energy consumption is required (LowEnergy). In "Series B", the high-end model, adaptive CC is only sold with radar, and some innovative third form of CC was introduced, but it is unclear whether or not it will be introduced to "Series A" in the future. While greatly simplified, this example presents typical problems occurring in a real-world multi-level organization of feature models.

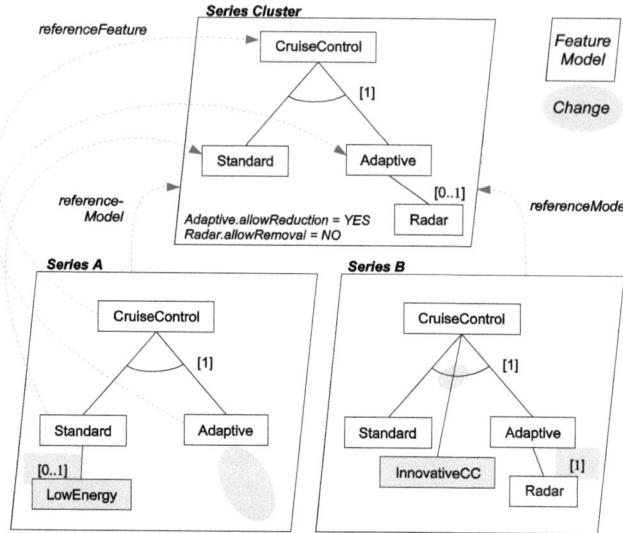

Figure 7.1: Example of a multi-level tree.

7.1 Plain Feature Models

The concept of multi-level feature trees can be seen as an add-on to traditional feature models. We therefore need to choose a feature modeling technique on which we can base the definition of multi-level feature trees. For the purpose of this thesis, the CVM feature modeling technique proposed above and formally defined in Section 4.5 is used here. Based on this technique, the concept of multi-level feature trees will be formally defined in the remainder of this chapter. The benefit of selecting this technique as a template is that it provides most of the advanced feature modeling concepts proposed in literature (e.g. features with a cardinality above 1). In choosing such a relatively complex technique, we will be able to also test the approach with these advanced concepts. In any case, the approach can easily be transferred to and used with other feature modeling techniques.

To not depart too far from an implementation perspective, we will also casually consider the meta-model representation of the CVM technique (cf. Appendix A). In this respect, the multi-level technique can be seen as a meta-model extension to the meta-model of a plain feature modeling technique. This is illustrated in Figure 7.2 which shows an excerpt of the CVM technique's meta-model (Figure 7.2.a) together with the multi-level extension (Figure 7.2.b). In summary, the formal definition below and the meta-model extension of Figure 7.2.b can be seen as two alternative definitions of the technique of multi-level feature models.

The precise details of the underlying feature modeling technique, the CVM technique in our case, are beyond the scope of this chapter and are not needed in the sequel. In particular, we do not need to choose a precise semantics here because the multi-level concept relates feature models solely on a syntactical level. Which precise semantics is applied makes no

7.2 Reference Feature Models

difference as long as the same semantics is used with both the reference and the referring feature model. This is another reason why the multi-level technique for CVM feature models presented in the following could be transferred to other feature modeling techniques very straightforwardly.

7.2 Reference Feature Models

A *reference feature model* is a normal feature model, except that there is some other feature model—called the *referring feature model*—that refers to it as its reference model. In Figure 7.1, "Series Cluster" is the reference model for the referring models "Series A" and "Series B". A feature model can only refer to one reference feature model at the most, but several feature models can refer to the same reference model. The reference feature model can itself refer to a third feature model as its reference model, e.g. if "Series Cluster" referred to a company-global reference model called "Company Cluster".

Furthermore, a feature in the referring feature model can point to a feature in the reference feature model as its *reference feature*. It is then called a *referring feature*. In the example, this is only shown for "Series A" and omitted for "Series B", so as not to clutter the presentation too much. A referring feature may only have a single reference feature and a reference feature may only have a single referring feature per referring model. This means the reference feature relation provides an optional one-to-one mapping from a referring feature model's features to those in the reference feature model.

To represent reference feature models and reference features on a formal level, we extend the definition of advanced feature models from Section 4.5.2 accordingly. Given $\mathcal{FM}$ as the set of all such feature models, we start with the relation

$$RefFM \subseteq \mathcal{FM} \times \mathcal{FM} \tag{7.1}$$

and require it to be defined such that the graph G defined by $G = (\mathcal{FM}, RefFM)$ is a forest of directed in-trees, i.e. for each connected component $C = (V_C, E_C)$ of G the following constraint applies:

$$|V_C| - 1 = |E_C| \tag{7.2}$$

This elegantly ensures that $RefFM$ is irreflexive, asymmetric, functional, and non-cyclic, as was explained in detail for the parent/child hierarchy of features in Section 4.5.1 (with the only exception that now the direction is bottom-up, i.e. we here have in-trees instead of out-trees). Now, for all $(FM, FM_{ref}) \in RefFM$ we call FM a(!) *referring feature model* of FM_{ref} and, conversely, FM_{ref} the(!) *reference feature model* of FM.

For a given pair of referring and reference feature models $(FM, FM_{ref}) \in RefFM$, we define a relation

$$RefF_{FM \to FM_{ref}} \subseteq F_{FM} \times F_{FM_{ref}} \tag{7.3}$$

and require it to be functional and injective. But it need not necessarily be left-total nor surjective, because there may be newly introduced features on the referring level without a reference feature and there may be features on the reference level not used as a reference feature. The relations $RefFM$ and $RefF$ were not defined as partial functions here because the concept can be extended to allow more than one reference model per referring model and more than one reference feature per referring feature, which will be discussed as an advanced consideration in Sections 10.2 and 10.3 below.

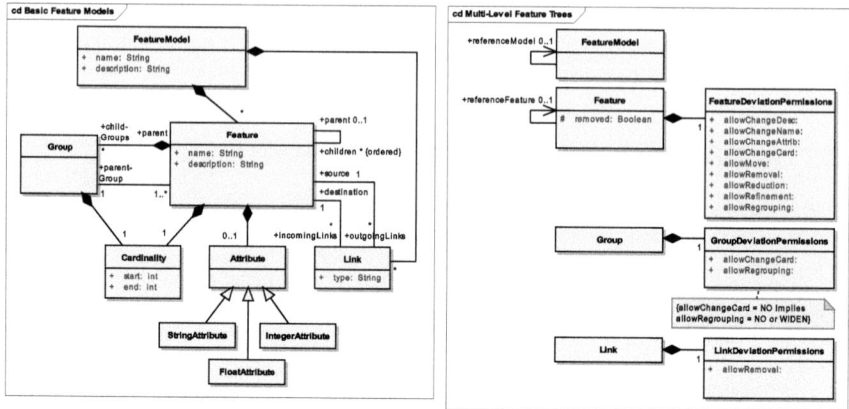

Figure 7.2: **a.** Meta-model for basic feature models (left) ; **b.** Meta-model increment for Multi-Level Feature Trees (right).

In a meta-model based definition of the multi-level concept this is realized as two additional associations. In the meta-model extension of Figure 7.2.b, this is expressed by the directed association named `referenceModel` and by the directed association `referenceFeature`, both with a cardinality of 0..1. Of course, this meta-model does not impose all the above restrictions on the reference relations; to achieve this some of the definitions above would have to be provided as additional constraints along with the meta-model, for example to avoid cycles of reference models. Since we want to put our primary focus on the formal definition, this is not presented in detail here.

Instead of an explicit association being used for the reference links, the names of the features could have been employed to find corresponding features in a reference model. But then features with the same name would "automatically" be associated with each other when an existing feature model is declared the reference model of another already existing feature model. In such a situation, however, it is preferable to only assume an association when the designer has actually decided to do so. The disadvantages of explicit associations—mainly the effort needed to edit them and keep them up to date—are only encountered in certain use cases and even then they can be eliminated with appropriate tool support. For example, when initially defining these associations, a tool could provide functionality to initialize them depending on a feature name matching; similarly, a tool could hide in the editor all reference feature associations between features with matching names to allow the user to easily grasp all exceptions to that rule. This will be further discussed in the context of case studies in Section 19.2.

Just as was explained for artifacts in general in Section 6.3, the concept of a reference feature model now allows for a hierarchically structured tree of feature models that reflects the subline structure of a complex product line. Such a tree of reference/referring feature models is called a *multi-level feature model tree* or *multi-level feature tree* for short.

At this point, the only thing left to be done is to provide a way to precisely define in a

7.3. Possible Forms of Deviation

reference model which deviations from it are allowed or disallowed. To do so, the possible forms of deviation will be examined in the next section.

7.3 Possible Forms of Deviation

Let F and R be two advanced feature models as defined in Definition 10, where R is the reference model for F, i.e. $(F, R) \in \mathit{RefFM}$. Furthermore, let f be a feature in F that refers to feature f_{ref} in R as its reference feature. To make it easier to think about the possible content of F and R, we assume that F was initially created as an exact duplicate of R, where all features in F refer to their corresponding feature in R as their reference feature, and that some changes have subsequently been made to F and R. Now let us examine how F and R can differ from each other. First, all differences in F compared to R are called *deviations*. We define:

Definition 15. Each divergence within a referring artifact with respect to its reference artifact is called a *deviation*. □

In Figure 7.1, these deviations are shaded in gray. We can now investigate in detail the various forms of deviations that may occur in a referring feature model (summarized below in Table 7.1 on page 85).

Basic Deviations

The simplest form of such a deviation is a difference in a basic attribute of a feature, such as its description. name is also one of these basic attributes because it is not used as an ID (see above). Similarly, there may be differences with respect to the attribution of a feature, i.e. whether the feature is an attributed feature or not. In particular, the referring feature f can be attributed, while the reference feature f_{ref} is not (or vice versa), or f has a different type from f_{ref}. Then, the cardinalities can differ between the referring feature and its reference feature. We distinguish two cases of differing cardinalities: the cardinality of the referring feature is a proper subset of the reference feature's cardinality or it is not a subset. Radar in "Series B" is an example of the first case.

Adding and Removing Features

Next, there may be a different number of features in the referring model than in the reference model. To be precise, we must distinguish four situations:

1. There is a feature in R for which no *referring* feature is defined in F because the feature in R was *added*.

2. There is a feature in R for which no *referring* feature is defined in F because the corresponding feature in F was *removed*.

3. There is a feature in F for which no *reference* feature is defined in R because the feature in F was *added*.

4. There is a feature in F for which no *reference* feature is defined in R because the corresponding feature in R was *removed*.

Radar in "Series A" is an example of no. 1 & 2, and LowEnergy of no. 3 & 4. Unfortunately situation no. 1 cannot be distinguished from no. 2, and no. 3 not from no. 4 when looking only statically at the two feature models at a certain point in time. But, from a methodological point of view, it makes a great difference whether a newly added feature in R has not yet been considered for inclusion in F—situation no. 1—or whether a referring feature has been (intentionally) removed even though the reference feature (still) exists—situation no. 2 above. In the first case, the designer of the referring model still has to make the decision as to whether to include the new feature or not, whereas in the second case this is not true. The same applies to the other two situations: a new feature in F has not yet been considered for representation in R as a reference feature, or its reference feature has been intentionally removed from R. To solve these problems, a feature that refers to a reference feature or that is referred to by one or more features as their reference feature is not actually removed from the feature model when deleted, but is only marked as deleted. This is the purpose of the removed attribute in class Feature in Figure 7.2.b .

Refinement and Reduction

What remains are differences in the structure of the feature trees other than added or removed features. These are a bit tricky because all possible forms of structural differences have to be covered without introducing too many types of deviation. First of all, the parent of f can differ from f_{ref}'s parent. Again, we distinguish two situations of differing parents: the parent differs but f_{ref}'s parent is still an ancestor of f (i.e. f has been moved down in the tree) or the parent differs "completely", including the case that f is a root feature (i.e. its parent is set to $null$).

On the other hand, the children of f can differ from those of f_{ref}. Here, we distinguish these cases:

1. f has a child for which there is no corresponding reference feature among the children of f_{ref}:
$$\exists f' \in childrenOf(f) : RefF(f') \notin childrenOf(f_{ref}) \tag{7.4}$$

   For example, this is the case for Standard in "Series A" and CruiseControl in "Series B" but not for CruiseControl in "Series A".

2. f_{ref} has a child for which there is no corresponding referring feature among the children of f:
$$\exists f'_{ref} \in childrenOf(f_{ref}) : \not\exists f' \in childrenOf(f) : \\ RefF(f') = f'_{ref} \tag{7.5}$$

   In the example, this is the case only for Adaptive in "Series A".

3. Like 2. but there is a corresponding referring feature at least among the descendants of f.

Deviation 1 is called *refinement* of f and means that a child feature was newly created as a child of f or moved from somewhere else within the same feature model to f. We do not have to distinguish between these two cases here because in the second case, and only in the second case, is there an additional deviation with respect to the parent of the moved feature.

7.3. Possible Forms of Deviation

Deviation 2 is called *reduction* of f and means that a child feature was moved somewhere else or that it was entirely removed from the model, while deviation 3 (also called reduction) means that it was moved down in its subtree.

Reordering

As another structural deviation, the children of a feature f can be rearranged within the list of its children. Of course, this requires the list of children to be ordered. Usually, feature-modeling techniques do not define the list of a feature's children to be ordered and do not attach any semantical meaning to the children's order. However, most tools for feature modeling actually allow a feature's children to be deliberately arranged. Otherwise, the order would be either random each time the feature model is loaded (which, of course, would be extremely confusing and completely unsuitable) or always fixed (e.g. in alphabetical order depending on the feature names). Practical experiences during the preparation of this thesis showed that the possibility of determining the order of child features is of great value during modeling and can make a feature model much more comprehensible, even if order does not have a semantical meaning with respect to configuration. This is especially true for rather flat feature trees, which often occur during the early phases of adopting product-line concepts. The author therefore decided to incorporate reordering as a form of deviation in this technique.

We can distinguish two cases: either the children of feature f are in the same order as their corresponding reference features among the children of f_{ref} or they are not. In the latter case, we say that they are reordered. More formally, the order of the children of feature f remained unchanged if

$$\forall f', f'' \in childrenOf(f), f'_R, f''_R \in childrenOf(f_{ref}):$$
$$f'_R = RefF(f') \land f''_R = RefF(f'')$$
$$\implies$$
$$(f' < f'' \Leftrightarrow f'_R < f''_R)$$

where relation $<$ is defined such that for two features f_1 and f_2 the expression $f_1 < f_2$ evaluates to *true* if and only if f_1 and f_2 are children of the same parent and f_1 precedes f_2 in this parent's list of children.

Note that the above definition does not consider how the child features are grouped. This is treated as a separate form of deviation (see below). In addition, the above definition takes care to only take into account the order of such child features as are present on both the reference and the referring level. This is very important because we do not wish to assume a reordering in cases where only a new child feature was added or a former child feature was removed. For example, consider CruiseControl in Figure 7.1. The fact that InnovativeCC was added in "Series B" does not mean that the children of CruiseControl have been reordered. In other words, we took care to define reordering such that if reordering is forbidden for a feature, it is still possible to refine or reduce this feature.

Feature Groups

Another form of deviation is related to feature groups. Here, we have to distinguish two cases: first, the grouping of existing features may be different, i.e. groups may have been created, deleted, shrunk, split or merged (let us call this *regrouping*), and second, a group's cardinality

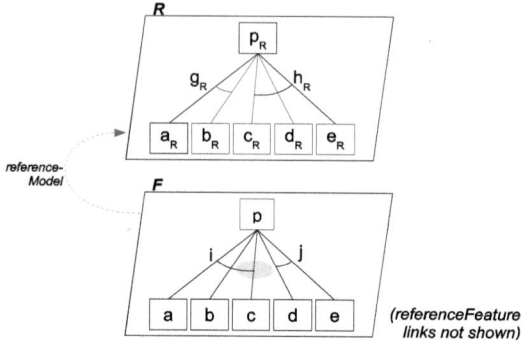

Figure 7.3: No corresponding group in F for the narrowed group h_R.

may be different. In Figure 7.1, the feature group below CruiseControl in "Series B" is an example of regrouping because InnovativeCC has been added. In this context, ungrouped features are treated as being in a single, implicit group of cardinality [0..*].

Similarly to refinement and reduction for features, we say that a group is *widened* if it includes a feature on the referring level that is not included in the group on the reference level (as in the example) and that a group is *narrowed* if a feature that is included on the reference level is no longer included on the referring level. In the case of widening, it does not matter whether the newly included feature was added to the referring model (as InnovativeCC in the example) or whether it was already present as a child of the group's parent feature. Correspondingly, in the case of narrowing, it does not matter whether the feature that is no longer included in the group was completely removed from the referring model or whether it was only excluded from the group but remained a child of the group's parent feature.

Following this terminology, it seems as though we could distinguish four cases: given a group g_{ref} on the reference level and its corresponding group g on the referring level, group g can be ...

1. unchanged with respect to g_{ref}

2. widened (but not narrowed)

3. narrowed (but not widened)

4. both widened and narrowed

Surprisingly, this is not true. In fact, we cannot distinguish between cases no. 3 and no. 4 because as soon as a group is narrowed, we can no longer tell whether the group is also widened or not. The reason for this is that a feature group does not have an identity beyond its set of grouped features. Therefore, when a feature group is narrowed, i.e. features are removed from the group, it is possible only in some cases to clearly find a "corresponding" group on the referring level for the group on the reference level.

This is illustrated in the example in Figure 7.3. Consider group h_R in reference model

7.3. Possible Forms of Deviation

R. In the referring model F, one of its features, namely c_R, is moved to group i. In such a situation, we cannot decide whether group j is to be seen as the group corresponding to h_R (in this case we would say that h_R was narrowed but not widened) or if group i is to be seen as the group corresponding to h_R (in this case we would say that h_R was both narrowed—because d and e were removed—and widened—because a and b were added).

One possible solution to this problem would be to explicitly link groups of the referring level to groups of the reference level, as done for features with the reference feature links. However, while simplifying the formalization of the approach, this would substantially increase the overhead of applying the approach, which is the reason why this solution proved unfeasible during the case studies.

A precise definition is therefore required of how to implicitly relate feature groups of the referring level to groups of the reference level. We say that a group g corresponds to a group g_{ref} in the reference model if both groups are located below corresponding features (or more precisely: if the reference feature of g's parent feature is g_{ref}'s parent feature) and if for all grouped features of g_{ref} there exists a referring feature among the features grouped by g, which means that no feature may have been removed, i.e. the group is not narrowed. Or more formally, for a feature model FM the relation $\leadsto_{FM}\, \subseteq F_{FM}/Group_{FM} \times F_{FM}/Group_{FM}$ defined as

$$g \leadsto g_{ref} \iff (RefF(parentOf(g)) = parentOf(g_{ref})) \,\wedge\, (\forall f'_R \in g_{ref}\; \exists f' \in g : RefF(f') = f'_R) \tag{7.6}$$

relates corresponding groups; for $g \leadsto g_{ref}$ we say that group g *corresponds* to group g_{ref}. Note that we identified $F_{FM}/Group_{FM}$ to be the set of all feature groups in feature model FM in Section 4.5.

Consequently, only three cases of regrouping remain for consideration: given a reference feature f_{ref} of referring feature f, the group g_{ref}—which groups several children of f_{ref}—is said to be ...

1. unchanged if there is a group g' grouping several children of f, such that (a) for each child of f_{ref} grouped by g_{ref}, there is a corresponding referring feature among the children of f which is grouped by g', and (b) for each child of f grouped by g', there is a corresponding reference feature among the children of f_{ref} grouped by g_{ref},

$$\exists g' \in childGroupsOf(f) : \forall f'_R \in g_{ref}\; \exists f' \in g' : RefF(f') = f'_R \,\wedge\, \forall f' \in g'\; \exists f'_R \in g_{ref} : RefF(f') = f'_R \tag{7.7}$$

or more concisely

$$\exists g' \in childGroupsOf(f) : g' \leadsto g_{ref} \,\wedge\, \forall f' \in g'\; \exists f'_R \in g_{ref} : RefF(f') = f'_R \tag{7.8}$$

2. widened only, if there is a group g' grouping several children of f, such that for each child of f_{ref} grouped by g_{ref} there is a corresponding referring feature among the children of f which is grouped by g',

$$\exists g' \in childGroupsOf(f) : \forall f'_R \in g_{ref}\; \exists f' \in g' : RefF(f') = f'_R \tag{7.9}$$

which can be simplified to

$$\exists g' \in childGroupsOf(f) : g' \leadsto g_{ref} \tag{7.10}$$

3. freely regrouped in any other case.

Note that no. 1 and 2 imply that f_{ref} is not reduced with respect to those children of f_{ref} that are grouped by g_{ref}.

In contrast to regrouping, a change in a feature group's cardinality is straightforward and treated in the same way as for features. The only exception is that a change in cardinality for a given feature group can only occur if the group is unchanged or only widened. Otherwise it is not possible—for the above-mentioned reason—to determine which two groups correspond to each other, and it therefore makes no sense to speak of a change in cardinality.

This detailed technical discussion about feature groups might give the impression that the multi-level concept were quite intricate with respect to handling grouping. However, from the perspective of an engineer working on a referring feature model, it all comes down to a simple rule: a given feature group may (a) remain completely unchanged, it may (b) be supplemented with additional features without any of the present features being removed or it may (c) be changed in any other way, including completely deleting or splitting it.

Feature Links

Finally, links between features have to be taken into account. Since a link is only identified by its source, destination and type, we only need to consider creation and deletion of links. When an existing link's type is changed or the link is moved from one source or destination feature to another, this can be treated as a deletion of the old link and creation of a new one.

Using these types of deviation, most of the differences of a feature model compared to its reference feature model can be described. A few minor differences are not covered, like the reordering of root features in the model's list of root features. Since such differences have no semantical meaning and are also of minor methodological relevance only, they are ignored by the multi-level technique presented here, i.e. a feature model differing from its reference feature model only with respect to such properties is deemed identical to it. But if such differences were actually significant in a certain use case, it would be straightforward to extend the concept appropriately.

Please note that we assumed that F started as a duplicate of R only to simplify the explanation. The definition of the possible deviations would also be applicable without changes if, say, F was created before R and R initially started as an empty model.

7.4 Restricting Deviations

The concept of multi-level feature trees is all about managing deviations in a referring feature model with respect to its reference feature model. To allow for this, a means has to be provided to allow and disallow certain forms of deviation from within the reference model. This is described in this section.

For each type of deviation, Table 7.1 lists an attribute that is responsible for specifying whether such a deviation is allowed or not (second column). The possible values of these so called *deviation permission attributes*, or *deviation attributes* for short, are listed in column 3. When a certain value is set, a constraint is imposed on the referring model, which is given in column 4. Please note that the deviation attribute's values are those specified in the reference model, whereas the corresponding constraints must be met by the referring model.

7.4. Restricting Deviations

Table 7.1: Overview of possible forms of deviation and the attributes allowing or disallowing them.

Form of Deviation	Permission Attribute	Values	Constraint
different name	allowChangeName	NO	$f.name = f_{ref}.name$
		APPEND	$\exists s \in \text{String} : f.name = f_{ref}.name + s$
		YES	true
difference in other basic attribute, such as a feature's description	allowChange...	as above	...
difference in feature attributtation	allowChangeAttrib	NO	$Type(f) = Type(f_{ref})$
		YES	true
different cardinality	allowChangeCard (in Feature and Group)	NO	$Card(f) = Card(f_{ref})$
		SUBSET	$Card(f) \subseteq Card(f_{ref})$
		YES	true
no referring feature for a reference feature (**Removal**)	allowRemoval (in Feature)	NO	$\exists f' \in F : RefF(f') = f_{ref} \wedge \neg f'.removed$
		YES	true
no reference feature for a referring feature (**Addition**)	-	always allowed	true
different parent, including $parent = null$ (**Move**)	allowMove	NO	$RefF(parentOf(f)) = parentOf(f_{ref})$
		SUBTREE	$RefF(parentOf(f)) = parentOf(f_{ref}) \vee (parentOf(f_{ref}), RefF(parentOf(f))) \in Predecessor$
		YES	true
referring feature f has a child without a corresponding reference feature among the children of f_{ref} (**Refinement**)	allowRefinement	NO	$\forall f' \in childrenOf(f) : RefF(f') \in childrenOf(f_{ref})$
		YES	true
reference feature f_{ref} has a child without a corresponding referring feature among the children of f (**Reduction**)	allowReduction	NO	$\forall f'_{ref} \in childrenOf(f_{ref}) : \exists f' \in childrenOf(f) : RefF(f') = f'_{ref}$
		SUBTREE	$\forall f'_{ref} \in childrenOf(f_{ref}) : \exists f' \in childrenOf(f) : f'_{ref} = RefF(f') \vee (f'_{ref}, RefF(f')) \in Predecessor$
		YES	true
order of children of f is different (**Reordering**)	allowReordering	NO	$\forall f', f'' \in childrenOf(f), f'_R, f''_R \in childrenOf(f_{ref}) : (f'_R = RefF(f') \wedge f''_R = RefF(f'')) \rightarrow (f' < f'' \Leftrightarrow f'_R < f''_R)$
		YES	true
difference in the grouping of the children of f_{ref} and f (**Regrouping**)	allowRegrouping (in Group)	NO	$\exists g' \in childGroupsOf(f) : g' \rightsquigarrow g_{ref} \wedge$
		WIDEN	$(\forall f' \in g' \exists f_R \in g_{ref} : RefF(f') = f_R)$
		YES	$\exists g' \in childGroupsOf(f) : g' \rightsquigarrow g_{ref}$
			true
no corresponding link l in referring model for link l_R in reference model (**Link Removal**)	allowRemoval (in Link)	NO	$\exists l \in F.links : l.src = l_R.src \wedge l.dest = l_R.dest \wedge l.type = l_R.type$
		YES	true

Sometimes there are more choices available than only completely allowing or disallowing a deviation. For the basic feature attributes `name` and `description`, it is possible to specify that only additional text may be appended and the original text may not be removed or altered. Changes in a `Feature`'s or `Group`'s cardinality can be restricted to partial configuration of the cardinality as defined in [CHE05b], i.e. the cardinality of the feature / feature group in the referring model must be a subset of that of the feature / feature group in the reference model. Finally, moving a feature can be restricted to moving it only in the subtree below it, i.e. moving it down the feature tree hierarchy. This can be specified either in the feature itself—by setting `allowMove` appropriately—or in its parent feature—by setting `allowReduction`. In the latter case, the setting also affects all the feature's siblings.

A special case is `allowChangeCard` in feature groups. Since we can only decide whether a group's cardinality has changed if the group is unchanged or only widened (as shown above), a change in the group's cardinality can only be restricted if at the same time `allowRegrouping` is set to either NO or WIDEN. This rule is captured in Figure 7.2.b by the constraint attached to class `GroupDeviationPermissions`.

A form of deviation that cannot be steered by the deviation permission attributes defined in Table 7.1 is the adding of feature links. The problem is that there is no place to attach the information that a certain link may not be added because the link in question is, of course, not present in the reference model. With a permission attribute attached to `Feature`, it would be possible to forbid the creation of any new outgoing and/or incoming link (no matter which feature is located at the other side of the link and of what type the link is). However, the author has not found any practical uses for such a far-reaching restriction. Another solution might be to add the link that is to be forbidden to the reference model and mark it as being only a placeholder for something that should not be added. But in this case, the basic feature-modeling technique would have to be changed in order to ensure that this link is ignored whenever the feature model is interpreted semantically. Since we want the multi-level approach to merely be an add-on to a plain feature-modeling technique without changing it, this is not a feasible solution. In practice, we have solved this issue on a semantic level: with links which have a semantic meaning that rules out a link we want to prevent—for example, a link of type "independent of" between f_1 and f_2 to rule out a link of type "needs" or "excludes". Of course, this requires an underlying feature-modeling technique that provides such types of links or allows custom link types to be added. Overall, the issue of preventing certain links proved to be of minor practical relevance. Preventing the removal of links is more important, but this is straightforwardly covered by the approach (see `allowRemoval` for links at the bottom of Table 7.1).

Except for link types used to rule out unwanted dependencies, we can say that the multi-level concept does not make any assumptions about what link types are available and what their precise semantics are: specifying a link of a certain type in a reference model and stating whether removing it is allowed or disallowed does not rely on the link type's meaning.

With these definitions in the reference feature model, it is possible to decide whether a referring feature model *conforms to its reference model* or not, i.e. whether all deviations from the reference model (if any) are allowed by that reference model or not. Now, three different states can be distinguished, called *conformance states* of the referring model:

1. The referring model is identical to the reference model and therefore conforms to it.

2. The referring model deviates from but still conforms to the reference model.

7.4. Restricting Deviations

3. The referring model does not conform to the reference model.

The third case is not technically forbidden, i.e. it is syntactically legal to bring a referring model into that state, and this should not be prevented by a modeling tool supporting multi-level feature trees. The modeler should only be urged to make the referring model conformant. This is mainly for practical reasons: when refactoring or altering a feature model, it is sometimes difficult to avoid nonconformant states in intermediate steps. However, in special cases it can also make sense to actually tolerate nonconforming referring models. This is a question of the role of the reference model, the referring model and their precise application in the actual development context. For example, when initially setting up a reference model with a rather strict policy, it may be desirable to let selected legacy product sublines stick to forbidden deviations in order to be able to adapt deviation permissions to the newer sublines and immediately enforce the new policy on them. In this case, the benefit of the multi-level concept with respect to the legacy sublines is not so much in steering their development but rather in spotting their deviations and pointing out these deviations to engineers who consider reusing subcomponents from them.

In the example, "Series A" is not conformant to "Series Cluster" because `Radar` was removed, which is disallowed (note the permission definition in the lower left corner of "Series Cluster"). If we swapped the values of `Adaptive.allowReduction` and `Radar.allowRemoval` in "Series Cluster", "Series A" would still be nonconformant. But then all children of "Adaptive" would be affected by the restriction.

The permission attributes introduced here bring about another form of deviation omitted in Table 7.1: a feature of the referring model may have its permission attributes set to values different from those of its reference feature

$$f.allowXYZ \neq f_{ref}.allowXYZ.$$

This is only of interest if the referring model is at the same time also used as a reference model because only in this case do the values of the permission attributes matter. Again, we can distinguish two cases of differing permission attributes:

1. The value is different and more restrictive (e.g. APPEND instead of YES or NO instead of APPEND in the case of `allowChangeDesc`).

2. The value is different and less restrictive (e.g. YES instead of APPEND or NO).

Making permission attributes more restrictive is always allowed; making them less restrictive is always disallowed. Thus, no additional permission attributes must be introduced for this form of deviation, which is why it was omitted from Table 7.1.

In summary, the concepts described in this section, namely reference feature models and multi-level feature trees, provide a means to organize a very complex product family as several hierarchically related product sublines, offering a compromise between having one large global product family or having many small, independent product families/lines.

Chapter 8
Multi-Level Requirements Artifacts

To allow artifacts to be organized in a multi-level fashion, it is necessary to adapt the multi-level approach for each type of artifact, as explained above. In this chapter, this is demonstrated for requirements artifacts. Since requirements artifacts are used in a multitude of very different forms[Poh07], ranging from simple textual descriptions in plain text documents to very sophisticated graphical modeling techniques such as in goal-oriented requirements engineering [RS77, vL01], it is not suitable to do this for requirements artifacts in general. Instead, we chose the data model of the commercial tool Telelogic DOORS as a concrete basis for the following discussion. The rationale behind this choice is the tool's great relevance to the automotive domain and its data model's high degree of flexibility. Several requirements engineering methods employ data elements that can be seen as a specialized form of DOORS requirements and this means that the adaptation of the multi-level approach at least also applies to these methods.

In this chapter, we follow the same procedure as in Chapter 7: first we present the structure of plain requirements artifacts in Telelogic DOORS, then we identify the possible forms of deviation before presenting a technique to define which deviations are allowed and which are forbidden.

8.1 Plain DOORS Modules

The data elements provided by Telelogic DOORS for managing requirements are quite similar to those of the feature-modeling technique presented in Section 7.1, which facilitates the task of transferring the multi-level concept.

The basic entity for requirements management in DOORS are DOORS *objects*. Usually, each such object represents a single requirement. Objects have several *attributes* and are hierarchically structured, i.e. objects may have a—single—parent object and one or more child objects, thus forming a tree. Objects are organized in *modules*, which are in turn contained in a *database* as the top-level container. The idea of modules is to allow to logically subdivide physical databases. The number of attributes, their names and types are freely configurable on a per-module basis; thus all objects in a module always have the same set of attributes of the same types. Beside these user-defined attributes, there are several *internal attributes*. The values of these are managed internally by DOORS and should not normally be modified by the user. Examples are ID, date of creation and date of last change. Finally, objects may be *linked* with other objects. These links may span different modules.

In the tabular editor of DOORS, attributes appear as individual columns and objects appear as lines. The fact that columns may be hidden and lines may be filtered can safely be ignored here; this mechanism only provides additional views on the data with no impact on a conceptual level.

8.2 Reference DOORS Modules

Since modules are simply logical subdivisions of databases, they can be structured relatively freely. Hence, they can be used to portray the organizational structure of a company and are therefore a suitable basis for the reference / referring artifact concept. However, in many typical use cases of DOORS, modules need to be used to further subdivide a project. It is therefore not enough to allow a single reference module for a referring module. Instead, it must be possible for a module to refer to several modules as their *reference modules*. A module that refers to at least one other module as its reference module is called a *referring module*. In the remainder of this chapter we assume that each referring module has at most one reference module; the more general case will be discussed later in Section 10.2.

8.3 Possible Forms of Deviation

The structure of objects in DOORS—i.e. a tree of objects with attributes and links—closely resembles that of feature models as described above in Section 7.1. Objects correspond to features (in optionally having a parent and several children) and links between objects correspond to feature links. Regarding the order of child objects, the situation is also very similar to that in feature models: even though requirements (i.e. child objects) should usually be formulated in such a way that order does not matter, this is often not the case in practice. But since order of child features is covered by the multi-level approach, this is not a problem. Feature cardinalities, feature groups and group cardinalities do not have a correspondence in DOORS, which simplifies the situation even further.

The situation is slightly more complex only with respect to attributes: in DOORS, the number of attributes and their type can be configured. This seems to correspond to non-basic feature attributes, which can also be allowed or disallowed for a certain feature and for which the type can be chosen (even though a feature may not have more than one such attribute). However, the situation is quite different: in a feature model, only the presence and type of a feature attribute—not its value—is part of the information captured in the model (as described in detail in Section 4.4), whereas in a DOORS module, an attribute's value is the primary information captured in the artifact. Thus, the attributes of DOORS objects correspond rather to the basic attributes of features, such as a feature's name or description, but with an important difference: In feature models, these basic attributes are fixed and are thus always identical on reference and referring level, while in DOORS the custom attributes may differ from reference module to referring module.

With these analogies in mind, we observe that the possible forms of deviation in DOORS modules are very similar to those in feature models. Nevertheless, we identified some important differences:

1. Objects do not have cardinalities.

2. Objects cannot be grouped, i.e. there is no correspondence to feature groups.

3. Objects do not have a concept like non-basic feature attributes.

8.4. Restricting Deviations

4. The number of basic attributes, their names and types may differ from referring module to reference module.

Differences no. 1 to 3 are trivial because the lack of the concepts of cardinality, feature group, and non-basic feature attribute simply means that the related forms of deviation are eliminated. Difference no. 4 introduces an additional form of deviation: the custom attributes in the referring module may differ from those in the referring module. The structural deviations—namely adding, removal, refinement and reduction—apply without change.

8.4 Restricting Deviations

The possible forms of deviation having been identified in the previous section, transferring the permission attributes is straightforward. I therefore refrain from copying Table 7.1 for DOORS requirements.

The only form of deviation that deserves closer examination is a difference in the set of custom attributes in the referring module with respect to the reference module. At first sight, this would appear to call for an additional deviation permission attribute. But it is more appropriate to solve this with a general rule (in much the same way as we did for "Adding" in feature models, see Table 7.1): *adding new custom attributes not present in the reference module or removing custom attributes of the reference module is always allowed; those attributes that are present on both levels must be of the same type.* Attributes not present on both levels are simply ignored by the multi-level concept. This solution is motivated by important use cases of the approach: often a referring module is created to use the requirements information for a special purpose or in a special context, e.g. an original equipment manufacturer (OEM) wishes to use it as a basis for negotiation with a supplier. In this case, it is necessary to be able to remove attributes (e.g. to hide internal meta-information from the supplier) or to add attributes for a purpose limited to the special context (e.g. an attribute for questions or other feedback from the supplier to the manufacturer).

In summary, the deviation permission attributes that apply to multi-level DOORS modules are:

- `allowChangeValue` (for each custom attribute present in both the referring and reference module)
- `allowRemoval` (for objects)
- `allowMove`
- `allowRefinement`
- `allowReduction`
- `allowReordering`
- `allowRemoval` (for links between objects)

What remains is a description of how these permission attributes are technically realized in DOORS. This will be outlined below when the prototypical implementation of the technique will be presented in Chapter 18.

By transferring the multi-level concept from feature models to DOORS modules, we are now in a position to also organize requirements in a hierarchical, multi-level fashion. The same could be done for other types of artifacts, such as design models or test-case specifications. Unfortunately, for some artifacts, in particular component diagrams, this proves to be a lot more challenging than for requirements because their structure differs considerably from that of feature models. However, this is a subject for future research and beyond the scope of this thesis, which was primarily focused on the basic idea of multi-level product line organization.

Chapter 9
Use Scenarios

This chapter describes some typical use scenarios for the multi-level approach encountered during the preparation of this thesis at Daimler AG. These scenarios are not intended as strictly alternative ways of applying multi-level artifact trees but rather give an overview of typical—often simultaneously occurring—situations in which they reveal their potential. The following main scenarios were identified and will be described later in this chapter:

1. Partial/selective coordination on superline level,
2. Full coordination on superline level,
3. Adding product sublines,
4. Bottom-up reuse,
5. Top-down reuse,
6. Integration of parallel innovations,
7. Incremental introduction of feature modeling,
8. Temporary working copy.

The first two scenarios deal with basic possibilities in setting up an overall multi-level hierarchy, in particular they deal with the question of which development artifacts of the sublines to include in the multi-level management on the superline level. Scenarios 3 to 7 then illustrate several important cases of application during the management and evolution of an already set up multi-level hierarchy. For the sake of clarity, these scenarios are all described for multi-level feature trees; but they are equally applicable to multi-level DOORS modules or other artifact types. Finally, the last scenario exemplarily shows that a multi-level hierarchy, once set up, can also be used for various other purposes beyond their primary intention.

9.1 Partial/Selective Coordination on Superline Level

When setting up a multi-level product line organization, a basic decision has to be taken: which artifacts of the sublines are to be included in the global management on the superline level? If only a limited selection of subline artifacts is to be centrally coordinated on the superline level, then either several individual artifacts or all artifacts of a certain type can be chosen. For example, only a single requirement specification artifact, the one for the climate control for instance, might be managed on the superline level; or all requirement specifications captured in the form of DOORS modules could be chosen. In both cases all other artifacts are developed and evolved separately and independently in each subline and are completely ignored on the superline level, i.e. they do not have a reference artifact on the superline level that may impose restrictions on them.

Minimal Comprehensive Coordination

One important special case of this scenario deserves a closer look: each subline has a single core feature model, that captures the subline's overall variability on a high level of abstraction, and these subline feature models are the only artifacts managed on the superline level, i.e. there is a single reference feature model. Feature models are arguably the most abstract technique to capture a complete system's core characteristics, both invariable and variable ones. Therefore this scenario is at the same time minimal in that it only includes a single artifact of each subline within the global superline management, *and* comprehensive, in that it completely covers all characteristics of the system and all of its subsystems, even if they are only considered on a highly abstract level as coarse-grained features. It can therefore be called *minimal comprehensive coordination on the superline level*.

Consequently, this special scenario allows to strategically steer on the superline level all core characteristics of the sublines, even if only in a very abstract form, but is entailed with a very limited organizational effort, because only a single artifact of each subline, i.e. its core feature model, has to be related to the superline level.

9.2 Full Coordination on Superline Level

Naturally, the counterpart of only including a single or very few artifacts of each subline in the multi-level management (the previous scenario) is to include all or most of them. Of course, all intermediate choices between these two extremes are equally conceivable, i.e. a third or half of the artifacts are chosen for global, multi-level management.

The important aspect to note here is that the different artifacts of the subline level need not be managed within the same superline. For example, it is possible to manage the requirements specification of the climate control subsystem of A-, C- and E-Class in a superline "Mercedes-Benz passenger vehicle", whereas the requirements specification of the wiper may be managed in a superline "Mercedes-Benz vehicle" and is thus shared with the commercial vehicle division. This situation is illustrated in Figure 9.1. In fact, the superlines of two different artifacts may be structured completely orthogonally. Figure 9.2 shows an example of such a situation: on the intermediate level, the climate control specification (white) is managed for passenger and commercial vehicles separately, while the wiper specification (gray) is managed separately for the European and U.S. market. Such an orthogonal structuring is possible because, as described above, the anchor point of the entire multi-level management is the individual artifact.

9.3 Adding Product Sublines

So far, the scenarios dealt with setting up an overall multi-level hierarchy. Now we turn to using and evolving such a hierarchy. The starting point for the description of this and the

9.3. Adding Product Sublines

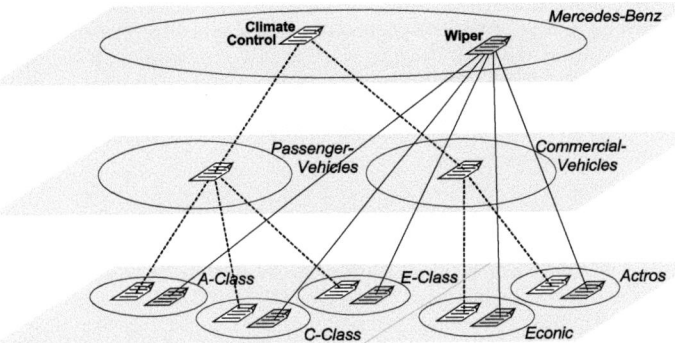

Figure 9.1: Two specification artifacts with a different multi-level structuring.

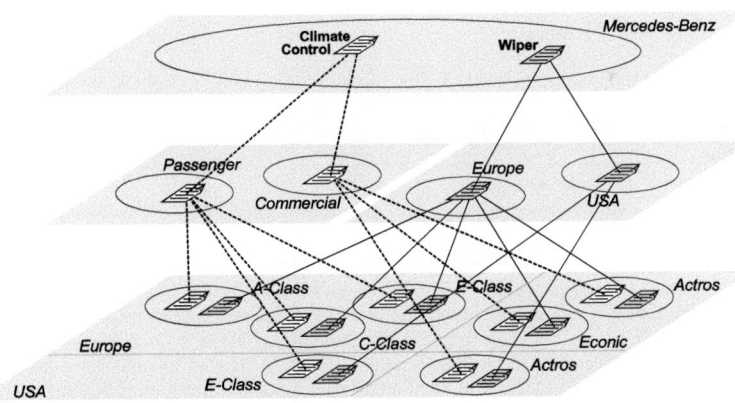

Figure 9.2: Two specification artifacts with an orthogonal multi-level structuring.

following scenarios is a tree of several product sublines, as shown in Figure 6.1. Each such product subline is represented by a feature model, which refers to the parent subline's feature model as its reference model. Together, they form a multi-level feature tree as described above.

A new leaf of such an already existing multi-level tree, i.e. a new product subline, is set up by simply creating a copy of the reference feature model or a sibling referring feature model and, for each feature in the copy, deciding whether or not to reuse it. If reused, a link from the feature in the copy to the corresponding template feature in the parent tree is created; if not reused, the feature is simply removed from the copy. This way, the reference links are already initialized appropriately and the new subline artifact is completely set up for being managed with the multi-level concept.

9.4 Bottom-up Reuse

In leaf product sublines, features for innovative functionality can be introduced locally at first. Then, when the new functionality has been consolidated and is to be used in more models, lines, etc., the corresponding features can be propagated up the tree hierarchy step by step to make them visible and valid in a broader context. The reason for introducing new changes locally at first may be that the new feature represents a stopgap solution (e.g. `LowEnergy` in Figure 7.1) for a problem that only exists locally or will be solved differently in other sublines. Then it makes no sense to clutter the global model with it. Another reason may be that it represents an innovation that may become useful in other contexts (e.g. `InnovativeCC`), but at the moment there is no time or reason to decide this and discuss it with the personnel responsible for the global model.

9.5 Top-down Reuse

Accordingly, features for innovative functionality may also be immediately introduced in the root reference feature model. This often makes sense when the innovation is driven by management decisions and is valid for many different product sublines at once, e.g. "all fellow passenger air-bags in all the company's models must be able to be switched off to avoid accidents with child car seats".

When using this mechanism, it is also possible to introduce new functionality in a step-by-step manner by first allowing many deviations from the globally introduced features and then making them more and more restrictive over time. This gives child sublines the chance to first employ a solution which is extensively adapted to the local needs and constraints and later evolve this into a solution which conforms to the global rule more closely.

As a middle course between this and the previous scenario, innovative features may also be introduced to a product subline somewhere below the root and above the leaves, e.g. "fuel cells should be available in C-, E- and S-Class from 2006 onward".

9.6 Integration of Parallel Innovations

Instead of propagating up the tree hierarchy an innovative feature that has no corresponding features in sibling product sublines (cf. "Bottom-up Reuse" scenario above), the concept can also be used to integrate parallel innovations. When two sibling product sublines have developed two versions of a new subsystem in parallel (e.g. a novel pedestrian safety system), the features related to this subsystem can be integrated by propagating up features that represent a common view of the variability of the new subsystem and defining the local situation for each subline with local deviations. Similar as for other scenarios, the local innovations can thus be integrated and evolved into a common form in a step-by-step process.

9.7 Incremental Introduction of Feature Modeling

In contrast to the above scenarios, which are all based on the assumption that a multi-level feature tree is already in use, there is also the interesting scenario of introducing them.

Multi-level feature trees do not have to be introduced all at once. Instead, they can be introduced in small steps. For example, let us assume that two departments are both working on climate control systems, one for the A-Class and Smart, the other for the C-, E- and S-Class. These two departments can, as a first step, build their own, local feature models. In a second step, they can define for them a reference feature model that is empty to begin with. Then, step by step, they see which parts of their local feature models are the same and propagate these features up to the reference model. This can be done not only for features that are completely identical but also for features that are only similar, because each department can still define deviations from the reference model to reflect its legacy situation. Next, they can try to reduce the number of such deviations over time so as to end up with a common feature model. In addition, other departments also working on climate control systems may join in at some point during the process. In simple situations, the local feature models may eventually even cease to be necessary.

Such a course of action is not only conceivable for individual departments but also for entire vehicle lines, groups, etc. (e.g. C- and E-Class or passenger vehicles and commercial vehicles) or individual subsystems.

9.8 Temporary Working Copy

For an existing feature model, a copy is created as a referring model to be used for a special purpose or in a special context, while the work on the base model is going on in parallel. For example, a manufacturer may want to use the copy as a basis for negotiating a contract with a supplier. While negotiation is taking place, the multi-level concept makes it easy to follow the changes to the base model, and afterwards it is possible to propagate changes that resulted from negotiation to the base model.

However, this last scenario does not employ the multi-level concept for a purpose it was primarily intended for. In fact, the multi-level concept is used here to support a traditional *branching*. The scenario was included mainly to illustrate that the concept has several additional benefits and can be utilized quite easily and flexibly for a range of other purposes.

Chapter 10
Advanced Considerations on Subscoping

This chapter is dedicated to a discussion of various advanced aspects and potential extensions to the basic concept of multi-level product line management. As in the scenario descriptions of the previous chapter this discussion will focus on multi-level feature models only to simplify the presentation; all statements are equally applicable to multi-level DOORS modules and other artifact types.

10.1 Temporal Changes

The idea of reference feature models is to define and strategically drive commonalities in their referring feature models, and thus between several product sublines. But with respect to temporal changes in the models over time, there may be a difference between the reference feature model and its referring models: it is possible that the referring models are only worked on for a limited period of time and are then replaced by other models, whereas the reference model is meant to last for a very long time or even forever. In the automotive domain, for example, such a situation usually exists on the lowest level of the product subline tree (Figure 6.1). The leaf sublines in that tree represent individual vehicle models that are only produced for a limited period and are then replaced by a follow-up model (e.g. "the C-Class C220 developed from 1996 onward and built from 1998 to 2001"). The sublines on higher levels are used to manage commonalities between these models and are therefore intended to be used much longer, if not forever.

Consequently, the multi-level approach and in particular the notion of reference feature models must cope with internally changing models and with adding, exchanging and removing entire referring models for the same reference model.

Changing referring or reference models internally does not affect the concept as described above. Since the definitions in Sections 7.3 and 7.4 are based only on two static models at a certain point in time and since referring models may also be brought into a nonconforming state, the content of both models can be changed freely as if the reference model relation were not in effect (except for deleting features as described above, i.e. setting Removed to true instead of actually removing the feature from the model). Then, after the changes have been applied, the question as to whether the referring model still conforms to the reference model is considered again based on the new content of the models.

Adding a referring model to an existing reference feature model can be done in two ways: (1) a new feature model can be created and added or (2) an already existing feature model can be added. In the first case, all features of the (existing) reference model R are duplicated in the newly created model F and are set to refer to the corresponding feature of R as their reference feature. More precisely, F is initialized so that

$$F.referenceModel = R$$

and

$$\forall f_{ref} \in R : \exists f \in F : RefF(f) = f_{ref}$$

In the second case, the—previously existing—added referring model is left unchanged at first. The modeler then has to specify manually which features of the referring model correspond to features of the reference model (she then has to set `referenceFeature` appropriately) or are to be seen as an add-on to the reference model (`referenceFeature` remains set to *null* for such features).

Detaching a referring model from a reference model is more straightforward. The referring model's `referenceModel` association is set to *null* and the same is done for all its features.

At this point, the temporal changes described above are already completely covered. There is only one problem: when work on a certain referring model ends (e.g. the corresponding vehicle model is no longer produced and maintained), the modeler has to decide either to detach the model from its reference model or to simply keep this link in effect. In the first case, all information on what features in the referring model correspond to what features in the reference model is lost, while in the second case future changes to the reference model will alter the conformance state of the—no longer maintained—reference model. The significance of the first problem (loss of feature → reference feature links) is not immediately obvious because work on the referring model has ended and so the information lost would not appear to be needed in the future. But the referring model may be duplicated in the future and used as the basis for work on a new product subline. In this case, the duplicate would have to be added to the reference model as an existing feature model as described above, which means that the modeler would have to define once more the feature → reference feature links lost before.

A simple solution to this problem is not to detach outdated referring models and to live with the fact that they all become nonconformant sooner or later owing to changes to the reference model. Another solution is not to let the referring model refer always to the newest version of the reference model but instead to a certain version or revision of it. If the reference model is then changed in the future, this does not affect the conformance state of the referring model because it still refers to the same version of the reference model as before. To allow such links to versions of reference feature models, the concept of multi-level feature trees was extended by version handling. For each feature model, all previous versions are recorded and can be retrieved in much the same way as source code can with systems like CVS [Ves06] or SVN [CSFP04]. At this point, no additional mechanism for branches is needed because feature models can be copied for this purpose (which is similar to the way SVN handles branches). More detailed treatment of this version management is beyond the scope of this paper.

10.2 From Multi-Level Trees to Multi-Level Hierarchies

Throughout the above introduction to multi-level product line management, it was assumed that each referring artifact may only have a single reference artifact. This way the explanations

10.3. Split and Merge

and examples could be kept as straightforward as possible. However, it is perfectly viable to also allow more than one reference artifact for a single referring artifact. The multi-level artifact tree as defined by the reference artifact relations is then turned into a general, non-tree graph. To take this into account we speak of a *multi-level artifact hierarchy* or *multi-level hierarchy* instead of a multi-level artifact tree.

This additional flexibility does not introduce any significant changes to the basic concept of multi-level management, because the detailed definition of deviations and deviation permissions relies not on the reference link of the entire artifact but on the reference links of individual elements within the artifact, and these may still only point to a single reference element (at least for now, this will also be liberalized in the next section). More concretely, a referring feature model FM may have two reference feature models FM_A and FM_B, but each individual referring feature within the referring model must refer to exactly one reference feature in either FM_A or FM_B.

So, allowing more than one reference artifact per referring artifact does not change the concept in principle. It just provides the possibility to merge in a single referring artifact the elements from several sources on the reference level, i.e. to package the elements differently into models. For example, it is possible to take one subtree in a referring feature model from reference feature model FM_A and another subtree from FM_B.

Note that in the reverse direction such an extension of the concept is not applicable: this would mean that we want to allow a single reference artifact to have more than one referring artifacts pointing to it, which is, of course, part of the initial idea behind multi-level artifact management.

10.3 Split and Merge

In the previous section we allowed a referring artifact to have more than one reference artifact but retained the restriction that each of the artifact's elements may point to at most one reference element. When abandoning also this second constraint, for example allowing a single referring feature to have more than one reference feature, then things become a bit more intricate.

Before looking into the technical details of this, let us first investigate the actual semantic meaning of such a construction by examining its potential practical motivation. When a feature, for example, has more than one reference feature, this means that two separate features from the superline level were semantically merged into a single feature in the subline. Since this in itself always represents a change in the lower-level artifact with respect to the reference artifact, we can perceive this as an additional form of deviation. In general terms we can define:

> **Definition 16.** When a referring element has more than one reference element, the referring element is assumed to comprise the semantic meaning of all reference elements. This form of deviation is called a *merge*. □

This formulation also points toward another supplementary form of deviation: instead of a single referring feature having more than one reference feature, it is also conceivable that several referring features point to one and the same superline feature as their reference feature. The practical motivation for this would be that a single feature's semantic meaning is distributed within the subline on several distinct features. Again, this necessarily constitutes a deviation in itself. We can thus define:

Definition 17. When several referring elements have the same reference element, the referring elements are assumed to jointly comprise the semantic meaning of the reference element. This form of deviation is called a *split*. □

These two additional forms of deviation are of particular practical relevance, which was one of the lessons learned from the N-Lighten case study, as discussed in detail in Section 19.2.

Having revealed the practical, semantic background behind split and merge, we can now turn back to the technical details of the concept. First of all, two new forms of deviation turned up, which means that, for example, a tool implementation of the multi-level concept would have to check these two additional deviations and present the result to the user. More importantly however, the fact that splitting and merging is now allowed also has an impact on the precise definition of the other deviations. For example, if a feature f with name "abc" has two reference features f_A with name "abc" and f_B with name "xyz", how do we decide if a change in f's name has occurred? As a general rule, we use a logical disjunction of the old definition evaluated separately for each referring feature (in case of a split) or each reference feature (in case of a merge). In the example this means that we assume that f's name has changed if its name is different from f_A's name *or* its name is different from f_B's name. In the above example this would be true. With this general, semi-formal guideline it is straightforward to adapt the definitions from Table 7.1 to support split and merge. The same applies to multi-level DOORS modules and other artifact types. Therefore, further details of split and merge need not be given here.

10.4 Statistics on Multi-Level Artifacts

The multi-level concept, which relates a reference artifact on the level of a superline to several referring artifacts within different sublines, is an ideal basis to reveal a multitude of interesting facts about the character of the referring artifacts and, through that, of the sublines as a whole.

Already the sheer number of deviations of a certain form can reveal significant information. For example, if a lower-level artifact contains many refinements and reductions this indicates that the hierarchical structure of the reference artifact was changed substantially in the referring artifact. Also the precise proportion between refinements and reductions is informative, as will be illustrated below with the statistics of the N-Lighten case study in Section 19.2.

More interesting than the plain amount of deviations of a certain form is, at this point, the possibility to formulate several additional statistic measures that can provide even more detailed information on the character of a certain subline. Quite a few of such values are conceivable and in each case there exist several alternatives for a detailed definition. Therefore only the two most apparent and important values will be defined here. They can be seen as an example of how to interpret and exploit multi-level statistics in general.

When looking at an existing multi-level hierarchy it is straightforward to find out which elements in a referring artifact were actually taken from the template of the reference artifact: exactly those for which a reference element link is defined. The others were newly introduced in the artifact and can therefore be considered as innovations. An implementation of the multi-level approach can easily provide the amount of referring and the amount of innovative elements. Based on this reflection, we can define

Definition 18. Given a reference artifact R with n_R elements and a referring artifact A with n_A elements of which n_{ref} have a reference link defined, the value

10.5. Abstract Multi-Level Technique for Generic Artifacts

cov_A^R defined as
$$cov_A^R = \frac{n_{ref}}{n_R}$$
is called *R-coverage* of A. □

A referring artifact's coverage is an adequate measure for how much information of the base module found its way into the referring module: a value of 1 signifies that all information of the superline is somehow represented in the subline artifact (but it may have been extensively changed, which is indicated by the number of deviations) whereas a value of 0 indicates that no information from the superline is left in the subline. Please note that this definition assumes that the advanced concepts of split and merge are not allowed; however, even if split and merge occurs in an artifact this definition is usually sufficiently accurate.

In addition to an artifact's coverage, we can easily formulate a measure for the artifact's inventiveness:

Definition 19. Given a reference artifact R and a referring artifact A with n_A elements of which n_{ref} have a reference link defined, the value $innov_A^R$ defined as
$$innov_A^R = \frac{n_A - n_{ref}}{n_A}$$
is called *R-innovation* of A. □

An artifact's innovation reflects how much additional information was introduced in a subline, compared to the information taken from the superline. A value of 1 means that the subline artifact consists of newly introduced information only, whereas a value of 0 shows that no information was newly introduced in the artifact.

As said before, more sophisticated measures could be formulated quite straightforwardly, following the example of the above two definitions. For instance, it would be interesting to have a measure similar to coverage which also takes into consideration the deviations in the subline artifact, i.e. a value of 1 indicates that all information from the superline was copied *without change* to the subline. Similarly it would be easy to formulate measures related to deviation permissions which indicate the degree of conformance.

10.5 Abstract Multi-Level Technique for Generic Artifacts

In Chapters 7 and 8 above, two concrete multi-level techniques were presented, which realize the idea of the multi-level approach for two artifact types: feature models and requirements specifications in the form of DOORS modules. It was said in Section 6.3 already that such a concrete realization of the multi-level approach is needed for each type of artifact that is to be organized and managed in a multi-level fashion. When transferring the technique for feature models to DOORS modules we have already seen that this need not be too much effort, because the basic structures of many types of artifacts show great similarities. However, from a scientific point of view, this situation is not completely satisfying. It would be preferable to define a generic multi-level technique on an abstract level that can directly be applied to artifacts of all sorts.

Such an abstract multi-level technique could be based on one of the common modeling languages for meta-modeling, for example the Meta Object Facility (MOF) defined by the

OMG [Obj06]. All the elements of a multi-level technique—i.e. precise definitions of reference links for entire artifacts and individual elements, of possible forms of deviations, of deviation permissions, and of the corresponding conformance constraints—would be formulated for the abstract meta language. Then, all artifacts that are specified in some modeling language, which is itself defined in this meta language, could immediately be incorporated into a multi-level management.

This was thoroughly investigated and also partly realized during the preparation of this dissertation which also lead to a Diploma thesis on this subject [Nei08]. However, due to the scope of this thesis as defined in Section 1.4, it is not possible to give a detailed presentation of such an abstract multi-level technique here.

The most interesting aspect to note in this context is that the high level of abstraction of such a generic multi-level technique has one important drawback: the technique, in particular the different deviations which are distinguished and the permissions' different legal values, cannot be tailored to the specific needs of an individual artifact type's context. For example, it was shown above that for changes in textual attributes many extra deviation permission values are conceivable in addition to the extreme cases of NO (no change allowed) and YES (any change allowed), e.g. a suffix may be appended. Naturally, such special adaptations won't be provided by a generic multi-level technique. A possible solution to this problem might be a generic extension mechanism to the multi-level technique, which allows the user to define her own, new deviations and deviation permission constraints in a form which can then be interpreted and evaluated by a generic multi-level tool. Such a generic multi-level framework was not yet investigated in detail and is left as a subject of future work[1].

---

[1] At time of writing, an academic/industrial research project called MESA-AV, which will supposedly be concerned with this matter, is already being planned.

Chapter 11
Discussion and Related Work

The multi-level approach is used for subscoping, i.e. to partition a large, global product line into several smaller product lines each with a reduced scope compared to the overall product line. These smaller product lines, or sublines, can then be developed and evolved relatively independently from the other sublines and the superline. But in order not to lose the advantages of a product line management on the global level, the multi-level techniques allow to strategically plan and manage the sublines' artifacts on the superline level. This chapter now briefly summarizes and complements the relations between this conception and other research efforts in the field, which were described throughout the preceding chapters.

First of all, the similarities and differences between the multi-level approach and version-handling systems, such as the Concurrent Version System (CVS) [Ves06] or Subversion (SVN) [CSFP04], deserve a closer look. Common to all these systems is a central data storage, usually referred to as the *repository*, in which different versions of development artifacts or other documents can be kept (Figure 11.1). It is possible to *checkout* the latest as well as all the former versions of an artifact and to *commit* a new version. If two or more teams need to edit an artifact without interference over a longer time, *branches* can be created in the repository. These branches can be updated independently from one another, i.e. new versions can be committed to the artifacts in each branch without the need for any synchronization with the other branches. A detailed discussion of the conceptual relation between the terms version, branch and variant has been given above in Section 2.6.

At first sight, the arrangement of a reference artifact and one or two referring artifacts seems to closely resemble the situation in the repository of a version control system. While it is not possible to regard a referring artifact as a newer version of the reference artifact, it is perfectly admissible to treat each referring artifact as a branch of the reference artifact[1]. Versions cannot be used here because if the reference artifact were realized as a prior version of the referring artifact, it would not be possible to edit—i.e. commit new versions to—the reference artifact and only a single referring artifact could be realized per reference artifact. On the other hand, these two problems can obviously be solved by applying branches.

However, the central objective of a multi-level product line organization is to define in the reference artifact which deviations from its content are allowed or disallowed in the referring artifacts. Applied to the situation in a version control repository, this would mean that one branch of the repository (representing the reference artifact) controlled how other branches (representing the referring artifacts) may or may not be modified. Such a conception is completely extraneous to ordinary version control. Nevertheless, version control systems might

---
[1] To be precise, also the reference artifact would be called a "branch" in this case, according to ordinary parlance in version control.

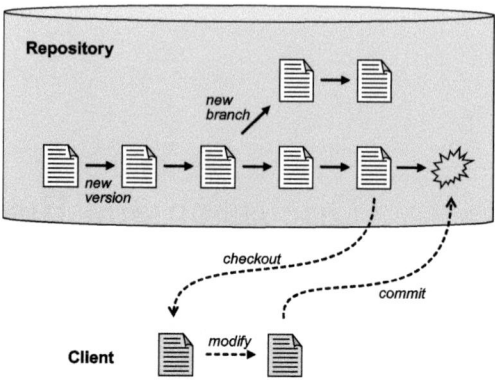

Figure 11.1: Common concepts in version control systems.

provide a solid technical basis for the actual implementation of a multi-level organization in practice; the core concepts of multi-level techniques however, i.e. deviation permissions and a mechanism to determine the conformance state of a referring artifact, are not provided by version control systems.

Staged configuration as defined by Czanrecki et al. in [CHE05a, CHE05b] is closely related to the multi-level feature models: to reduce complexity when working in the context of a particular product subline, a partially configured version of the superline's feature model could be used. This fact and the relation between staged configuration and the multi-level approach was already thoroughly discussed in Sections 6 and 7. To just recapitulate the key point here, by using staged configuration only a specialization of the global feature model can be achieved, e.g. by "narrowing" cardinalities or by masking unnecessary features, whereas other forms of local amendments are often needed, especially structural changes like adding child features or moving features within a tree hierarchy. In addition, the step-wise introduction of innovative variabilities from within a single subline is poorly supported by this mechanism.

Another approach of Pohl et al. that also aims to make highly complex product families more manageable is described in [BLP05]. The difference is that this approach tries to achieve its goal by introducing views on a single, global variability model, whereas the approach proposed here tries rather to avoid a global, extremely large variability model by interrelating formerly independent models. Also, there is no way to strategically drive the content of one view from within another (which would be the correspondence to deviation permissions) and it is not possible to introduce changes locally without affecting the global model. On the other hand, views are a simple but powerful concept and are probably in line with many software product family use cases.

In addition, multi-level feature trees are related to hierarchical and n-dimensional product lines as introduced in [TH03]. However, the approaches differ on a very fundamental point: hierarchical product lines are made up of sublines in a strict sense, i.e. a valid product of a subline is always a valid product of the higher-level product line, whereas in multi-level feature trees a valid product of a referring feature model does not necessarily have to be a valid product of the corresponding reference feature model, because very far-reaching deviations may be allowed. Basically, this is the same situation as in staged configuration described above and in Sections 6 and 7. Also, multi-level feature trees are more closely geared to the specific problems that arise from complex organizational structures and to the process of initiating product-line oriented development in these contexts.

An approach with a very similar objective as the multi-level approach was proposed by Tavakoli in [Tav06]. This work is interesting in several respects. Independently from the research presented here, the same challenge and objective as described above for subscoping and the multi-level approach (Chapter 6) was identified in the domain of automotive software development. This provides further evidence of these issues' great practical relevance. Also, despite several important differences, the basic direction of the proposed solution is quite similar: just as the multi-level approach provides means to organize several sublines under the umbrella of a single, higher-level superline, the solution proposed in [Tav06] provides means to manage the variability in several model-range-specific requirements specifications on a higher level and across the individual model ranges ("baureihenübergreifende Variabilität"). The actual technical solutions, however, are fundamentally different. The multi-level approach tries to make the individual sublines as independent of each other as possible and distributes the entire information across several artifacts (i.e. one artifact per subline plus another for the superline); this way, variability that only occurs between sublines completely disappears from the subline artifacts (Section 6.4). The solution proposed by Tavakoli, on the other hand, incorporates all information in a single artifact for all model ranges and distinguishes between variability within a single model range and variability between model ranges by way of dedicated variability modeling means. Also, there are no such notions as deviation permissions, leading to legitimate or illegitimate deviations, or as local deviations, supporting local innovations and stop-gap solutions without complicating the global picture. A thorough comparison with a discussion of advantages and disadvantages of each solution was published by Tavakoli and myself in [TR07].

Finally it is worth mentioning that all these related approaches have in common that they target an individual type of artifact only, namely feature models (except for the last case which focuses on requirements specifications). The multi-level approach however, while also originating from the context of feature modeling, was carefully devised to be applicable to other artifact types as well. During the preparation of this thesis, requirement specifications were investigated under this respect (cf. Chapter 8 and 18). Considerations on formulating a completely generic multi-level technique directly applicable to all sorts of artifacts can be found in Section 10.5.

A brief work-in-progress report on multi-level feature trees was given in [BBP+05]. An abridged, early version of the overall multi-level approach was introduced in [RW06] and a full account of the approach was published in the Requirements Engineering Journal [RW07]. The preceding chapters of this thesis are a revised version of that article.

Part III
Configuration Links

Chapter 12

Configuration Links — Motivation and Basic Idea

The adoption of product line oriented software development in the automotive domain is still faced with significant challenges, as described in detail in Section 5.1. In this part of this thesis, I argue that a promising way to deal with several of these challenges on the basis of feature modeling is to include *configuration* in the focus of feature modeling. This means that feature models are not only used to define the common and variable characteristics of the line's products, but also to define under which circumstances each such characteristic, i.e. feature, will be selected or deselected for a product. Thus, configuration is not seen as a manual, interactive process taking place when an actual product is derived and delivered; instead it is predefined during domain engineering. Such an early specification of feature configuration is called a *configuration predefinition* or simply *preconfiguration* in the following. Of course, a certain degree of manual configuration will always remain, but there are a number of important uses for predefined configuration, especially in industrial contexts.

The technical concept proposed here for incorporating configuration definitions in feature modeling is called *configuration link*. Such a configuration link is a directed association between two feature models FM_{src} and FM_{dest}. It defines the configuration of model FM_{dest} in terms of a given configuration of FM_{src}. In other words, whenever a configuration of FM_{src} is provided, a configuration of FM_{dest} can be deduced by applying the configuration link. Such a mechanism can be a highly valuable instrument in a wide variety of situations during the development and evolution of complex industrial product lines, as will be substantiated in Chapter 14. However, this broad range of use cases with very diverse demands in expressiveness and usability, requires the mechanism used to define a configuration link to be extremely flexible. The concept must be suitable for defining the configuration of a complex core feature model—for example that of an automotive manufacturer—with well over a thousand features and at the same time must be applicable to situations where a configuration link between two quite small and very similar feature models needs to be defined.

Predefining the configuration of a feature model on an abstract level instead of manually configuring it is not an entirely novel idea. There are several traditional ways to achieve this. For example, each feature can be supplied with a logical expression which evaluates to true if and only if the corresponding feature is selected for a certain product instance. The main point here is that the predefinition of feature model configurations is proposed to become a first-order activity in product line engineering, equally important as feature modeling itself, having a great impact on the overall organization of a complex product line. Also, none of the traditional approaches to preconfiguration provides the necessary degree of flexibility;

especially in very complex cases they prove infeasible. Therefore a novel concept is proposed here.

The remainder of this part is structured as follows: in the next section, an overview of traditional techniques of configuration specification is given. Following that, Section 12.2 then highlights important limitations of these traditional techniques, providing the motivation for configuration links which are presented in the last section as a solution to these limitations (Section 12.3). This chapter deals with configuration links on a conceptual level only, showing the basic idea behind this concept; a thorough formal definition of configuration links is given in Chapter 13. The subsequent Chapter 14 then describes the abovementioned diverse ways how configuration links can be applied in complex product line settings and how they thereby help solve the challenges of these domains. Chapter 15 then elaborates on several advanced considerations on configuration links.

12.1 Traditional Techniques for Feature Configuration Definition

Numerous procedures have been used to predefine the definition of a feature model, i.e. to define for which product instances each feature is to be selected or deselected. For the overview given in this section, they are divided into the following five basic approaches:

1. List of selected features (per product)

2. Selection criteria for features

3. Links from features to a product model

4. Links from a product model to features

5. Combination of 2. and either 3. or 4.

In some cases, where there are only a small number of individual products, simply listing the selected features for each product is perfectly feasible. The product engineer explicitly states for each individual product and for each feature whether or not it will be included. At first glance, this may seem to apply to only a small number of trivial cases because if the number of products is small, there may appear to be no need for product family engineering concepts at all. But this is not true. Even if the number of delivered products is as low as three or four, there may be hundreds of features that need to be considered and therefore elaborate domain engineering could well make sense. Another situation in which this first approach is often sufficient is where there is no distinction between a customer-driven configuration and an internal preconfiguration by development engineers and management personnel.

However, in more complex situations in which there are a huge number of individual products or in which a preconfiguration is required, feature selections cannot be defined for each product/feature combination explicitly. A very straightforward solution is to attribute each feature with a logical statement (e.g. [CE00]), which will henceforth be called *selection criterion*. This selection criterion refers to attributes of the individual products such as country (the country where the product will be offered), chassis (station wagon, etc.) or engine. If and only if the selection criterion evaluates to true will the corresponding feature be selected. This approach is highly flexible and scales fairly well and a slightly simplified form of it has proved viable in development projects at Daimler AG. But it also has some

12.1. Traditional Techniques for Feature Configuration Definition

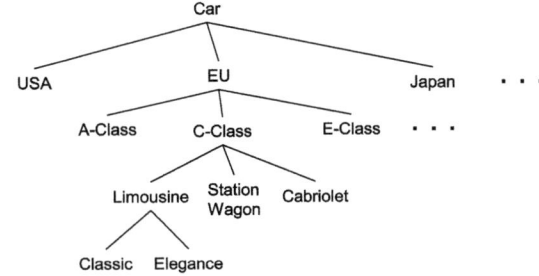

Figure 12.1: Example of a product model in tree form.

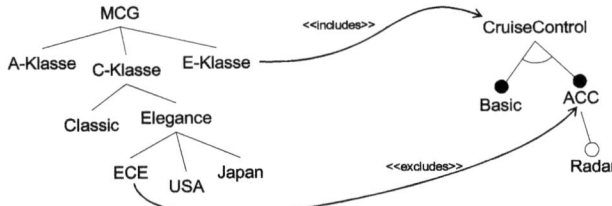

Figure 12.2: Feature selection with links from a product model to the feature model.

severe methodological shortcomings, which are outlined in Section 12.2. Apart from these, there is the disadvantage that what products will be on offer is no longer defined, i.e. what combinations of product attributes are valid.

The other two approaches (3. and 4. in the above list) solve this problem by providing a *product model* in addition to the feature model to be configured. This is a model of all available individual products, usually organized in tree form, see Figure 12.1.

Feature selections can then either be defined by a link from the product element to an included feature (the link is called "includes") or vice versa (then called "included in"), see Figure 12.2. Similarly, "excludes" or "excluded by" links can be used to state that a feature is not part of a product. Since lower-level product elements now inherit the "includes"/"excludes" links from their ancestors—or lower-level features inherit the "included in"/"excluded by" links—not all feature selections have to be defined explicitly. But, from that perspective, this approach is still less efficient than the selection criterion approach.

Note that the product tree can also be considered part of the feature tree itself, which makes no difference from a conceptual point of view. The products then simply become features, i.e. a "U.S. station wagon" becomes a feature a certain product may have. The "includes" or "included in" links can be realized by "needs" links. The advantage is that this solution manages with fewer element and link types, while the separation of models helps to

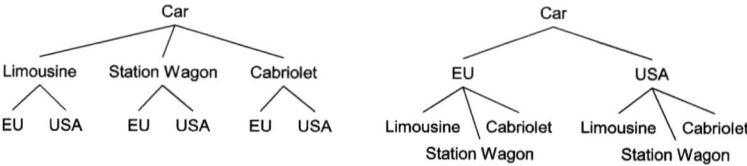

Figure 12.3: Spreading of information in product trees.

prevent misunderstandings and enforces a certain methodological approach connected to the idea of product models.

Finally, the approaches can be combined by having the selection criteria refer to a product model in addition to (or instead of) product attributes (as detailed in [RW05]).

12.2 Limitations of Traditional Configuration Definition

Listing all selected features for each possible product individually is obviously not feasible if the number of products is very large. This is especially true in the automotive domain, [BLPW04, WW02]. There, the products have to be distinguished at least by the market the car is being built for (e.g. EU, US, Japan, ...), the vehicle line (e.g. A-Class, C-Class, E-Class for Mercedes-Benz), the body type (e.g. Limousine, Station Wagon, Cabriolet), the engine types, the transmission types, and a style category (e.g. Classic, Elegance), cf. Section 5.1. If we assume that there are on average three values for each parameter, we get approx. three to the power of six, i.e. some 700 different products, which is still a conservative estimate. Of course, this figure must be reduced somewhat because not all combinations reflect products actually being offered. But even if this reduced the number by 50%, there would still be about 350 products left to be configured. And this does not even take into account the customer configuration.

When using a product model in tree form, the various product criteria (such as country, body type, etc.) are put in a certain order depending on what criteria are applied on each of the tree's levels. This means that the elements representing the values of criteria on lower levels are spread over multiple branches of the tree.

> **Example 4.** Let us assume that we have two product criteria: country (with values EU and USA) and body type (with Limousine, Station Wagon, and Cabriolet). When the body type is used for distinction on the tree's first level and the country on the second level, we obtain multiple elements that only when taken together represent a certain market (see left tree in Figure 12.3). In the example, we thus have three elements representing the U.S. market and another three for the European market. No matter how the product tree is organized, this situation remains basically unchanged. The only thing that changes is the criterion for which the value elements are spread (compare left and right tree in Figure 12.3). □

This separation creates the problem that statements such as "all cars for the U.S. market have cruise control" cannot be defined directly but have to be partly defined at different locations in the product tree, i.e. an "includes" link has to be defined for each USA element. Technically, this makes no difference. But from a methodological point of view, it is desirable to document feature selection considerations as closely as possible because there is a rationale behind each of these considerations that has to be documented and taken into account when changing the product tree or the feature selections later on, e.g. when a new body type is being added to the product tree.

This problem of product trees can be avoided by using feature selection criteria that refer to product attributes (approach no. 2 in the above list). But then a similar problem arises. What if we wished to define that not only the feature CruiseControl is expected as standard equipment in all cars in the U.S., but also some other features such as automatic transmission? Of course, we could define this in the selection criteria of the corresponding features. But the fact that all these selections share the same rationale is lost.

Moreover, the selection criteria of these features will also be influenced by other considerations and it is not documented how the different considerations for a single feature led to the feature's final selection criterion which was recorded.

Example 5. If we wished to state that a certain feature F will be included in all cars for the entire North American market for some reason (perhaps because all competitors offer it as standard equipment or it is traditionally expected by all customers there), and at the same time it has to be included in Canadian cars for some other reason (perhaps owing to special Canadian legislation), the final selection criterion for feature F will only state that the feature is included in the U.S. and Canada—at least in the optimal but unrealistic case that no other considerations influence the criterion even further. When the motivation for one of the individual selection statements is no longer justified or when a market is split in two (e.g. the French- and English-speaking parts of Canada), it is difficult—if not impossible—to decide how this change affects such a "combined" selection criterion. □

The same applies to the other forms of feature selection definition. Of course, all this additional information could be put into separate documentation on the feature model, but this would lead to a new source of inconsistency and many similar problems that typically arise when separately and informally capturing modeling information.

In the automotive domain, such complex and "orthogonal" considerations affecting a single feature's selection are very common in the preconfiguration of products [Gri03] and therefore a more sophisticated form of modeling is needed.

12.3 Configuration Links as a Solution

In summary, the basic problem of traditional approaches is that they model the context in which each feature is selected, either by a logical expression or by links: one such context definition is provided per feature. The actual entity of interest, however—during definition and evolution of configuration information—are *configuration considerations* such as "All North American, i.e. U.S. and Canadian, cars have adaptive cruise control because our competitors offer it as standard equipment there", or "Canadian cars have adaptive cruise control because local legislation requires it.". Since a single one of these considerations may well span several features and the actual considerations are usually highly redundant (as in the example), the per-feature context definition is not a suitable form for documenting them.

116   Chapter 12. Configuration Links — Motivation and Basic Idea

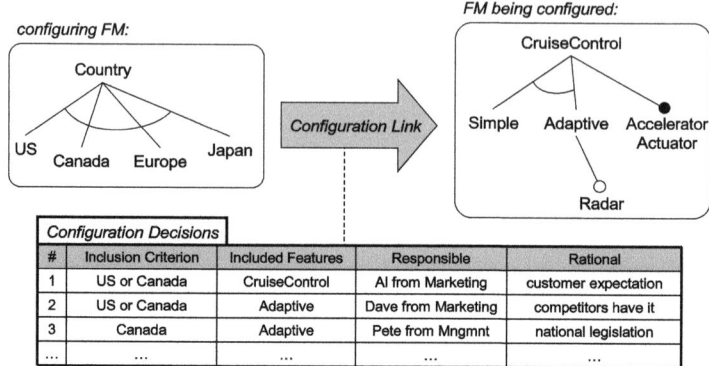

Figure 12.4: Defining feature configurations with configuration decisions.

The configuration definition concept proposed here therefore focuses on configuration considerations as first-order entities of modeling. To achieve this, a dedicated entity called *configuration decision* is introduced. Each configuration decision captures a single configuration consideration. It is provided with a context in which it is valid (e.g. "all North American, i.e. U.S. and Canadian, cars"), a specification of the features selected and deselected in this context and additional meta-information such as a motivation (e.g. "our competitors offer it") and a person responsible for the configuration decision. With this meta-information, it is possible to detect and resolve conflicts that always occur when defining and evolving the configuration of complex feature models. In summary, we obtain:

Definition 20. A *configuration decision* for a feature model *FM* captures a single consideration on how *FM* has to be configured by stating that under certain circumstances some of the features in *FM* need to be selected and/or others need to be deselected; in addition its motivation and the person in charge of changing it is specified. □

Two apparent observations should be noted here: firstly, an appropriate solution is required to specify the "certain circumstances"; in the next chapter we will simply use feature models for this purpose, thus limiting the amount of entities introduced by the concept. Secondly, the fact that a configuration decision's motivation and person in charge was mentioned in the definition, emphasizes the importance of this meta-information for the concept from a methodological perspective.

To illustrate all this, let us consider a small example of such a configuration link, as illustrated in Figure 12.4. Let us assume that there are three considerations that influence the configuration of the cruise control feature model:

1. All North American cars[1] must have cruise control because this feature is expected by customers in this market as standard equipment (marketing decision).

---
[1]Comprises the U.S. and Canadian markets.

12.3. Configuration Links as a Solution

2. All North American cars must be equipped with adaptive cruise control because it is standard equipment for our main competitor (marketing decision).

3. Canadian cars must include adaptive cruise control. This is required by national legislation (management decision).

This situation is modeled as three configuration decisions as shown in the table in Figure 12.4. Each configuration decision has an *inclusion criterion*, a logical expression stating for what product instances the decision is valid. If and only if the inclusion criterion evaluates to true the configuration decision will take effect during configuration. From a conceptual point of view, such an inclusion criterion thus defines a set of product instances which is thereafter referred to as the configuration decision's *product set*. Next, for each decision several features of the configured feature model are listed that are included or excluded (the latter case is not shown in the example) in all product instances that are in the decision's product set. Finally, each decision is supplied with a person in charge and a rationale. When a certain configuration of the configuring feature model is provided, then the configuration of the configured feature model can be derived by combining the configuration decisions that are valid for the product instance that corresponds to the configuration feature model's configuration.

The benefit of documenting the individual configuration decisions separately becomes obvious when considering the redundancy of the considerations in the example. When using one selection criterion per feature, the three considerations would all be compiled into a single rule: North American cars are equipped with adaptive cruise control. However, when one of the considerations changes or ceases to apply, the clear separation of concerns is of great importance in order to establish the effect of this change on the configuration in general. For example, when the competitor changes his product range and no longer offers adaptive cruise control as standard equipment, the motivation of configuration decision no. 2 becomes obsolete. In this case it is very important to know that there were other reasons to ship North American cars with adaptive cruise control. Similarly, when new considerations come up, it is possible to detect conflicts with existing ones; then the rational of the conflicting configuration decision can be consulted or the person in charge can be contacted in order to resolve the conflict.

A configuration link may also only partly configure the destination feature model. In this case, configuration links from more than one source feature model may be used to incrementally configure a single destination model in a step-by-step fashion. Similarly, a single configuration link may connect more than one source feature model to more than one destination feature model. In such a case, the configuration of the destination model(s) depends not only on the configuration of a single source feature model but on the configurations of several.

Chapter 13

Formal Definition of Configuration Links

In order to formally define the concept of configuration links, a formalization of plain feature models is needed as a basis. Therefore the definitions described in Section 4.5 are briefly recapitulated in the coming section. Then, configuration links will be defined in two steps: first in a limited version only for basic feature models without cloned features (Section 13.2) and then for more sophisticated feature models with cardinalities above 1 and other advanced modeling means (Section 13.3). The reason for this separation is that the advanced feature modeling concepts introduce a great deal of additional complexity and it is helpful for the assessment of both configuration links as well as those advanced concepts to be able to compare these two versions. Also, the description of two versions of the concept provides the opportunity to illustrate and discuss several alternatives in defining configuration links and to justify the choices made in the advanced version. This discussion is given in Section 13.4. The basic version can be seen as a minimal version of the concept whereas the advanced version is the one actually proposed for use in practice in this thesis.

13.1 Plain Feature Models

As stated in Definition 9, a basic feature model is an ordered 4-tuple $FM = (F, Parent, Man, Alt)$ that meets several requirements. F is a finite set, called the set of features in FM. $Parent$ is a binary relation over F such that the graph defined by $G_{FM} = (F, Parent)$ is a forest of directed out-trees. Man is a subset of F called the set of mandatory features in FM, and Alt is an equivalence relation over F with

$$(f_1, f_2) \in Alt \land f_1 \neq f_2 \implies \exists p \in F : (p, f_1) \in Parent \land (p, f_2) \in Parent \quad (13.1)$$

For F, $Parent$, Man, and Alt we also write F_{FM}, $Parent_{FM}$, Man_{FM}, and Alt_{FM} respectively.

Conversely, an advanced feature model (cf. Definition 10) is a an ordered 6-tuple $FM = (F, Parent, Inherit, Group, Card, Type)$ where again F is a finite set and $Parent$ is a binary relation over F such that G_{FM} is a forest of directed out-trees. The binary relation $Inherit$ over F defines inheritance relationships such that the graph $G_{FM}^{Inh} = (F, Inherit)$ is an acyclic digraph. $Group$ is an equivalence relation over F to which (13.1) applies as for Alt above. The equivalence class $[f]_{Group}$ of f is called the feature group or simply group of f. Given $\mathcal{C}$ as the set of all valid cardinalities, the (left-total) function $Card_{FM} : F_{FM} \cup F_{FM}/Group \setminus \{M \mid |M| = 1\} \to \mathcal{C}$ defines cardinalities for features and groups. With $\mathcal{V}$ as the set of all legal values, the partial function $Type_{FM} : F_{FM} \to \Pi(\mathcal{V}) \setminus \phi$ defines types of parameterized features: for each $(f, T) \in Type$, f is called a parameterized feature and T is called the type of f.

13.2 Configuration Links for Basic Feature Models

Before links between configurations can be defined, we first require the notion of configurations of feature models. In a second step, this is then used to define configuration links (Section 13.2.2). At the same time, the formalization of feature configurations provides a formal semantics for feature models.

13.2.1 Configurations

In the most simple case, a configuration C_{FM} of a feature model FM can be defined as a subset of the set of features in FM:

$$C_{FM} \subseteq F_{FM} \tag{13.2}$$

Each feature in F_{FM} which is contained in C_{FM} is said to be "selected in C_{FM}", all other features are supposed to be "deselected in C_{FM}". However, with this formalization it is impossible to describe partial configurations, because, according to the fundamental principle of set theory, an element—here: a feature—can only be either contained or not contained in a set ("tertium non datur"), there is no way to express the third case of a feature not being configured yet. In addition, there is a practical problem with the conception behind this formalization: when the feature model is being changed through adding new features to F_{FM}, then existing configurations would immediately define these new features as deselected. However, from a practical standpoint, it would be preferable to see that, with respect to configuration, no decision was taken for these features yet.

For these reasons we choose a more elaborate formalization of a feature configuration. A *feature configuration* C_{FM} of feature model FM is defined as a partial function:

$$C_{FM} : F_{FM} \to \{\top, \bot\} \tag{13.3}$$

Now a feature f is called ...

- "selected in C_{FM}" $\iff (f, \top) \in C_{FM}$,
- "deselected in C_{FM}" $\iff (f, \bot) \in C_{FM}$, and
- "unconfigured in C_{FM}" $\iff \nexists\, b \in \{\top, \bot\} : (f, b) \in C_{FM}$.

For convenience we define

$$C_{FM} \vdash f \iff (f, \top) \in C_{FM} \tag{13.4}$$
$$C_{FM} \nvdash f \iff (f, \bot) \in C_{FM} \tag{13.5}$$

and say "C_{FM} selects f" for $C_{FM} \vdash f$ and "C_{FM} deselects f" for $C_{FM} \nvdash f$. If the configuration is obvious or irrelevant, we simply write $\vdash f$ and $\nvdash f$ respectively. A configuration C_{FM} of a feature model FM is also called an *FM-configuration*, for short. According to a common language use in product line engineering, the term "product instance" or simply "product" may be used instead of configuration. Similarly, we can say a feature is "present" in some product instead of saying it is selected in the configuration (accordingly "not present" instead of deselected).

13.2. Configuration Links for Basic Feature Models

At this point it is important to note that

$$\not\vdash f \iff \neg \vdash f \tag{13.6}$$

Saying that f is deselected is not the same as stating that f is not selected. The reason is the third case of f being unconfigured. In that case, $\not\vdash f$ is false whereas $\neg \vdash f$ evaluates to true. This immediately suggests another convention

$$C_{FM} \vDash f \iff \neg\big((f, \top) \in C_{FM} \lor (f, \bot) \in C_{FM} \big) \tag{13.7}$$

which can be used to denote that a feature is unconfigured.

Obviously not all configurations conform to the constraints implied by a feature model. A configuration C_{FM} is called a *valid configuration* of feature model FM if and only if

$$\forall (p, c) \in Parent_{FM} : C_{FM} \vdash c \Longrightarrow C_{FM} \vdash p \tag{13.8a}$$
$$\forall (p, c) \in Parent_{FM} : c \in Man_{FM} \Longrightarrow (C_{FM} \vdash p \Rightarrow C_{FM} \vdash c) \tag{13.8b}$$
$$\forall f \in Man_{FM} : isRoot(f) \Longrightarrow C_{FM} \vdash f \tag{13.8c}$$
$$\forall g \in F_{FM}/Alt_{FM} : |g| > 1 \Longrightarrow (C_{FM} \vdash parentOf(g) \Rightarrow \exists c \in g : C_{FM} \vdash c) \tag{13.8d}$$
$$\forall (f_1, f_2) \in Alt_{FM} : f_1 \neq f_2 \Longrightarrow \neg(C_{FM} \vdash f_1 \land C_{FM} \vdash f_2) \tag{13.8e}$$

Otherwise the configuration is called *invalid*. The first line states that whenever a child is selected, also its parent needs to be selected. Predicate (13.8b) means that all mandatory children need to be selected if their parent is selected. Note that this clearly shows that mandatory does not mean that the corresponding feature must be present in all configurations; instead it only means that it is required whenever its parent is selected. However, mandatory root features need to be selected in all configurations, which is expressed in (13.8c). The constraint implied by making a child mandatory can be seen as an inverse of the constraint implied by the parent-child relationship. Finally, predicate (13.8e) states that never two alternative features may be selected at the same time.

Also note that the above predicates are carefully formulated such that the undecided state is treated as deselection. For example, (13.8e) could not be formulated as $\forall (f_1, f_2) \in Alt_{FM} : f_1 \neq f_2 \Longrightarrow (C_{FM} \vdash f_1 \Rightarrow C_{FM} \not\vdash f_2)$, because this would fail if f_1 was selected and f_2 was undecided while succeeding for f_1 being selected and f_2 being deselected, and thus the undecided state would be treated differently than the deselected state.

13.2.2 Configuration Links

Based on the definition of a feature model and a configuration thereof, we can now define configuration links. For basic feature models without cloned features this is rather straightforward. We start with configuration decisions.

Let S and T be two feature models with $F_S \cap F_T = \phi$. Let further $\mathcal{C}_S$ be the set of all possible configurations of feature model S. Then a *configuration decision* $D_{S \to T}$ from S to T out of the set $\mathcal{CD}_{S \to T}$ of all configuration decisions from S to T is defined as an ordered 3-tuple $D_{S \to T} = (R, Inc, Exc)$ with

$$R \subseteq \mathcal{C}_S \tag{13.9a}$$
$$Inc, Exc \subseteq F_T \tag{13.9b}$$
$$Inc \cap Exc = \phi \tag{13.9c}$$

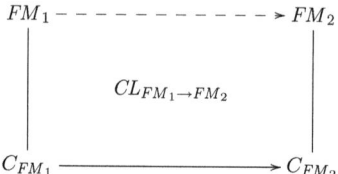

Figure 13.1: Relations defined by a configuration link $CL_{FM_1 \to FM_2}$.

The set R of S-configurations affected by configuration decision D, its *range*, is denoted by R_D. The set *Inc* is called the *set of included features* of D and is denoted by Inc_D, Exc the *set of excluded features*, denoted by Exc_D. S is called source feature model or simply source of D; T is called target feature model or target. For $D_{S \to T}$ we simply write D where the source and target feature models are obvious. As a short form, we define ...

$$c \in D \iff c \in R_D \qquad (13.10)$$

Now, a *configuration link* $CL_{S \to T}$ from feature model S to feature model T can be defined as

$$CL_{S \to T} \subseteq \mathcal{CD}_{S \to T} \qquad (13.11)$$

Again, we call S the *source feature model*, or simply *source*, of configuration link CL and T its *target feature model* or simply *target*. Note here that it is already an important design decision to define a configuration link as a *set* of configuration decisions instead of a sequence, which means that the order of configuration decisions cannot have an impact on their effect.

Further note that a configuration link constitutes, precisely speaking, a link between two configurations, i.e. configurations of two feature models. Conceptually however this may as well be seen as a link between the two corresponding feature models. This is illustrated in Figure 13.1: the configuration link $CL_{FM_1 \to FM_2}$ can be used to derive an FM_2-configuration C_{FM_2} from any given FM_1-configuration as indicated by the drawn-through arrow in the figure; conceptually speaking, this establishes a configuration related link from FM_1 to FM_2, shown as a dashed arrow, because it semantically relates the two feature models.

In order to derive a configuration of the target feature model from a given configuration of the source feature model by way of a configuration link $CL_{S \to T}$, we define an operation χ with

$$\chi : \mathcal{CL}_{S \to T} \times \mathcal{C}_S \longrightarrow \mathcal{C}_T \qquad (13.12)$$

To keep the main definition below from becoming too complex, we need two auxiliary relations. Given a configuration link $CL_{S \to T}$, they are defined as ...

$$Inc^* \ \subseteq \ \mathcal{C}_S \times F_T \qquad (13.13)$$
$$c \ Inc^* f \iff \exists \ D \in CL_{S \to T} \ : \ c \in D \ \land \ f \in Inc_D \qquad (13.14)$$

$$Exc^* \ \subseteq \ \mathcal{C}_S \times F_T \qquad (13.15)$$
$$c \ Exc^* f \iff \exists \ D \in CL_{S \to T} \ : \ c \in D \ \land \ f \in Exc_D \qquad (13.16)$$

13.3. Configuration Links for Advanced Feature Models

This means that an S-configuration c is Inc^*-related to feature $f \in T$ if and only if there exists a configuration decision in $CL_{S \to T}$ that *directly* defines f as being included (correspondingly for Exc^*). However, this does not prove whether f will really be included in a final configuration of T. For this, the parents of f in the feature tree and the exclusions defined by other configuration decisions need to be considered as well. This is the next relation's task.

Relation $Sel_{CL_{S \to T}}$ now specifies whether a certain feature f is selected in a configuration of T which was derived by way of a configuration link $CL_{S \to T}$ from a certain configuration of the source feature model S:

$$Sel_{CL_{S \to T}} \subseteq \mathcal{C}_S \times F_T \tag{13.17}$$

$$c\ Sel_{CL}\ f \iff (\ isRoot(f) \vee c\ Sel_{CL}\ parentOf(f)\ ) \wedge \\ [(c\ Inc^* f\ \wedge\ \neg\ c\ Exc^* f) \vee isMandatory(f)] \tag{13.18}$$

Based on this, we define an operation χ as

$$\chi : \mathcal{CL}_{S \to T} \times \mathcal{C}_S \longrightarrow \mathcal{C}_T \tag{13.19}$$

$$\forall f \in F_T : (\ \chi(CL_{S \to T}, c_S) \vdash f \iff c_S\ Sel_{CL_{S \to T}}\ f\ ) \wedge \\ (\ \chi(CL_{S \to T}, c_S) \nvdash f \iff \neg (c_S\ Sel_{CL_{S \to T}}\ f)\ ) \tag{13.20}$$

and introduce as an abbreviation

$$CL_{S \to T}(c_S) = c_T \iff \chi(CL_{S \to T}, c_S) = c_T \tag{13.21}$$

Now, we say $CL_{S \to T}(c_S)$ is the T-configuration *derived* from c_S by *applying* configuration link $CL_{S \to T}$.

Based on these definitions, we could deduce various conclusions and formulate further observations. However, to not unnecessarily protract the presentation, this will only be shown for advanced feature models below.

13.3 Configuration Links for Advanced Feature Models

As for basic feature models before, we first look at configurations and then, in a second step, define the concept of configuration links on top of that.

13.3.1 Configurations

The whole picture gets a bit more intricate as soon as advanced feature modeling concepts are considered. While the concept of parameterized features can be added quite straightforwardly, cloned features and feature inheritance introduce a new level of complexity. The reason for this is that as soon as you have a cloned feature in your feature model, there is no longer a bijective relation between features in the feature model and features in the configuration: on the level of configuration you may have several features for a single feature of the feature model and you have to distinguish between them. Consider the following example (illustrated in Figure 13.2):

> **Example 6.** In a feature model of a product line of cars, the feature Wiper has cardinality [1..2], i.e. each configuration must have at least one wiper but may also have two. Wiper has a single child feature RainSensor of cardinality [0..1]. In case a configuration selects Wiper twice, e.g. a front wiper and a rear one, the RainSensor needs to be configured for each Wiper separately. □

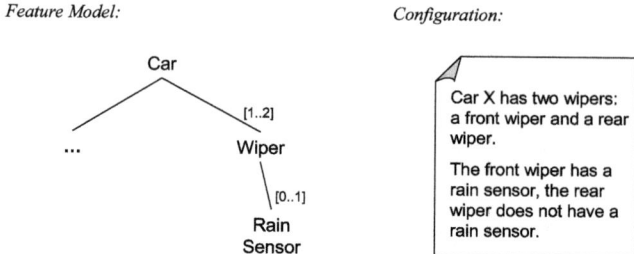

Figure 13.2: Relation between a feature model with a cloned feature and its configuration.

The formalization of a configuration must provide for expressing cases like this one. An interesting thing to note about this situation is that the configuration not only states that there are two wipers, but also that one is the front and the other the rear one. This has a lot in common with class instantiation, and in fact, when using cloned features you are essentially doing class modeling, as was pointed out in [CKK06]. These observations on cloned features are equally applicable to feature inheritance.

So we first need a way to uniquely identify features of the configuration. To this end, we introduce the notion of a configured feature identifier. But before that we need a construct to identify a single instance of a cloned feature: For an advanced feature model FM, an ordered pair $is = (f, i)$ is called an *instance specification* if and only if

$$f \in F_{FM} \qquad (13.22)$$
$$i \in \mathcal{IN} \cup \{ \texttt{NoInstance} \} \qquad (13.23)$$
$$\neg\, isCloned(f) \implies i = \texttt{NoInstance} \qquad (13.24)$$

with $\mathcal{IN}$ being the set of all allowed instance names, $\texttt{NoInstance} \notin \mathcal{IN}$. This means an instance specification provides a feature and optionally an instance name; but an instance name may only be supplied if the feature is a cloned feature (cf. (13.24)). For convenience, we write $f(is)$ for f and $i(is)$ for i and denote the set of all possible instance specifications for feature model FM with $\mathcal{IS}_{FM}$.

Before we can proceed we need a variation of the *Parent* relation that takes inheritance into account. We therefore define $Parent^{Inh}$ as a binary relation over F_{FM} with

$$(p, c) \in Parent^{Inh} \iff (p, c) \in Parent \,\vee \\ (\exists f \in F_{FM} : (p, f) \in Inherit \wedge (f, c) \in Parent^{Inh}) \qquad (13.25)$$

This auxiliary relation achieves this by relating a parent feature to all its children, both direct and inherited ones.

13.3. Configuration Links for Advanced Feature Models

Given an advanced feature model FM, a finite sequence $CFID = (is_0, is_1, ..., is_{n_{max}})$ with $n_{max} \in \mathbb{N}_0$ is called a *configured feature identifier* if and only if

$$\forall\, n \in \mathbb{N}_0, 0 \leq n \leq n_{max} : is_n \in \mathcal{IS}_{FM} \tag{13.26}$$

$$\forall\, n \in \mathbb{N}_0, 0 \leq n \leq n_{max} : \begin{cases} isRoot(f(is_n)) & \text{for } n = 0 \\ (f(is_{n-1}), f(is_n)) \in Parent^{Inh} & \text{for } n > 0 \end{cases} \tag{13.27}$$

$$\forall\, n \in \mathbb{N}_0, 0 \leq n < n_{max} : isCloned(f(is_n)) \implies i(is_n) \neq \texttt{NoInstance} \tag{13.28}$$

This means that all elements in the sequence need to be valid instance specifications (first line), their features must form a path starting with a root feature ((13.27)), and for all but the last specification an instance must be provided if they refer to a cloned feature ((13.28)). The exception that the last instance specification need not provide an instance even if it points to a cloned feature allows a configured feature id to point to a cloned feature itself, instead only to one of its instances.

Similar as before, we denote the set of all valid configured feature identifiers for a feature model FM with $\mathcal{CFID}_{FM}$. In addition, two auxiliary definitions will prove helpful later on: Given a configured feature identifier $cfid = (is_0, is_1, ..., is_{n_{max}})$ we introduce the following two abbreviations

$$f(cfid) \iff f(is_{n_{max}}) \tag{13.29a}$$
$$i(cfid) \iff i(is_{n_{max}}) \tag{13.29b}$$

To illustrate the meaning of configured feature identifiers we consider once more Example 6:

Example 7. The `RainSensor` of the front wiper would be referred to with the following configured feature identifier:

$$FrontRainSensor = (\quad (\texttt{Car}, \texttt{NoInstance}),$$
$$(\texttt{Wiper}, \texttt{"frontWiper"}),$$
$$(\texttt{RainSensor}, \texttt{NoInstance})\ )$$

The first element is an instance specification for root feature `Car`, all others form a path. The second element must provide an instance name because it is not the last element in the sequence and `Wiper` is a cloned feature. In this example we provided the string `"frontWiper"` as an instance name. □

Given a configured feature identifier it is straightforward to find its parent. We define the partial function *parent* as

$$parent : \mathcal{CFID}_{FM} \to \mathcal{CFID}_{FM} \tag{13.30}$$

$$\forall\, (is_0, ..., is_{n_{max}}) \in \mathcal{CFID}_{FM} : n_{max} > 0 \implies$$
$$parent\big((is_0, ..., is_{n_{max}})\big) = (is_0, ..., is_{n_{max}-1}) \tag{13.31}$$

As you can see it is only defined for non-root ids.

Obviously the notation of a configured feature identifier as a sequence of ordered pairs as in Example 7 is not very practical. Therefore we introduce a dedicated notation for configured feature identifiers, similar as above in Section 4.5 for cardinalities. It is defined by the following EBNF grammar.

$$ConfiguredFeatureID \longrightarrow InstanceSpec\ (\ "."\ InstanceSpec)* \qquad (13.32\text{a})$$
$$InstanceSpec \longrightarrow [\ InstanceName\ ":"\ ]\ FeatureName \qquad (13.32\text{b})$$
$$InstanceName \longrightarrow Name\ |\ String \qquad (13.32\text{c})$$
$$FeatureName \longrightarrow Name\ |\ String \qquad (13.32\text{d})$$
$$Name \longrightarrow Char\ (Char\ |\ Digit)* \qquad (13.32\text{e})$$
$$Char \longrightarrow "a"\ |\ \ldots\ |\ "z"\ |\ "A"\ |\ \ldots\ |\ "Z"\ |\ "\_" \qquad (13.32\text{f})$$
$$String \longrightarrow \text{string literal as defined in the Java language} \qquad (13.32\text{g})$$

Instance and feature names can be *Strings* to allow for feature names containing white-space or special characters. As for cardinalities before, not all words of this grammar are legal configured feature identifiers; in particular constraints (13.26) to (13.28) need to be met but are not checked with this grammar. In Chapter 17, this grammar will be used to generate a parser for configured feature identifiers with the parser generator javacc [AP03, Jav08].

Example 8. By applying this notation, the configured feature identifier from Example 7 can be formulated as:

```
Car.frontWiper:Wiper.RainSensor
```

To form a legal configured feature id we must provide an instance name for each cloned feature in the path except for the last element; for this we *may* provide an instance if it is a cloned feature. □

Note that in the actual implementation of this concept, which accompanies this thesis, several usability advancements are provided for the notation of configured feature identifiers beyond what is defined by the above grammar. Most importantly, not an absolute path, i.e. one that starts with a root, needs to be provided, as long as the incomplete path uniquely specifies the configured feature and provides instances for all cloned features among the predecessors of the last feature in the path. With this second improvement, specifying `frontWiper:Wiper.RainSensor` would suffice in Example 8, but not `RainSensor` because in that case no instance would be provided for `RainSensor`'s cloned predecessor `Wiper`.

With $\mathcal{CFID}_{FM}$, the set of all valid configured feature identifiers for feature model FM, we now have an appropriate domain for a configuration function for advanced feature models, corresponding to C_{FM} we defined above for basic feature models. However, we do not have a suitable codomain for this function yet. For basic feature models we used $\{\top, \bot\}$, which was sufficient because all that can be done with a feature of a basic feature model during configuration is to select or deselect it. When configuring advanced feature models however, many different activities are on option:

1. a feature can be selected

2. a feature can be deselected

3. the cardinality of a feature can be narrowed (e.g. change `[0..*]` to `[2..8]`)

4. an instance of a cloned feature can be created

13.3. Configuration Links for Advanced Feature Models

5. the value of a parameterized feature can be set

The first two include the selection and deselection of a feature which is inherited by the parent from another feature, which is the reason why feature inheritance does not appear as a special case in this list. The third activity obviously includes the first two as special cases, i.e. setting the cardinality to [1] actually means selecting a feature while setting it to [0] effectively deselects it. When comparing the last activity, setting a value, with the activity of narrowing a cardinality an inconsistency can be noticed: while allowing to set a cardinality by narrowing it in a sequence of consecutive configurations, we only allow to set a value in one step. To make this more consistent and to connect parameterized features more seamlessly with staged configuration, we allow to narrow the type, i.e. to narrow the set of legal values, of a parameterized feature. In summary, we get the following revised list of configuration activities:

1. the cardinality of a feature can be narrowed

2. an instance of a cloned feature can be created

3. the type of a parameterized feature can be narrowed

Now, to actually set a value in a parameterized feature, its type is simply narrowed down to a single value, which may, of course, be done stepwise.

Based on these considerations we can now formalize an advanced feature model's configuration: A feature configuration C_{FM} of an advanced feature model FM is defined as a partial function

$$C_{FM} : \mathcal{CFID}_{FM} \longrightarrow \mathcal{C} \times \Pi(\mathcal{IN}) \times \Pi(\mathcal{V}) \tag{13.33}$$

with

$$\begin{aligned} C(\textit{cfid}) = (c, i, t) \iff &\; c \subseteq \textit{Card}_{FM}(f(\textit{cfid})) \land \\ &\; (\neg\, \textit{isCloned}(f(\textit{cfid})) \implies i = \phi\,) \land \\ &\; (\,\textit{isParameterized}(f(\textit{cfid})) \implies t \subseteq \textit{Type}_{FM}(f(\textit{cfid}))\,) \land \\ &\; (\neg\, \textit{isParameterized}(f(\textit{cfid})) \implies t = \phi\,) \end{aligned} \tag{13.34}$$

Therefore, the new cardinality and type have to be subsets of the feature's cardinality and type. In case of non-parameterized features, the new type must be the empty set ϕ. Instance names may only be specified for cloned features. Note that the new cardinality and type need not be proper subsets; this allows for not configuring some of these properties while configuring the others. For example, if only the value of f should be set, then the cardinality can be set to $c = Card_{FM}(f)$ and thus remains unchanged.

When interpreted this way the set $\mathcal{C} \times \Pi(\mathcal{IN}) \times \Pi(\mathcal{V})$ used as co-domain above can be seen as the set of all conceivable activities during the configuration of a feature model. For convenient reference we define

$$\mathcal{CA} \iff \mathcal{C} \times \Pi(\mathcal{IN}) \times \Pi(\mathcal{V}) \tag{13.35}$$

and call $\mathcal{CA}$ the *set of configuration activities*. Note that this set is independent of the feature model currently being configured. Since it will be of great importance below we define several abbreviations for a $ca \in \mathcal{CA}$ with $ca = (c, i, t)$:

$$Card(ca) \iff c \qquad (13.36a)$$
$$Inst(ca) \iff i \qquad (13.36b)$$
$$Type(ca) \iff t \qquad (13.36c)$$

Given a configuration C_{FM} and a configured feature identifier $cfid$, we further introduce the following abbreviations

$$Card_C(cfid) \iff Card(C_{FM}(cfid)) \qquad (13.37a)$$
$$Inst_C(cfid) \iff Inst(C_{FM}(cfid)) \qquad (13.37b)$$
$$Type_C(cfid) \iff Type(C_{FM}(cfid)) \qquad (13.37c)$$

Note how these abbreviations follow the scheme already used for feature models: the cardinality of feature f in feature model FM is denoted with $Card_{FM}(f)$ while the cardinality of the configured feature $cfid$ as specified by configuration C_{FM} is denoted with $Card_C(f)$, and so on.

Apparently the configuration of an advanced feature model is somewhat more complex than that of a basic one. However, what remains unchanged is that in the end we mainly want to know whether a certain feature has been selected or not. For this we introduce a partial function $\sigma : \mathcal{CFID}_{FM} \longrightarrow \{\top, \bot\}$ with

$$\sigma(cfid) = \top \iff (\ isRoot(cfid)\ \lor\ \sigma(parentOf(cfid)) = \top\ )$$
$$\land \begin{cases} Card_C(cfid) = [1] & \text{if } Card_{FM}(f(cfid)) = [0..1] \\ \top & \text{if } Card_{FM}(f(cfid)) = [1] \\ \bot & \text{if } Card_{FM}(f(cfid)) = [0] \\ Inst_C(cfid) \ni i(cfid) & \text{if } isCloned(f(cfid)) \end{cases} \qquad (13.38)$$

$$\sigma(cfid) = \bot \iff (\ \neg isRoot(cfid)\ \land\ \sigma(parentOf(cfid)) = \bot\ )$$
$$\lor \begin{cases} Card_C(cfid) = [0] & \text{if } Card_{FM}(f(cfid)) = [0..1] \\ \bot & \text{if } Card_{FM}(f(cfid)) = [1] \\ \top & \text{if } Card_{FM}(f(cfid)) = [0] \\ Inst_C(cfid) \not\ni i(cfid) & \text{if } isCloned(f(cfid)) \end{cases} \qquad (13.39)$$

From here we follow the nomenclature we introduced above for basic feature models and say a configured feature identified by $cfid$ is ...

- "selected in C_{FM}" $\iff (cfid, \top) \in \sigma_C$,
- "deselected in C_{FM}" $\iff (cfid, \bot) \in \sigma_C$, and
- "unconfigured in C_{FM}" $\iff \not\exists\, b \in \{\top, \bot\} : (cfid, b) \in \sigma_C$.

and define for convenience

$$C_{FM} \vdash cfid \iff (cfid, \top) \in \sigma_C \qquad (13.40)$$
$$C_{FM} \not\vdash cfid \iff (cfid, \bot) \in \sigma_C \qquad (13.41)$$

13.3. Configuration Links for Advanced Feature Models

and say "C_{FM} selects cfid" for $C_{FM} \vdash \mathit{cfid}$ and "C_{FM} deselects cfid" for $C_{FM} \not\vdash \mathit{cfid}$.
A configuration C_{FM} is called a *partial configuration* if and only if

$$\exists\ \mathit{cfid} \in \mathcal{CFID}_{FM} : (\neg C_{FM} \vdash \mathit{cfid}\ \wedge\ \neg C_{FM} \not\vdash \mathit{cfid}) \vee \\ |\mathit{Type}_C(\mathit{cfid})| > 1 \tag{13.42}$$

Otherwise it is called a *full configuration*.

13.3.2 Configuration Links

Before being able to define configuration decisions on the level of advanced feature models—similar as we did above for basic feature models—we need an additional concept, called configuration step. A configuration step can be seen as the smallest unit of an overall configuration activity, for example setting a single value or narrowing a certain feature's cardinality. For an advanced feature model FM it is defined as a 4-tuple

$$cs_{FM} = (\mathit{cfid}, c, i, t) \tag{13.43}$$

with

$$\mathit{cfid} \in F_{FM}\ ;\ c \subseteq \mathcal{C}\ ;\ i \subseteq \mathcal{IN}\ ;\ t \subseteq \mathcal{V} \tag{13.44}$$

that meets the following constraints

$$c\ \subseteq\ \mathit{Card}_{FM}(f(\mathit{cfid})) \tag{13.45}$$
$$i \neq \phi \implies \mathit{isCloned}(f(\mathit{cfid}))\ \wedge\ i(\mathit{cfid}) = \texttt{NoInstance} \tag{13.46}$$
$$t \neq \phi \implies \mathit{isParameterized}(f(\mathit{cfid}))\ \wedge\ t \subseteq \mathit{Type}_{FM}(f(\mathit{cfid})) \tag{13.47}$$

This means that the cardinality and type specified by a configuration step need to be subsets of the cardinality and type of the feature that the configured feature identifier cfid is pointing to, i.e. the cardinality and type may only be narrowed by a configuration step. This further means that instance names may only be provided for configured feature identifiers that refer to a cloned feature but not an instance of that cloned feature (cf. predicate (13.46)). The reason for this restriction is that it makes no sense to create an instance for a non-cloned feature or for an existing instance of a cloned feature.

The set of all configuration steps for feature model FM is denoted with $\mathcal{CS}_{FM}$ while $\mathcal{CS}$ denotes the set of all configuration sets.

Apart from the configured feature identifier a configuration step consists of an element of $\mathcal{CA}$ and, correspondingly, the rational behind the above constraints is the same as described before for predicate (13.34). In other words, the information captured in a single configuration step corresponds exactly to the information captured in a configuration for a single configured feature identifier, i.e. a narrowed cardinality, a set of instance names and a narrowed type. The reason why we cannot go without the concept of a configuration step and just use a partial configuration is that, when dealing with configuration decisions below, we need to handle several—possibly contradicting—configuration steps for a single configured feature identifier. This is not possible with a (partial) configuration because a configuration was defined to be a function, i.e. it can only relate each configured feature identifier to a single configuration information.

Again, a dedicated notation for configuration steps would come in handy. We thus define:

$$ConfigurationStep \longrightarrow ConfiguredFeatureID \\ (\ Cardinality \\ |\ (\ "="\ String\ ) \\ |\ (\ "\$"\ InstanceName\ )\ ) \tag{13.48}$$

When supplying a cardinality, then a configuration step is formed for narrowing the corresponding feature's cardinality. The notation with "=" is used to denote a configuration step for setting a value and with "$" an instance is created. Not all forms of configuration steps can be denoted with this notation, esp. the narrowing of a type (instead of setting a value) cannot be expressed with this notation.

As a preparation to dealing with several configuration steps for a single configured feature identifier, we need to define what happens when such configuration steps are combined. This is achieved with a function $+_{CS} : CS \times CS \longrightarrow CS$, with

$$(cfid, c_a, i_a, t_a) +_{CS} (cfid, c_b, i_b, t_b) = (cfid_c, c_c, i_c, t_c)$$

$\Longleftrightarrow$

$$cfid_c = cfid \tag{13.49}$$

$$c_c = \begin{cases} c_a \cap c_b & \text{when } c_a \cap c_b \neq \phi \\ \{0\} & \text{otherwise} \end{cases} \tag{13.50}$$

$$i_c = i_a \cup i_b \tag{13.51}$$

$$t_c = \begin{cases} t_a \cap t_b & \text{when } t_a \cap t_b \neq \phi \\ Type_{FM}(f(cfid)) & \text{when } t_a \cap t_b = \phi \wedge isParameterized(f(cfid)) \\ \phi & \text{otherwise} \end{cases} \tag{13.52}$$

Note that consequently $+_{CS}$ is only defined for two configuration steps for the same configured feature identifier. For $+_{CS}$ we write $+$ where this is unambiguous. As another abbreviation we say

$$\sum_{i=n}^{m} cs_i \Longleftrightarrow cs_n +_{CS} cs_{n+1} +_{CS} \ldots +_{CS} cs_m \tag{13.53}$$

The fact that $+_{CS}$ is commutative (which can easily be shown because it is defined by way of the commutative set operations union and intersection) will be of importance below when showing that the order of configuration decisions is irrelevant. Also, the fact that we defined the combined cardinality of two non-intersecting cardinalities as $\{0\}$ is significant because this realizes the precedence of exclude over include, as will be shown below.

Equipped with these utensils we are now prepared to define configuration decisions and links. Let S and T be two advanced feature models with $F_S \cap F_T = \phi$. Let further C_S be the set of all possible configurations of feature model S. Then a configuration decision $D_{S \to T}$ from S to T out of the set $CD_{S \to T}$ of all configuration decisions from S to T is defined as a pair $D_{S \to T} = (R, Steps)$ with

$$R \subseteq C_S \tag{13.54}$$

$$Steps \subseteq CS_T \tag{13.55}$$

13.3. Configuration Links for Advanced Feature Models

As above, the set R of S-configurations affected by configuration decision D is called the decision's *range* and is denoted by R_D. The set *Steps* is called the *set of configuration steps* of D and is denoted by $Steps_D$. Note that we here no longer have a separation between inclusion and exclusion, as was the case with configuration decisions for basic feature models. As before, S is called source feature model or simply source of D; T is called target. For $D_{S \to T}$ we simply write D where the source and target feature models are obvious. As a short form, we define ...

$$c \in D \iff c \in R_D \tag{13.56}$$

Now, a *configuration link* $CL_{S \to T}$ from an advanced feature model S to another advanced feature model T, out of the set of all such configuration links $\mathcal{CL}_{S \to T}$, can be defined as

$$CL_{S \to T} \subseteq \mathcal{CD}_{S \to T} \tag{13.57}$$

Again we define a configuration link as a *set* of configuration decisions instead of a sequence. We can do so because the order of configuration decisions shall not have an impact on their effect. We will see below why we can safely treat configuration decisions that way.

The following auxiliary function $Cfg_{CL_{S \to T}}$ now specifies how a certain feature f of feature model T is configured in a T-configuration which was derived by way of a configuration link $CL_{S \to T}$ from a certain configuration of the source feature model S:

$$Cfg_{CL_{S \to T}} : \mathcal{C}_S \times \mathcal{CFID}_T \longrightarrow \mathcal{C} \times \Pi(\mathcal{IN}) \times \Pi(\mathcal{V}) \tag{13.58}$$

It is defined by

$$Cfg_{CL_{S \to T}}(cfg, cfid) = (c, i, t)$$

$$\iff$$

$$(cfid, c, i, t) = \sum_{cs \in CL_{S \to T} \,\wedge\, id(cs) = cfid} cs \tag{13.59}$$

This function already provides the semantic of configuration links by showing how the link's configuration decisions influence the configuration of the target feature model; what remains to be defined is a function to obtain an entire target configuration from a source configuration (see χ below). At this point it becomes apparent why it was legal to ignore the order of configuration steps in the definition of a configuration link, because their effect relies entirely on the commutative function $+_{\mathcal{CS}}$.

Finally, in order to derive a complete configuration of the target feature model from a given configuration of the source feature model by way of a configuration link we define an operation χ as

$$\chi : \mathcal{CL}_{S \to T} \times \mathcal{C}_S \longrightarrow \mathcal{C}_T \tag{13.60}$$

$$\chi(CL_{S \to T}, cfg_S) = \{ \; (\; cfid, \; Cfg(cfg_S, cfid) \;) \; | \; cfid \in \mathcal{CFID}_T \; \} \tag{13.61}$$

and introduce as an abbreviation

$$CL_{S \to T}(cfg_S) = cfg_T \iff \chi(CL_{S \to T}, cfg_S) = cfg_T \tag{13.62}$$

Now, we say $CL_{S \to T}(cfg_S)$ is the T-configuration *derived* from cfg_S by *applying* configuration link $CL_{S \to T}$.

For two configuration links $CL^a_{S_a \to T_a}$ and $CL^b_{S_b \to T_b}$ with $T_a = S_b$ we define

$$CL^a_{S_a \to T_a} \circ CL^b_{S_b \to T_b} \in \mathcal{CL}_{S_a \to T_b} \tag{13.63}$$

$$(CL^a_{S_a \to T_a} \circ CL^b_{S_b \to T_b})(cfg_{S_a}) \iff CL^b_{S_b \to T_b}(CL^a_{S_a \to T_a}(cfg_{S_a})) \tag{13.64}$$

Since we defined configuration links as ordinary sets of configuration decisions, and since we defined how conflicting configuration decisions are combined (cf. (13.49)–(13.52)) we can safely apply ordinary set operations such as union, intersection and set-minus to them as long as the source and target feature models of all configuration decisions match.

13.4 Comparison of Basic and Advanced Forms

The previous two sections provided a detailed definition of configuration links in two forms: a basic and an advanced one. In this section these two versions are now compared to each other and, based on that, it will be discussed which is preferable for use in practice or if both versions are required in order to be able choose for each project the one most appropriate. As was revealed in the introduction of this chapter already, we will see that the basic version can be abandoned and the advanced version can arguably be deemed suitable for all application contexts.

But let us start with the differences between the versions. First of all there is this obvious difference that the basic version does not support cloned features, feature inheritance and parameterized features. Closely related to that, the basic version gets by with definitions and rules of significantly less complexity with obvious advantages for understanding and applying the concept. Similarly, the effect of a configuration decision is simply defined by two sets of features, one for those features included by the decision and the other for the excluded ones. The advanced version of the concept needs a comparatively complex set of configuration steps for this.

In addition to these rather apparent differences, there is a more subtle, yet very important difference to note. It is related to how a configuration is defined and how the validity of such a configuration is assured. As illustrated in Figure 13.3, the basic approach is to define a configuration function C_{FM} that directly specifies the selection or deselection of a feature, represented as the set $\{\top, \bot\}$. The validity of such a configuration is then enforced by stating several constraints that must be met (cf. propositions (13.8a) through (13.8e)). In the advanced version a different solution was chosen: here the co-domain of the configuration function is the set of all possible configuration activities and thus this function defines a configuration activity to be taken for each configured feature. Then, as a separate step, function σ was provided to *interpret* the configuration activities defined by C_{FM} in terms of selection and deselection of features[1]. This allows to incorporate some of the validity constraints from above into the definition of σ and thus ensure by definition that these constraints are met. Namely this is the case for the constraints related to the hierarchical tree structure of the feature model as captured in propositions (13.8a) to (13.8c). When comparing these to the definition of σ in (13.38) f. it can be seen how they correspond to each other. However, this is not the case for the last validity constraint (13.8e). It remains as a criterion to distinguish valid from invalid configurations.

---

[1] Note that the domain of σ is actually $\mathcal{CFID}_{FM}$, not $\mathcal{CA}$. The arrow in the diagram for σ is intended to indicate that it relies on C_{FM} and can be seen as an add-on to C_{FM}.

13.4. Comparison of Basic and Advanced Forms

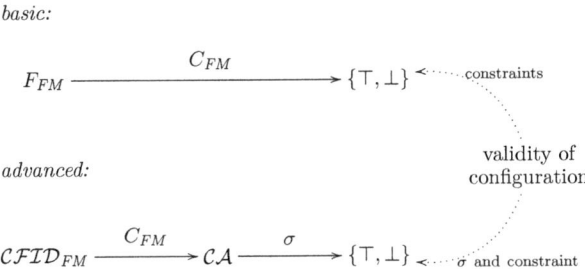

Figure 13.3: Comparison of how configurations were defined in the simple and the advanced versions of the concept.

The main reason for this separation of the configuration definition in the advanced version is that the configuration activities defined by C_{FM} do not directly constitute a statement on selection or deselection of a feature and therefore yet have to be interpreted in that sense. When doing so it is a good opportunity to take into account some of the validity constraints as pointed out before. However, there is also an important methodological implication of this: when defining a configuration by way of configuration decisions there is no need to ensure that the outcome is always valid in the sense of the aforementioned validity constraints. Instead, many sources of invalidity are handled by σ and interpreted in a safe way such that the engineer editing the configuration decisions is released from the duty of ensuring this. Of course, this in turn requires that the engineer is supplied with simple guidelines and rules to be able to foresee the effect of this "safe interpretation" of his configuration specifications. This is described in detail in the next section.

This comparison of the two options of defining configurations clearly shows how the concept of configuration links is closely linked to that.

At this point we can come back to the question of how to treat the two versions of the concept. Is the additional complexity of the advanced version actually worth the effort and also tolerable during dissemination and practical application of the concept? Or would it be possible to confine oneself to the basic version? Another possibility to be considered is using the basic version whenever it is sufficient and reverting to the advanced concept when its strengths are actually required.

To begin with, abandoning the advanced version completely in favor of the basic approach is not an option because the advance feature modeling concepts of, most importantly, parameterization, but also cloned features and feature inheritance, are not dispensable in embedded systems domains and in particular in the automotive domain, as was pointed out in Chapter 4. One the other hand, it was said there that the use of these advanced concepts (esp. that of cloned features) should be limited to those cases where they are actually required. This would suggest the solution of having both versions of the configuration link concept available and choosing between them depending on the current situation. However, when looking at the advanced version and examining how it handles the special case of an advanced feature model that does not make use of any advanced feature modeling concept, it can be noticed that most of the additional complexity is avoided. Most importantly:

- The configured feature ids are in that case just alternative elements for the features without introducing additional complexity (i.e. F_{FM} and $\mathcal{CFID}_{FM}$ are isomorphic).

- The configuration steps of a configuration decision are limited to the two cases of setting the cardinality to [0] or [1], because there are only optional features with cardinality [0..1] to be configured when not using any advanced concepts. These two cases correspond exactly to the two set of included and excluded features in the basic version of the concept.

This means that in the standard case of non-parameterized and non-cloned features the advanced version of the concept more or less comes down to the basic version and its additional complexity is not of much harm. A tool could easily hide the additional complexity by providing a flexible parser for configured feature identifiers that accepts incomplete paths as long as they uniquely identify the configured feature or by presenting the a configuration decision's configuration steps as two sets of feature that are included and excluded by the decision.

In summary this means that we can now safely dismiss the basic version of the concept as given in Section 13.2 and view the advanced version as the only, general definition of configuration links for both basic and advanced feature models. In the remainder of this thesis we will therefore refer the advanced version only.

13.5 Contradictory Configuration Specifications

As pointed out in Chapter 12 above, an important design goal of configuration decisions and links is to allow for redundancy in configuration specifications. As a consequence, these specifications will certainly contain a substantial amount of contradictions. In order to be practically feasible, a concept which fosters the use of redundancy therefore needs to treat these contradictions in a clear and understandable way such that an engineer can easily and unambiguously foresee the effect of configuration specifications, especially in contradictory cases.

This section is therefore dedicated to a discussion of such contradictory specifications of configuration. This will be investigated in two steps: first, possible forms of contradictions are examined and categorized and, second, it will be investigated how these contradictions are treated and—where appropriate—resolved by the concepts defined above. We won't need to amend the above concepts; instead they where already carefully defined in a way that correctly handles the problem cases identified here. This section therefore also intends to explain these design decisions.

Before identifying possible contradictions and investigating how they are treated, we need to explain what is meant by a contradiction in this sense.

Definition 21. A *configuration contradiction* occurs whenever

   a. two or more configuration steps of a configuration link, which are both in effect for the same source configuration, state conflicting configurations which cannot both be put into practice at the same time, OR

13.5. Contradictory Configuration Specifications

b. a single configuration step states a configuration which is not allowed by the feature model to be configured, i.e. the target feature model of the configuration link.

Such a contradiction may but need not constitute an erroneous inconsistency in the configuration specification. □

The simplest example of a contradiction is one configuration step specifying a cardinality of [0] and another one of [1] for the same configured feature. It is important to note that the use of the term "contradiction" instead of "inconsistency" shall emphasize that not every contradiction is to be seen as an error in the configuration specification. Instead, for each contradiction we have two possibilities: it can be seen as an ...

1. inconsistency, i.e. an error in the configuration specification, or as an

2. intended, legal contradiction that is resolved by the concept of configuration links in a predefined way by deciding which of the conflicting configuration specifications will be granted priority.

For the sake of completeness it should be noted that, in the second solution, the contradiction can also be resolved by defining that not one of the conflicting configurations is chosen but that some third possibility is used which is different from all specified conflicting configurations (example will be given below).

So, what contradictions may possibly be encountered in a configuration specification which is formulated by way of a configuration link? In the simplest case, a configuration may state a value for the new cardinality or type which is not a subset of the cardinality or type of the feature in the target feature model. For example, this would be the case if a configuration link targeting the feature model from Figure 13.2 contained a decision narrowing the cardinality of Wiper to [0], because, according to the feature model, this is not a legal cardinality for Wiper. This trivial case of a contradiction is handled by the concept through the definition of configuration step: when the specified cardinality or type is not legal or if an instance is created for a non-cloned feature, then we do not have a configuration step at all, because this would violate constraint (13.34) which is part of the definition of configuration step. Strictly speaking, we do not even have a contradiction according to the above definition of this term, because it refers to configuration steps.

Apart from this trivial case, the most important contradictions fall into three categories. First, there may be two or more configuration decisions stating conflicting properties for the same configured feature. Two cardinalities $c_1, c_2 \in \mathcal{C}$ conflict if and only if neither $c_1 \subseteq c_2$ nor $c_2 \subseteq c_1$ is true, even if their intersection is non-empty. Exactly the same applies to types, which were defined above as sets of legal values of a parameterized feature. With respect to instance creation, we cannot produce a contradiction of this category, because there is nothing like the deletion of an instance. The creation of several instances of the same cloned configured feature through several configuration decisions has a simple additive semantic. The question whether a legal number of instances was created does not fall into this category and is further discussed below.

The second category comprises those contradictions that show up when considering the tree hierarchy of the target feature model. Such contradictions may only appear between configuration decisions targeting two different configured features, so we have a clear distinction from the first category. The contradictions of this category all have the same structure: a

Chapter 13. Formal Definition of Configuration Links

Table 13.1: Overview of typical forms of contradictions in a configuration link $CL_{S \to T}$ (with $p, f, c \in T$ and p *Predecessor* f and f *Parent* c).

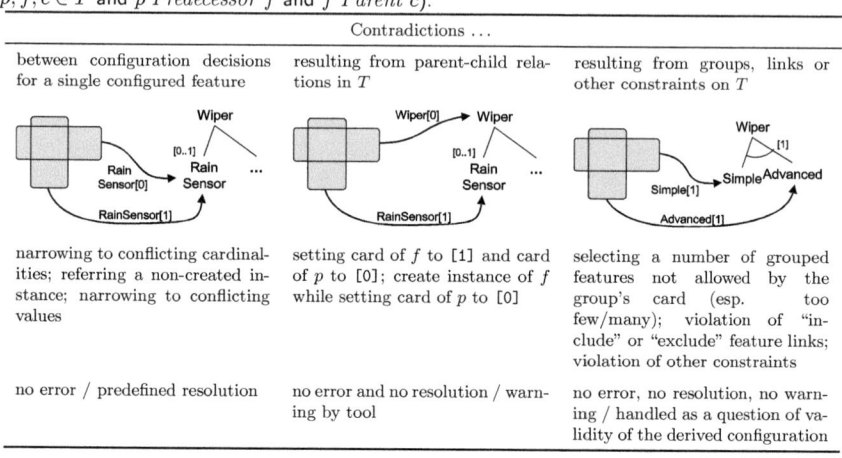

Contradictions ...		
between configuration decisions for a single configured feature	resulting from parent-child relations in T	resulting from groups, links or other constraints on T
narrowing to conflicting cardinalities; referring a non-created instance; narrowing to conflicting values	setting card of f to [1] and card of p to [0]; create instance of f while setting card of p to [0]	selecting a number of grouped features not allowed by the group's card (esp. too few/many); violation of "include" or "exclude" feature links; violation of other constraints
no error / predefined resolution	no error and no resolution / warning by tool	no error, no resolution, no warning / handled as a question of validity of the derived configuration

predecessor's cardinality is set to [0] while the successor is set to [1]. From a methodological point of view, this is the most important kind of contradiction and it is therefore particularly important to find reasonable means to cope with such situations. Note that the inverse of this case, i.e. a parent is set to [1] while a mandatory child is set to [0] is *not* a contradiction of this category but instead is an example for the trivial case identified above, because setting the mandatory child to [0] would be a direct violation of the child's cardinality of [1]; because this is avoided by definition (see above) we can therefore not encounter such a case within a configuration link as defined in the previous section.

The final category encompasses all other contradictions that do not fall in one of the other two categories and are not covered by the trivial case. Such contradictions arise in situations where one or more configuration decisions state a configuration which violates some other constraint implied by the target feature model. These can be (1) the cardinality of a feature group (i.e. invalid number of grouped features selected), (2) the cardinality of a cloned feature (i.e. invalid number of instances), or (3) some general, additional constraint defined for the target model, including the special case of feature links of type "include" and "exclude".

This completes our brief survey of possible contradictions. The three groups identified here are summarized in Table 13.5. So we can now turn to finding appropriate ways to deal with these contradictions. As already indicated above, we will find that the definition of configuration links and their associated concepts were already formulated such that this is achieved; we did not discuss these considerations above to not clutter the presentation too much.

We also already explained how the abovementioned trivial case is prevented by definition. The definition of configuration step makes sure that these problem cases are avoided. So, when talking about a configuration step, configuration decision or configuration link, we can be sure that we have none of these cases. In a tool, this would mean that when the user enters a configuration decision containing such a configuration step which not conforms to

13.5. Contradictory Configuration Specifications

the definition, an error would be shown for this configuration decision and it would be ignored when applying the configuration link. The tool implementation provided along with this thesis is doing just that. Apart from invalid cardinalities or types, the tool also treats unknown features or ambiguous configured feature identifiers in the same way.

If we treated category 1 contradictions in the same manner as errors, then it would be very difficult to define redundant configuration decisions. An engineer would carefully have to define the decisions such that never an include overlaps an exclude. This would be extremely difficult an would mean that the configuration decisions would again become reliant upon each other, because the inclusion criterion of a decision which includes a certain feature f would need to be adapted when a decision is being added that excludes f for some special cases. Consequently it is clear that contradiction of this kind need to be resolved by the concept. This is done by operation $+_{\mathcal{CS}}$ in propositions (13.49) through (13.52). Conflicting cardinalities are resolved to their intersection or, if the intersection is empty, to [0]. In particular the important special case of a contradictory configuration of an optional feature (setting cardinality to [0] and [1]) is resolved to [0], which means that excluding features has a higher priority than including them. Or differently: A single configuration decision excluding a feature overrides any number of decisions including it. For types the situation is similar yet different: conflicting types are resolved to their intersection but, when the intersection is empty the conflicting configurations have no effect at all. The reason for treating the empty intersection differently for cardinalities and types is that with types there is no meaningful default value that could be used.

The second category of contradictions, i.e. such induced by the hierarchy of parent/child relations, is arguably the most important. If a child was configured to be selected while one of its predecessors is configured to be deselected, this would clearly constitute a contradiction. However, the question is when a non-root feature is actually being configured to be selected. This could be the case when its cardinality is narrowed to [1]. But in fact, a feature's cardinality is to be interpreted relative to its parent. For mandatory features this was emphasized strongly in Section 4.5: when a feature is mandatory this means only that it is mandatory with respect to its parent, i.e. it is present in all products in which its parent is present, not that it is present in each and every product. Consistently, narrowing a non-root feature's cardinality to [1] by way of configuration only means that it will be selected whenever the parent is selected. With this interpretation, setting a feature to [1] while setting a predecessor to [0] is not a paradox really. To make a long story short: the cardinality set for a feature f by way of configuration links is to be interpreted with respect to f's parent.

Example 9. Consider a feature model with a feature CruiseControl having a single child Radar, both features have cardinality [0..1]. By specifying a configuration decision that sets Radar's cardinality to [1] for all US cars except A-Class, for example, then this only means that the US cars other than A-Class are equipped with a wiper if(!) they have a CruiseControl. In other words, in order to make the Radar actually appear in a product instance, the same or another configuration decision needs to set the cardinality of feature CruiseControl to [1] for a certain condition, e.g. all US cars. □

This behavior is realized by how we defined configurations of advanced feature models and the selected / deselected relations σ, $\vdash$ and $\nvdash$ (cf. propositions (13.38) to (13.41)). At this point we should briefly consider whether this solution is actually suitable in practice. In many circumstances it proved very versatile to define the selection of features this way, i.e. always relative to their parents. However, there are cases where you want to state that a certain feature should be actually present in a certain configuration; but this can easily be expressed by setting the cardinalities of all predecessors to [1] (which can conveniently be achieve through the *requires* function). Then, a contradiction with another configuration decision setting one of the predecessors to [0] is simply treated as a category 1 contradiction. Since this results in a prioritization of the exclude over the include and therefore in an exception to what was intended, a tool can aid the engineer in spotting such contradictions. But they are not to be seen as an error.

Note that in this discussion of category 2 contradictions we only considered optional and mandatory predecessors, i.e. such with a cardinality of [0..1] or [1]. When there are cloned features among the predecessors, the observations remain unchanged in principle, the only difference is that an appropriate instance of the predecessor needs to be created instead of setting the predecessor's cardinality to [1]. But this is also covered by the *requires* function. In addition, the problem of another configuration decision negating the configuration of the predecessor cannot occur here, because this would again require the deletion of instances which is not possible. So this case is a bit less problematic.

The last type of contradictions is related to a violation of some secondary constraint implied by the target feature model (groups, links, etc.). These cases are not at all avoided, prohibited or resolved by way of the concept's definition. It is rather perfectly legal to specify configuration links that result in such invalid configurations. It lies in the responsibility of the tool to aid the engineer in spotting and resolving such issues (see below). The advantage of this solution is that it keeps the basic concept of configuration links as simple as possible and limits side-effects between configuration decisions to a minimum.

The survey of possible contradictions and their resolution presented in this section can also serve another purpose: as a list of critical problem cases that may occur during the definition and evolution of large configuration link repositories. It is therefore an ideal basis for finding appropriate supportive analyses and functionalities that need to be provided by a tool in order to allow for the application of the concept in complex real-world projects.

13.6 Required Refinements for Implementation

The formalization of configuration links given in Section 13.3 above is intended to provide a sound and precise definition of the fundamental idea behind the concept. To not blur the presentation with unnecessary detail and thereby jeopardize that intention, it was not planned as a comprehensive formal specification for an implementation. However, this means that several details had to be left out or has to be defined on a fairly abstract level which is not sufficient as a basis for implementation. In this section, these aspects are briefly discussed.

As a by-product this makes a very nice example for such things that can be expressed in a set-theory-based formalization very straightforwardly and elegantly but, at the same time, diminish the formalization's value for guiding the implementation, leading to a certain gap between the formalization and implementation.

The refinements in this section can arguably be deemed indispensable for an implementation of the concept whereas the advanced considerations discussed in Chapter 15 are dealing with rather optional additions.

13.6. Required Refinements for Implementation

Inclusion Criterion

The inclusion criterion of a configuration decision was formalized as a set of configurations for which the decision shall be in effect. Implemented naively, this would mean that all those configurations would need to be recorded. While being a compact and precise formal explanation of the inclusion criterion's purpose, this is apparently not suitable for implementation in non-trivial cases.

Therefore a more concise means of expression needs to be found. To achieve this the inclusion criterion can, as its name already suggests, be represented as an expression in propositional logic. The syntax and semantics of conjunctions, disjunctions and negation can be lent from the standard definitions of a propositional calculus [KK06] without change. The same applies to precedence rules. However, for the atomic formulae we have to define syntax and semantics. For the syntax we can here reuse the definition of configuration steps from page 129, which means that in the inclusion criterion configuration steps can be used to express certain conditions with respect to the configuration of the source feature model. For the semantics we define for a given feature model FM a function

$$evaluate : \mathcal{C}_{FM} \times \mathcal{CS}_{FM} \longrightarrow \{true, false\} \qquad (13.65)$$

with

$$\begin{aligned} evaluate\bigl(cfg, (cfid, c, i, t)\bigr) = true \iff\ & Card_{cfg}(cfid) \subseteq c\ \wedge \\ & Type_{cfg}(cfid) \subseteq t\ \wedge \\ & i \subseteq Inst_{cfg}(cfid) \end{aligned} \qquad (13.66)$$

This means that a configuration step used as a proposition evaluates to true with respect to a certain configuration when that configuration narrows the cardinality and type of the corresponding configured feature to the same extent or even more and all instances specified in the configuration step are also created by the configuration for the corresponding configured feature.

However this does not take into account the parent-child relations. It is possible to test with this mechanism, for example, whether a configuration is setting the cardinality of a certain configured feature to [1]. But in most cases this is not of interest; instead the selection state as defined by function σ above is usually the primary concern. This could be achieved by way of a logical conjunction of configuration steps that test for the configured feature in question and all its predecessors if the cardinality is set to [1]. Of course this is tedious when done manually. Therefore an implementation of the concept must provide a means of expression to conveniently test the selection state of a configured feature as defined by σ. In the accompanying demonstrator this is the purpose of the unary operators "sel" and "desel".

Types of Parameterized Features

Similar as for the inclusion criterion, the type of a parameterized feature was at first defined in a very simple fashion: as a set of legal values. Again such an enumerative approach is not feasible when it comes to implementation. Therefore we also need a refined type definition mechanism. In the prototypical implementation of the concept a fairly straightforward solution was devised. All values of parameterized features are represented as strings; a type then simply restricts the allowed string values in various ways. The following forms of restrictions are supported:

- Boolean: the string value is restricted to the two strings "true" and "false".
- Integer: the string must be a sequence of digits, optionally prepended with "-"; in addition a minimum and maximum value may be specified.
- Float: the string must be a sequence of digits, optionally prepended with "-" or containing "."; again, a minimum and maximum value may be specified.
- String: the string is not restricted at all; optionally a pattern may be specified in form of a standard regular expression that the string value must match.
- Enum: the string is restricted to a finite set of explicitly specified string values.

In principle, it does not make sense to have a parameterized feature with boolean type, because the feature is itself a boolean property due to the two states of being selected or deselected. This type was added because in the implementation the type mechanism described here is also used for user attributes (user customizable attributes for features and other elements, such as a project specific "Status").

Since this type mechanism does not really constitute a novel scientific contribution and is more or less exchangeable without affecting the fundamental idea of the concept of configuration links, no further formalization of the type system is given here. In Appendix A, where the implementation of the data model is documented, you can find some more information on how these types were realized.

Configuration Links as n:m Associations

We above defined configuration links to have exactly one source and one target feature model, which means we thought of them as 1:1 associations so far. This is not a problem in principle because when several (target) feature models need to be configured, it is possible to simply provide a separate configuration link for each of them. Conversely, when the configuration of a (target) feature model depends on more than one (source) feature model, it would be possible to merge them into a single feature model and use this as the source of the configuration link then. This merging is can be performed without any difficulties because we allowed a feature model to have several roots (at least as long as features are not shared among feature models, i.e. each feature $f \in \mathcal{F}$ is always contained in a single feature model only). However, when actually applying configuration links in practice this is not really feasible. As we will see when looking at the use cases in the next chapter, more complex n:m relations between feature models are very common.

Moreover, in the use case of compositional variability (see next chapter), it is often even necessary to use a single feature model several times as source or target. More precisely, it may be desirable to specify several (target) configurations of a single (target) feature model within a single configuration link or to base the specification of a target configuration on several (source) configurations of a single (source) feature model. This is exemplified in Figure 13.4. It shows a configuration link for specifying how the front and rear wipers in a car's wiper system are configured depending on the configuration of the feature model BodyElecFM of the overall body electronics system. Two things are noteworthy. First, the configuration

13.6. Required Refinements for Implementation

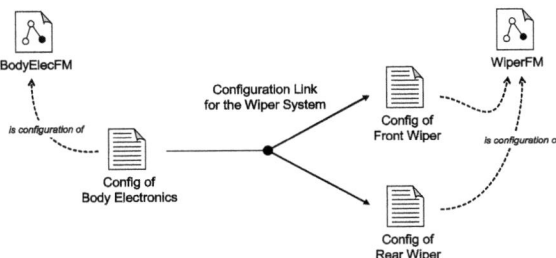

Figure 13.4: Example of a configuration link representing a 1:2 association.

link relates a source configuration to two target configurations and, second, the two target configuration are configurations of the same feature model, i.e. WiperFM.

In order to support such situations it is not sufficient to extend a configuration link to have several source and target features, because then WiperFM could not be used twice as target. Instead, *feature model prototypes* need to be introduced which work much like Parts in UML2 composite structures. They are typed by a feature model and provide a name to reference that feature model in the context of their owner, here the configuration link. Each configuration link is then attributed with a set of source feature model prototypes and a set of target feature model prototypes. In the example we would therefore have three feature model prototypes: one typed by BodyElecFM and named something like "Config of Body Electronics" and two typed by WiperFM and called "Config of Front Wiper" and "Config of Rear Wiper". The first is registered as source prototype, the latter two as target prototypes.

Another required addition is that now configured feature identifiers in a configuration link need to refer to one of the feature model prototypes in order to uniquely identify a configured feature. The ids in the configuration steps must refer to a target prototype while those in the inclusion criterion (as introduced in the previous section) must refer to a source prototype.

Again, the further details are an issue of implementation and do not affect the essential idea behind configuration links. They are therefore omitted here. Appendix A provides some more insight into these matters.

Chapter 14
Use Scenarios

As announced before, this chapter describes the various scenarios in which configuration links between feature models can be applied, in order to give an impression of their great variety and to indicate how the concept can help meet several important challenges described in Section 5.1. These scenarios are not strictly alternative forms of usage but instead highlight the potential benefits to be had from the concept; they can be combined with each other, and in a very complex product line setting even all of them may actually be made use of.

14.1 Factoring Out Customer-Invisible Variability

Not all configuration is carried out by the customer. Some configuration decisions will depend on circumstances beyond the influence of the customer. For example, configuration may depend on the country the car is being built and sold in, or it may depend on which of three suppliers that can deliver a certain subsystem is currently offering the best price. Similarly, configuration may be needed for a subsystem that is reused from a system outside the scope of the product line; here, configuration may be needed even if there is no variability within that subsystem in the current product line. In order to separate this configuration, which is invisible to the customer, an additional feature model can be introduced that captures all these non-customer-related circumstances—e.g. it has a feature Market with child features NorthAmerica, Europe, EastAsia—together with a configuration link from this feature model to the product line's core feature model, which partly configures the core model depending on the non-customer-related circumstances. Then, this configuration is clearly separated from customer configuration.

14.2 Prepackaging Customer Configuration

Often, a product line's core feature model, though located on a very high abstraction level, is quite closely related to the details of software and hardware design and contains many technical aspects. Also, not all of the configuration space defined by customer-controlled features is actually available to the end customer. This could be specified with additional dependencies in the core feature model, but often the configurations not provided to the end customer are not forbidden from a technical point of view and this should not be misleadingly suggested, as would be the case with additional dependencies. In short, it would be desirable to provide a basis for end customer configuration as an orthogonal view of the technical core feature model. With an additional feature model that only captures features for end customer configuration and a configuration link that maps a configuration of this feature model to the technically oriented core feature model, this can be achieved. This way, the variability presented to the end customer can be completely diversely packaged and organized. In addition, very different customer configuration feature models can be presented to the end customer, even if they map to the same technical core feature model, e.g. because the same technical platform is used for two model lines.

The previous two use scenarios are aimed at making the complexity of the core feature model manageable. This is achieved by factoring out certain aspects of configuration and keeping them separate from the core model. The following scenarios are instead aimed at the variable design artifacts in the product line infrastructure and designed to show how these artifacts are related to each other and to the core feature model.

14.3 Hierarchical Organization of Product Line Artifacts (Artifact Lines)

The basic idea of this scenario is that each development artifact in the product line infrastructure may be viewed as a small product line in its own right. Similarly, several artifacts may be combined and managed together as a single small-sized product line. Of course, the instances of these subordinate product lines are different in nature from the instances of the overall product line: in the first case, we have an initialized, non-variable development artifact, such as a test-case description or a requirements specification, while in the latter case we actually have a product, e.g. an automobile. To emphasize this fact, we refer to these small-sized "product lines" of development artifacts as *artifact lines*. Each such artifact line is provided with its own feature model. This feature model is used to publish an appropriate view of the artifact's variability to the actors interested in instances of this artifact. This makes the one or more artifacts in the artifact line independent from the global core feature model of the overall product line. The link between the artifact line and the overall product line is achieved by way of a configuration link from the core feature model of the overall product line to the artifact line's feature model. Artifact lines may, in turn, be composed of other, lower-level artifact lines by linking the feature models of the lower-level lines to the higher-level line's feature model with configuration links.

In this way, variability exposed by artifact lines may be partly hidden, diversely packaged or presented in a different form. This concealment of the details of variability within an artifact has remarkable similarities with information hiding and can therefore be referred to as *configuration hiding*. Following the terminology of interfaces of classes and components, this means that the core feature model of the overall product line can be seen as a description of *required variability*, whereas the lower-level feature models describe *provided variability*. This configuration hiding is key to supporting the diverging life-cycle of individual development artifacts and fostering their reuse. In addition, such hierarchical management of variability is an effective instrument for reducing the combinatoric complexity of product-line engineering, as pointed out by Krueger in [Kru06].

14.4 Coupling Core Feature Models to Artifact Level Variability

In product line settings, variability occurs on two basically distinct levels: first, in the core feature model the variability of the overall product line is described by defining the common and variable characteristics of the products within the product line's scope and the depen-

14.5. Variability in Component Hierarchies (Compositional Variability)

dencies between them; second, within each artifact it has to be specified at what locations variability occurs (i.e. variation points) and in what different forms the artifact can appear at each of these locations (i.e. several variants per variation point). These two levels have to be linked together, which means that it must be specified for each variation point what variant to choose depending on a certain configuration of the core feature model. If the artifact variability mechanism applied (e.g. variation points with variants in UML models, requirements with an attribute "optional", preprocessor macros in C-Code) can be expressed as a feature model (e.g. a feature for each variation point with child features for each variant), the coupling of the core feature model to the artifact variability can simply be expressed through a configuration link. A detailed description of this scenario with a discussion of which properties a feature-modeling technique must have in order to be able to express as many artifact variability mechanisms as possible is given in [RTW07b].

14.5 Variability in Component Hierarchies (Compositional Variability)

As shown above, the artifacts of a product line infrastructure can be hierarchically organized with configuration links. However, some artifacts are themselves internally structured in a hierarchical manner, most notably component diagrams. In this case, configuration links can also be used within these artifacts. Let us consider component diagrams as an example: each component is supplied with a feature model as part of its public interface (note that this constitutes a significant change to the component model, of course). Composite components then use configuration links to map configurations of their public feature model to the public feature models of their contained, lower-level components. This way, when designing a composite component, the developer has the choice between invariably binding the variability published by contained components, simply propagating this variability up the containment hierarchy or to diversely packaging it. During the preparation of this thesis, the term *compositional variability* was used for such a treatment of variability within a component hierarchy.

This scenario can be combined with the previous one such that the definition of the internal structure of a composite component may contain variation points and thus introduce variability beyond that provided by the contained lower-level components. This scenario was examined in detail in the European research project called ATESST [ATE08], as will be described in detail in Chapter 19. A more detailed discussion of this use case was published in [RTW09].

14.6 Manufacturer/Supplier Interaction

As described in Section 5.1, the fact that a multitude of different companies are usually involved in the development of large-scale industrial systems is an important challenge for product line engineering. Configuration links can be of value here, too. The contribution of the supplier is simply treated as an artifact line as described in scenario 3 above. This artifact line's feature model then serves as an interface to the embracing product line organization of the manufacturer in which the supplier's product line is to be integrated. If the supplier and manufacturer do not wish to disclose all details of their feature models, they can introduce an intermediate feature model that represents only the variability of interest in this specific manufacturer/supplier relation.

Summary

These use scenarios illustrate the most important basic styles of application of configuration links. In principle, the feasibility of the concept and technical realization of configuration links has to be evaluated for each of these scenarios separately. In this thesis, I focused on the use cases "customer configuration", "coupling core feature models to artifact level variability", and "compositional variability". An overview of these efforts will be presented in Part IV.

Chapter 15

Advanced Considerations on Configuration Links

The concept of configuration links as defined in Chapter 13 can be extended in many interesting ways. Most of them are aimed at increasing the understandability and maintainability of a large number of configuration decisions with their complex interdependencies and were identified during the evaluation of the concept as outlined in Part IV later in this thesis.

When introducing a new concept it is generally not advisable to include all such ideas for extension in the first version of the concept right from the start. This would make the concept more difficult to understand and assess. Also, in the early phases of introduction of a new concept, the experience with it is probably not sufficiently consolidated in order to always find and choose the best technical solution for incorporating the extension into the concept. As a consequence, far-reaching changes to the concept at a later stage will often result from that. Moreover, the practical experience in the automotive domain during the preparation of this thesis shows that however consolidated a methodology is, when applying it to non-trivial industrial projects there always arise tricky, project-specific situations that demand workarounds and pragmatic solutions. When setting up new methods it would be very dangerous to try to provide a technical solution for each and every conceivable problem. This would lead to an enormously complex methodology and those nifty concepts are most often not correctly understood and applied by the end-user anyway. The right procedure must instead be to provide a lean methodology with a few basic concepts that cover the core problems to be solved and make it flexible and extensible to allow for pragmatic, project-specific solutions.

For all these reasons, the concept of configuration links as proposed in this thesis was not enriched with all of the following extensions. Instead, only some of them were incorporated while the others are only documented here for reference and to save the experience from the evaluation.

15.1 Equivalences

When editing configuration decisions you often encounter a situation where a feature of a target feature model has a directly corresponding feature in a source feature model. The following example illustrates this.

> **Example 10.** The feature model of the core controller in the wiper system contains a feature `Rain-Controlled`, meaning that the controller has to consider input from a rain sensor when selected. In the overall feature model of the

complete system there is a feature `RainSensor`, which states whether the car is equipped with a rain sensor and the wiper is to be turned on automatically in case of rain. When mapping the global feature model to the wiper controller's feature model, then `Rain-Controlled` would need to be selected if and only if `RainSensor` is selected. □

Of course this could simply be modeled with a single configuration decision with an inclusion criterion that evaluates to true when `RainSensor` is selected and a single configuration step setting `Rain-Controlled`'s cardinality to [1]. However, interpreted logically, this specifies only an implication from source to target. But what we actually have is an equivalence, so the implication from target to source—i.e. the information "only if"—gets lost.

Obviously this constitutes a special case of a configuration decision. It is also obvious that this additional information is worth being captured in the specification of a configuration link. The only question is how to introduce this into the concept in a practical way with minimal impact and overhead. Fortunately there is a very elegant solution. Each configuration decision is supplied with an additional attribute called "equivalence" and the semantic is defined as follows.

> **Definition 22.** An *equivalence* is a configuration decision which is specially marked as such. In that case, the following constraint applies: no configured feature identifier that appears in the configuration steps of the equivalence may appear in any other configuration decision of the containing configuration link. □

In the above example this means that when the configuration decision that configures `Rain-Controlled` is marked to be an equivalence, no other configuration decision in the same configuration link may refer to that feature, i.e. the feature's configuration may not be influenced by any other circumstances except those captured in the equivalence. In other words, the feature `Rain-Controlled` becomes an exclusive target for the single configuration decision which was marked to be an equivalence.

The nice thing about this definition is that it leaves the core concept from Chapter 13 completely untouched and can be realized entirely on the tool level, i.e. the constraint from Definition 22 can be enforced by the editor with which configuration decisions are managed. Also this definition explains quite clearly the meaning of an equivalence which refers to more than one cfid on the target side: simply all those cfids become exclusive then. Other alternatives for the realization of equivalences that were considered proved to become quite intricate in such situations.

A final remark should be added regarding the logical interpretation of equivalences. From saying that feature f_{trgt} should be selected if and only if feature f_{src} is selected you cannot deduce that f_{trgt} should be deselected if and only if f_{src} is deselected, because there are several other cases, in particular the state of undecided. Of course, often this will be intended but it need not be modeled explicitly because when the (partial) configuration is interpreted in terms of selection and deselection of features the undecided state will be treated as deselect (see σ above).

15.2 Aggregating Configuration Decisions and Exclusive Folders

Whenever a lot of entities have to be managed it makes sense to provide means to aggregate several of these entities to indicate that they are somehow related to each other or share a common property or purpose. That is true for files on a hard disk, for example, and in the same way for configuration decision in a complex configuration link. In the accompanying demonstrator this was achieved by adding *configuration decision folders*. The most important thing to say about these folders is that there is nothing important to say about them: they have, in principle, absolutely no impact on the effect of the configuration decisions of the configuration link. In other words, when applying a configuration link, the folders are completely ignored.

Configuration decision folders should support user customizable attributes, because often project-specific meta-information must be supplied on the level the folders.

However, an (optional) enhancement to that is conceivable which may be seen as an exception to the rule that folders have no impact on semantics. Each folder may be supplied with a set of configured feature identifiers with the following meaning:

> **Definition 23.** A configuration decision folder with a non-empty set of exclusive configured feature identifiers is called an *exclusive folder*. Then, within the same configuration link, the specified configured features *and all their successors* may only be referred to, i.e. may only be configured, within that folder. □

This mechanism can be used to assure that certain sub-trees of a complex target feature model are only touched by a certain department or team. Also the organization of a complex configuration link's decisions becomes a lot more stable during maintenance and evolution and also far more understandable.

Just as equivalences, these exclusive folders can be realized entirely on the tool-level and therefore they do not add complexity to the core concept.

15.3 Relating Configuration Decisions

Often several configuration decisions are semantically very closely related to each other. One might be an exception of the other or they may share a very specific purpose. Usually the number of decisions is very limited in these cases, maybe between 2 and 5. If the engineer wants to model the fact that these decisions belong together, he can, of course, put them in a new configuration decision folder, as introduced in the previous section. However, this is not satisfiable because it adds an additional element and hierarchical level to the presentation in the editor window, and, more importantly, it does not capture the situation very well: folders aggregate a comparatively large number of decisions that are loosely related to each other and that are all of equal significance. With the close relations discussed here it is often the case that the related decisions play different roles, for example when a relation indicates an exception, then one decision is the standard and the other the special case. This cannot be expressed with folders.

It is therefore a reasonable option to introduce a mechanism to express such relations. They would have to be directed and allow for more than one start and end (i.e. directed n:m associations). They should further be typed by a simple string value; actual types can be defined by end-users on a per-company or per-project level. Finally, they should provide for a textual description and support user attributes.

Even though this is, at time of writing, not implemented in the demonstrator, several types of relations were identified during the experiments with the concept.

- *Exception To*: the decisions at the start of the relation formulate an exception to those at the end. If the exception is an inclusion (not an exclusion) then this is of particular significance because most probably the inclusion criteria of the end decisions had to be changed in order to realize the exception, which means that if the rationale for the exception becomes obsolete, the standard case needs to be adapted.

- *Relies On*: the start decisions may somehow become invalid if one or more of the end decisions are changed or removed.

- *Replaces*: the start decisions were added to replace the end decisions which have become obsolete. Usually the end decisions will be set to inactive here and are still contained in the configuration link only for reference or because they may become valid again at a later point in time.

- *Hindered By*: as before, but for some reason the replacement could not be performed yet. Usually the start decisions should be set to inactive here. Also this may be used that there is some problem with the definition of the end decisions that has to be resolved before the start decisions can be activated.

- *Other*: a relation not covered by any of the other types.

In all cases, the relations have no impact on the configuration specification in a configuration link and therefore do not affect the core concept. They are just meant to make the interrelated configuration decisions more understandable and to reveal dependencies that have to be taken into account when changing one of them.

15.4 Prioritization of Configuration Decisions

As mentioned several times already, the concept of configuration links, each made up of numerous configuration decisions, does not try to avoid redundancy but instead encourages a redundant definition of overlapping configuration considerations. As a consequence there will often appear contradictions between individual configuration decisions. Section 13.5 was devoted to a detailed description how such contradictions are by default resolved according to the concept of configuration links. Such a resolution means that it is defined which configuration decision is granted priority and is therefore put in effect. The most important resolution rule is that an exclude has priority over an include. Sometimes however, these default prioritizations are not suitable. In particular, it often seems desirable to have one configuration decision which states that a certain target feature is to be excluded for a broad range of source configurations and define one or more exceptions from that standard case for which the feature is to be included.

> **Example 11.** In all Canadian cars the cruise control does *not* have a radar; but Canadian S-Class cars of body type "Comfort" are equipped with a radar. This cannot directly be specified as two configuration decisions, because the exclude of the first would always have priority over the include of the second, even for Canadian S-Class cars of type "Comfort". □

In principle there are two ways to approach this problem. First, it is possible to append the negation of the inclusion criterion of the second decision—the one capturing the exception—to

15.4. Prioritization of Configuration Decisions

the inclusion criterion of the first; in the example the inclusion criterion of the first decision would thus become something like "all Canadian but not 'Comfort' S-Class cars". Obviously there is a severe drawback to this: the configuration decisions are no longer defined independently from one another, because some information associated with the second needs to be put into the first. The advantage, on the other hand, is that no modifications to the core concept are necessary.

Alternatively, as a second way of approaching this problem, we can introduce a new mechanism to prioritize individual configuration decisions. Countless different techniques are conceivable for achieving this. The following two give an impression of their variety:

1. An additional boolean attribute of configuration decisions indicates, when set to true, that all includes specified by this decision shall overrule any excludes which may somewhere be defined in the configuration link for the same configured feature(s). Alternatively this attribute could be put in the configuration steps.

2. Each configuration decisions is attributed with a numeric value, its priority. The default is 1. Whenever a contradiction between two decisions arises, the one with the higher priority is put in effect; if their priorities are equal, the defaults apply as defined by the core concept (cf. Section 13.5).

The advantage of these techniques is that they reflect very well the actual situation to be modeled and the configuration decisions are defined independently from one another: the first, standard decision has priority 1 no matter whether or not 'include'-exceptions are defined for it. Also this situation is not uncommon when defining configuration links so it may seem worth adding an additional mechanism for it. Finally, on the implementation level, such an extension would not be very difficult to realize.

Despite all these observations in favor, it is here proposed to not provide an additional mechanism for decision prioritization. First of all, such a mechanism would constitute a profound alteration of the overall functioning of configuration decisions. It would become more difficult to foresee the actual effect of several decisions being applied together. More importantly, providing a concept for flexible prioritization would even encourage the engineer to model complex interactions between configuration decisions; by not supporting them directly, it is instead possible to foster a more consistent overall modeling of decision interactions, i.e. the user is encouraged to describe the situation to be modeled with inclusions as standard cases and exclusions as exceptions to them. Generally there is a certain degree of freedom how to formulate configuration decision and so the situations where includes need to be prioritized over excludes can thus be avoided to some extent. Finally, in the cases where this cannot be avoided, it is still possible to model an "include"-exception case with the standard mechanisms of the concept, as shown above. And in the previous section we have also seen that with relations between decision it can be highlighted very well that some information from one decision made its way into the inclusion criterion of another.

In summary, an explicit prioritization of configuration decisions is certainly a candidate for further extensions of the concept, but presently it seems more advisable to use the core mechanisms for that and apply meta-information in form of configuration decision relations in order to make up for the minor disadvantages of this procedure.

15.5 Configuration Decision Events

When defining the configuration decisions in a configuration link, the user not only defines its inclusion criterion and configuration steps, but also describes the rationale behind the configuration captured in the decision and names the person responsible for all further considerations associated to this configuration decision. The documentation of this meta-information is an important aspect of the methodological considerations behind the concept of configuration links (cf. Chapter 12). In particular, the purpose of the rationale is to clearly define the justification of a certain configuration decision in order to be able to decide, at a later point in time, whether the configuration decision is still valid or whether it needs to be removed or altered. At first it was assumed that such a validation of a certain configuration decision would be performed at certain points in time during the life-cycle of a product line in form of a general review of all configuration links and their decisions. However, while working on the case study and the examples, it became apparent that while formulating the rationale it is often very easy to identify certain circumstances under which this individual configuration decision needs to be revisited for modification. Therefore, this is an excellent opportunity to define so-called *configuration decision events* which can later, when the corresponding event occurs, point the engineer to the decisions that need reassessment.

The circumstances under which such a reassessment becomes necessary can be related to many different things, both within the scope of the system or outside (e.g. a change in legislation). This is because the considerations that are captured in configuration decisions are usually of very diverse nature (as indicated in 12). Consequently, there will not be a few isolated points in time where all or almost all configuration decisions need to be reviewed but instead there will be very frequently the need to review just some individual decisions. In such a situation, it is a great advantage to not always having to do a complete review but being able to directly revisit the individual configuration decisions associated with the corresponding event. This allows to keep the configuration links up-to-date in relatively short intervals.

As another consequence of the great diversity of such events, the mechanism for defining them must not be too restrictive in order to be flexible enough to support all kinds of events. In particular, it is not effective to provide a fixed set of predefined events. On the other hand, the definition of events cannot be carried out completely informally, because then the same conceptual event could be named and described very differently across several configuration decisions and would therefore not be easily identifiable any more. The conception of configuration decision events therefore calls for a mechanism which represents a reasonable compromise between strictly formal and completely informal, as is the case so often in software engineering.

A good starting point would be to have events as dedicated entities, each supplied with a name and a textual description to start with, and to associate configuration decisions to these events (with n:m associations). Again, it would be very important that these new event elements support user customizable attributes, because most meta-information on events will be project specific.

Further refinements to these events are beyond the scope of this thesis, because they lie beyond the core concept of configuration links. They can be seen as one mechanism to support project and company organization, communication and various other processes. We will briefly come back to this issue at the end of this thesis when discussing the potential for further research work.

15.6 Flexible Parameter Assignments

Currently, the core concept of configuration links only allows to assign literally specified values to a parameterized feature. Several stages of refinement are conceivable here:

1. Copying values from a parameterized feature on the source side to one on the target side.
2. As 1., but instead of simply copying the value it may also be possible to modify it (e.g. multiply a float by 3, convert a temperature from Celsius to Fahrenheit or append a suffix to a string).
3. Making the target configuration dependent on whether the value of a parameterized feature on the source side is greater than or lower than a certain value.
4. Making the target configuration dependent on whether two or more parameterized features on the source side have equal values or have values that are in some way related to each other (e.g. one being equal to twice the other).

In fact, refinements 3. and 4. are already supported by the core concept as formalized in 13.3, but not by the more implementation-oriented realization proposed in 13.6. In other words, the last two refinements are a challenge only with respect to implementation, in a set-theoretical formalization they can be realized rather straightforwardly.

Chapter 16
Discussion and Related Work

The idea of configuration decisions as defined in the preceding chapters originated in the ITEA project EAST-EEA, which ended in 2004, [EAS08, WRW+04]. The work presented here is an extensive refinement, extension and generalization of this initial idea. In particular, the initial conception was only targeted at the use scenario of "end-customer variability" (Section 14.2).

Naturally, the main body of related literature consists of the feature modeling techniques proposed so far, such as FODA [KCH+90], FORM [KKL+98], cardinality-based feature modeling [CHE05b, CK05], etc. as well as recent contributions to a consolidation and integration of feature modeling concepts, e.g. [Gom04, AMS06, SHTB06]. These different techniques and the different concepts and notations they provide were already discussed throughout Chapter 4. In addition, the precise details are of no particular interest here because configuration links were carefully defined to be compatible with most existing feature modeling concepts and techniques. This was achieved by not defining configuration links on the basis of one of the existing techniques but instead using the CVMfeature modeling technique introduced in Section 4.5, which was designed to be as flexible as possible such that most existing approaches can be seen as a specialization of it.

More specific approaches and publications related to configuration links usually only linked to a single or a few of the use cases of configuration links as identified in Chapter 14.

To begin with, traditional techniques for configuration management as commonly used in the automotive domain [Say84, CAD03, SZ06], for example the configuration management support in the DIALOG product management system of Daimler AG [AS02], are closely related to the "compositional variability" use case (cf. Section 14.5), because they, of course, also constitute a form of variability management. These techniques usually deal with configuration parameters on a global scale only: configuration parameters are defined at a global level and are immediately available at all levels of the component hierarchy in identical form. It is often not possible to newly introduce a parameter in the context of an individual component—e.g. a wiper controller—which is then differentiated for each use of this component in the complete system—e.g. for the front and rear wiper controller—and it is impossible to hierarchically organize the binding of these parameters or to change their structuring and presentation. In other words, such "flat" variability management with plain configuration parameters takes no account whatsoever of the hierarchical structuring of the component-based design. Obviously, most of the benefits of compositional variability management are therefore not available when following such an approach. On the other hand, compositional variability management by way of configuration links as proposed above contains this global scenario as a special case by way of globally public features, thus supporting it for application contexts where this is deemed

Table 16.1: Comparison of configuration links and KOALA [vO04].

	Compositional Variability with ...	
	Configuration Links	KOALA
variability of internal structure	n/a	function binding, switches, optional interfaces
exposure of internal variability	feature models	diversity interfaces
variability mapping	configuration link	diversity spreadsheets

desirable; it is even possible to freely combine the global style of variability management with the hierarchical one within a single system.

Some development techniques from the automotive domain with support for configuration management (e.g. the TITUS design technique [TIT96, EKLM97]) enable the values of the configuration parameters to be set in a hierarchical fashion, thus extending traditional configuration management as discussed in the previous paragraph. However, in these cases only flat lists of configuration parameters are supported (instead of feature trees in our case) and, more importantly, the structuring and packaging of these parameters or their semantic connotation cannot be changed from one hierarchy level to the next. Such approaches to hierarchical configuration management can also be seen as a special case or as one constituent of compositional variability management with configuration links.

Let us now turn from the configuration management domain to the variability management field. There, the basic idea of managing variability in a hierarchical manner is not new. Van Ommering et al. propose to organize the variation within a component hierarchy by defining and binding variability at each hierarchical level, similar as described above for the "compositional variability" use case (for an overview refer to [vO04]). In fact, their KOALA component model can arguably be seen as an alternative technical realization of compositional variability as defined above: the internal structure of composite components can be defined in a variable form with *function binding*, *switches*, and *optional interfaces*; the component's internal variability is exposed through *diversity interfaces*; and the variability mapping is achieved by way of so-called *diversity spreadsheets* (summarized in Table 16.1). However, in KOALA these means of expression are tightly coupled with the other elements of the component model, e.g. the communication ports, which means that even with respect to the variability interface and mapping all variation specification is tightly coupled with the component model. The procedure proposed here is different in that it takes up the established technique of feature modeling for this purpose. With their tree structure and clear modeling means for expressing variability, feature models are an ideal tool for publicly specifying a component's inner variability, especially on the higher levels in the system design. In addition, such a standardized, more abstract technique provides advantages in more heterogeneous application scenarios, i.e. when the variability management covers other types of artifacts as well, such as requirement specifications on analysis level or test case definitions. Section 5.1 highlighted how ubiquitous such heterogeneity is in the automotive domain. The notion of compositional variability thus aims to generalize the elements and benefits of KOALA's variation management and reconcile them with the well-established technique of feature modeling, thus strengthening the ability for a shift in viewpoint from lower to higher levels and retaining variability management as an orthogonal dimension of software and system development.

Another proposal to manage variability in a hierarchical manner was described by Krueger in [Kru06] how modularization and hierarchical decomposition can be used to cope with combinatoric complexity in product lines of software-intensive systems. The hierarchical organization resulting from compositional variability with configuration links is different in that it only relies on feature models and some mapping between them, while in [Kru06] the additional concept of matrices is introduced to allow the hierarchical composition of modules. In addition, configuration links are designed to allow variability to be presented in a completely orthogonal manner in order to provide the benefits discussed in Section 14.5, which is not the case for matrices.

The approach presented in [ABB+02] by Atkinson et al. also deals with variability management in component structures. However, it is very different in focus and nature because it utilizes decision tables (cf. Section 3.4) instead of feature models. A more detailed discussion of this work is therefore not required here.

In summary, the difference between the framework proposed in this thesis and the other research efforts related to the "compositional variability" use case is that the concept of configuration links tries to make no assumptions about the nature and content of the artifacts and does not aim to embrace the entire system family with a single consistent methodology. Instead it embraces many different types of artifacts and use cases with a single flexible, basic concept. While other system family oriented component approaches try to bring together variability management and a certain development paradigm, i.e. component-oriented design [Szy02], the framework above tries to separate variability management from the employed development methods as strictly as possible. In other words, the above framework does not replace these other approaches but provides a parenthesis to combine them with other development methodologies, such as requirements engineering or test methods. Furthermore, modularization and decomposition is, according to the broader use scenarios of configuration links, motivated also by the partitioning of development artifacts and organizational units rather than only of subsystems or subcomponents.

As an approach to predefine the configuration of a feature model and to cope with the complexities of such a configuration predefinition, configuration links are also related to *staged configuration* of Czarnecki et al., as presented in [Cza04] and further detailed in [CHE05a, CHE05b]. According to staged configuration, the process of configuring a feature model is organized in a number of consecutive steps, each further specializing the feature model or parts of it. For example, a feature is selected by narrowing its cardinality to [1] and deselected by narrowing it to [0]. However, this approach is not sufficient to solve all the problems of traditional technique for configuration predefinition identified in Section 12.2. This is particularly true for the spreading of selection considerations over several features' selection definitions and the need for an explicit documentation of "orthogonal" and overlapping considerations. This applies especially to non-technically motivated feature selections (driven by product strategy, marketing, legislation, etc.). However, staged configuration certainly has the advantage of being more straightforward to use and far easier to implement in a tool framework. In some application contexts staged configuration will therefore probably be sufficient. Whether only staged configuration or only configuration links are applied, or a combination of the two, probably depends on the specific needs of the user during product engineering, but this was not examined in detail during the preparation of this thesis; instead it was deemed sufficient to show that there are at least some areas of application which clearly demand a more sophisticated preconfiguration management than staged configuration can offer.

Another approach for complex preconfiguration management devised by Pohl et al. is presented in [BLPW04]. It solves several of the limitations described in Section 12.2 but does not separate different feature selection considerations in the actual preconfiguration specification. This has the advantage of increasing the complexity of the selection definition not as much as configuration decisions do. On the other hand, the main advantage of configuration decisions is not provided by that approach, which is relevant especially in very complex cases as typically encountered in the use scenarios from Sections 14.2 and 14.4. Thus, the two approaches might be seen as two alternatives mainly addressing the same problem.

Finally, it should be noted that there are a multitude of other techniques and approaches, both from research and practice, which somehow relate to one or more of the use scenarios identified in Chapter 14. The summary above only highlighted those efforts which specifically deal with variability. An example for those others that cannot be discussed in more detail here might be the Requirements Interchange Format RIF [Her07] initiated by the German Herstellerinitiative Softwaretechnik [HIS08]. It is also aimed at facilitating the manufacturer/supplier interaction, as the use scenario from Section 14.6, but tries to achieve its goals in a far more pragmatic way without a dedicated variability management.

An early, very limited version of configuration links, which were intended for the use case from Section 14.2 only, was published in [RW05]. A discussion of the basic idea of configuration links, but with an emphasis on the requirement of a unified feature modeling technique instead of configuration links, was presented in [RTW07b]. A very detailed discussion of the "compositional variability" use case from Section 14.5 was published in [RTW09].

Part IV

Evaluation

Chapter 17

Prototypical Implementation of a Variability Management Framework

As a preparation for extended examples and case studies, as well as a first evaluation effort in its own right, the concepts introduced in the previous two parts of this thesis were prototypically implemented in form of a demonstrator tool. Since these concepts represent extensions to traditional feature models, the demonstrator also had to provide for basic feature modeling functionality. Roughly speaking, it can thus be characterized as a feature editor with several additional, innovative functionalities. However, two of these additional functionalities actually shift the focus of the demonstrator from pure feature modeling towards a more general management of variability:

- The concept of variable entities, which allows to define and manage a complex network of interrelated configurations and supports the derivation of dependent configurations within this network.

- The possibility of defining variability information by way of a formal language similar in syntax to a programming language, called Variability Specification Language (VSL), which does not introduce new entities or concepts but still opens a broad range of application options, as will be described later in this chapter.

Therefore the implementation provided along with this thesis in fact constitutes a prototypical tool framework for variability management in a more general sense.

In addition to that, another prototype was implemented in order to demonstrate and experiment with multi-level requirements artifacts as defined in Chapter 8. This demonstrator, based on the requirements-engineering tool DOORS from Telelogic, is independent from the one mentioned above and will be described separately in the following chapter.

17.1 Yet another feature editor ?

There already exist several tools that provide feature editing functionality, available both as commercial products (e.g. pure::variants [PS08]) as well as in the form of research prototypes (e.g. CaptainFeature and FMP [AC04] or XFeature [XF08]). It therefore only makes sense to come up with a new implementation of feature editing if this is justified by factual necessities.

The primary motivation for implementing the prototypical VM framework with its own feature editor was the fact, that the feasibility of the underlying concepts, especially of subscoping and of configuration links, is closely linked to how they are embedded in the overall feature-editing facility and it was therefore necessary to experiment with different forms of editing functionality. In addition, when building on an existent research demonstrator there would always be the risk that its development is broken off or that the team working on the demonstrator decides to introduce fundamental changes to the tool's architecture or concepts which could lead to irreconcilable conflicts with assumptions made in the own project. Finally, building basic editors for your own newly introduced domain specific methodologies became a lot easier thanks to latest achievements in model driven development, for example the Eclipse Modeling Framework (EMF), the Graphical Editing Framework (GEF), and associated projects.

17.2 Key Capabilities of the Framework

The key functionality of the prototypical VM framework can be divided into the four areas of (a) feature editing, (b) multi-level feature trees, (c) configuration links, and (d) configuration networks. Support for feature editing comprises the following:

- feature modeling for advanced feature models as defined in Section 4.5:
    - essential feature editing capabilities (creating and deleting features, moving features within the feature tree hierarchy, cut / copy / paste, editing basic properties of features such as name, description, cardinality)
    - optional and mandatory features
    - cloned features
    - feature groups
    - feature inheritance (often called "feature references" in literature)
    - feature links (for dependencies such as "needs" and "excludes")
    - parameterized features
    - a type system for checking the validity of values of parameterized features during configuration

- explorer-style tree views as well as graphical views of the feature models (cf. Section 17.4.1)

- creation and editing of configurations of feature models (cf. Section 17.4.2)

- exporting configurations in a simple text format (optimized for simple parsing)

- customizable user attributes for project-specific meta-information (which can be attached to most elements)

- a simple constraint framework allowing various constraints to be defined (e.g. "feature names must not be empty and should start with an upper-case letter")

- support for various well-known feature-modeling techniques, such as FODA [KCH+90], FORM [KKL+98], pure::variants, realized through constraints which ensure that only the capabilities of these techniques are employed in a feature model in order to maintain compatibility with certain methods or tools (Section 5.3; only implemented partly to demonstrate the idea)

17.2. Key Capabilities of the Framework

- saving/loading in XMI format

Multi-level feature trees are supported by the implementation through the following core functionalities:

- defining reference feature models (Section 7.2)
- propagating features from a referring model to a reference model and vice versa (see Chapter 9)
- determining the conformance state of a referring model (Section 7.4)
- finding deviations in a referring model with respect to its reference model (Sections 7.3 and 7.4)

The area of configuration links relies on the following functionalities:

- essential editing of configuration links and their configuration decisions (creation, deletion, cut / copy / paste, etc.)
- direct editing of inclusion criteria and the included and excluded features of configuration decisions
- assisted editing of inclusion criteria and the included and excluded features within a preview of the source and target configurations (cf. Section 17.4.3)
- exploring configuration decisions and their impact on the target configuration(s) comfortably, including special markers that highlight the areas where configuration decisions affect the target configurations (cf. Section 17.4.3)
- testing the interaction of several selected configuration decisions or a complete configuration link seamlessly while editing is in progress ("test-drive mode", cf. 17.4.3)
- basic supportive analyses, for example when an include is defined a warning is shown if an exclude is already defined for the same configured feature
- configuration derivation, i.e. application of configuration links to existing configuration(s) of the link's source feature models, resulting on one or more target configurations

Lastly, the area of configuration networks comprises:

- definition of variable entities, i.e. definition of complex networks of interrelated configurations, optionally including a containment hierarchy
- creating, editing and deriving such networks of configurations
- support for splitting the definition of the networks of configurations across several file servers, allowing to span these networks across several teams, departments, units or even companies
- support for version management and collaborative editing of these networks of configurations, based on the version control system Subversion, [CSFP04]

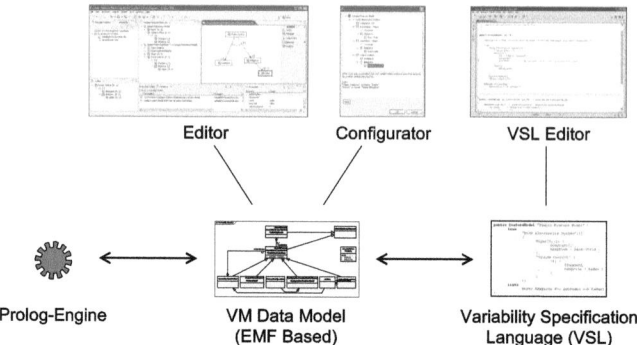

Figure 17.1: The main constituents of the variability management framework.

It should be noted at this point that the last two items are of enormous complexity. Of course, not all issues that arise from a collaborative variability management in complex organizational structures could be investigated in the course of this thesis. However, the proposed concepts together with their prototypical implementation should provide a solid and promising basis for this, which should also prove quite flexible and extensible when actually applied in a certain organizational context, as will be illustrated below in Section 17.4.4. Beyond that, suggestions for further research work on this topic are given at the end of this thesis.

17.3 Constituents and Architecture of the Demonstrator

From a user perspective, the variability management framework is divided into five main constituents, which are illustrated in Figure 17.1. Each of them has its specific purpose and plays a certain role in the overall framework.

Data Model The data model for variability management is the core of the entire framework and is the exact implementation of the formalization provided in Section 4.5 and the variability management information model as specified in Appendix A. It provides the necessary functionality to programmatically manage variability related information in memory, for example setting of an entity's values, management of bidirectional associations and containment, event notification or XMI import and export. It was partly generated with Eclipse EMF by using the information model from Appendix A as a meta-model input to the EMF code generator.

Editor The (main) editor provides a means to interactively navigate and manipulate variability management information.

Configurator In order to create and edit configurations of feature models, a dedicated configurator is provided. It supports partial configurations with undecided states and management of entire networks of feature model configurations, called entity configurations.

Variability Specification Language (VSL) A language to specify variability information, similar in syntax to programming languages such as Java. It provides an al-

Figure 17.2: The architecture of the framework implementation.

ternative way to capture variability related information and also an alternative way to manipulate it by directly editing the specifications in a standard text editor. A parser is provided that transforms VSL specifications to instances of the data model. Also the reverse direction, exporting information from the data model to VSL, is supported.

VSL Editor A text editor with specific support for VSL (e.g. syntax highlighting)

Prolog-Engine A connection to a Prolog engine was implemented which allows to analyze (but not manipulate) feature models in Prolog. This was used for experimentation during the refinement of the concepts of multi-level feature trees and configuration links, which proved very helpful. However, the final consolidated version was then implemented without making use of the Prolog engine. So the significance of it is somewhat reduced now and it is provided only as a by-product of the experimentation phase; the framework does not rely on it.

Several important parts of the framework implementation are not shown in this list because they are not directly tangible for the user. We therefore add another perspective to investigate some further implementation details. Figure 17.2 shows a technical view of the overall architecture. The framework is designed as an Eclipse plug-in. It is based on the Eclipse Modeling Framework EMF [BSME03] for implementing the data model and on the Graphical Editing Framework GEF [Ecl08] for the graphical editing functionality.

17.4 Details on Selected Capabilities

In this section, several selected capabilities of the framework implementation will be presented in some more detail. However, it is not the purpose of a doctoral thesis to provide a complete reference manual for an accompanying research demonstrator. The goal is just to highlight some capabilities of particular interest and give an impression of the framework's scope and its look and feel.

17.4.1 Feature Modeling

Figure 17.3 shows a simple feature model in both the explorer-style view and a graphical feature diagram view. Regarding the graphical view for feature trees, the implementation follows the model/diagram pattern used by most modeling tools such as Rational Rose or Enterprise Architect: for a feature model, several *feature diagrams* may be defined that provide views of the model. This means that some parts of the model, i.e. some features, may show up in the diagram while others do not, and when they appear in more than one diagram, all the diagrams show the same model objects. When they are changed in one diagram, the change will also appear in all the other diagrams.

17.4.2 Creating and Editing Configurations

As mentioned above, a configurator is provided to support configuration of feature models. In order to actually use a feature model it is usually necessary to configure it, i.e. select and deselect its features and provide values for parameterized features that are selected.

Chapter 17. Prototypical Implementation of a Variability Management Framework

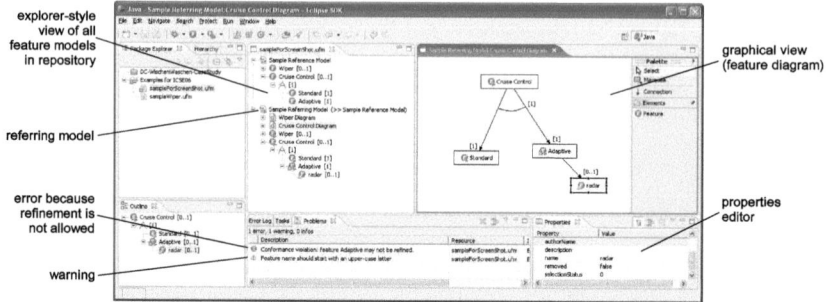

Figure 17.3: The two views provided by the prototypical feature editor.

A feature configuration is an element in a variability model just as a feature model is. It is possible to have as many configurations of the same feature model as required. To create a new feature configuration from within the editor the user may right-click on the feature model to be configured and then select "Configure ..." from the context menu. The configurator will show up in a separated window, as shown in Figure 17.4.

In the top area of this window the configuration can be edited. The lower area provides additional information on the currently selected feature. While editing in this dialog the data model in the editor remains unchanged; only if the user clicks "Ok" on exit the changes will be committed to the model.

As can be seen in the figure, optional features are presented with a check box (e.g. Cruise Control or Radar). The check box has three states: undecided, selected and deselected. For example, the radar is deselected in the picture which is indicated by the red cross. Optional features that are in a feature group of cardinality [1] are presented with radio buttons to indicate that they are alternative (e.g. Standard and Advanced below the cruise control).

Cloned features with a cardinality greater than 1 (e.g. Wiper[0..2]) are special in that they cannot be selected or deselected. Instead, instances have to be created for them. To achieve this, the user right-clicks on the cloned feature and selects "Create instance ..." from the context menu. In the example, two instances of Wiper were created: frontWiper and rearWiper. Instances can be deleted again via the context menu.

The value of a parameterized feature can be set by right-clicking the feature and then selecting "Set Value ..." from the context menu. In the example Radar was not yet supplied with a value which is indicated by the label "<undefined>".

17.4.3 Editing Configuration Decisions

To conveniently edit configuration decisions in a configuration decision model a special view is provided in the editor, called "Configuration Preview" (to open it, select in the main menu of Eclipse the item "Window > Show View > Other ..." and select "Configuration Preview" in the dialog). It is also possible to use a special "Configuration Specification" perspective in Eclipse to easily jump from a window layout for feature editing to one for editing configuration decisions.

A running Eclipse with a window layout optimized for configuration decision editing could

17.4. Details on Selected Capabilities

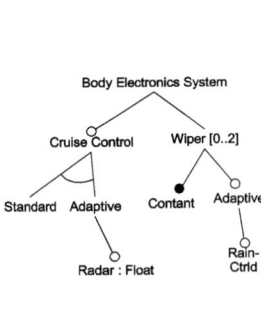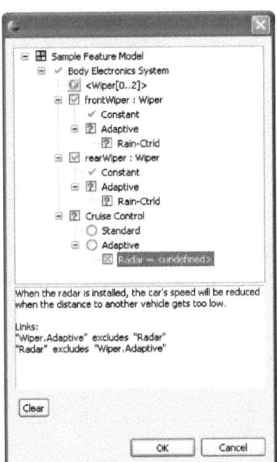

Figure 17.4: Editing the configuration of a sample feature model.

look like the one from Figure 17.5.

The left side of the configuration preview shows configurations of all *source* feature models of the configuration decision model while the right side shows configurations of the *target* feature models. Editing works exactly as described in the previous section for the configuration dialog.

The configuration preview has two distinct modes of operation:

1. An *editing mode*, active if a single product decision is selected in the editor window.

2. A *test drive mode*, active if either a single product decision model(!) or several product decisions are selected in the editor window.

In the first mode, it is possible to edit the currently selected configuration decision by manipulating the left and right side of the preview. The right side shows the impact of the selected configuration decision on the configurations of the target feature models. When changing the configurations of the right side in the preview, then the attributes "included features" and "excluded features" of the selected configuration decision are updated accordingly. Yellow markers highlight the places in the configuration where the selected configuration decision actually has an impact. In the example, the selected configuration decision (line number 8 in the editor window) has the following impact: Adaptive is selected and the Radar is selected. If you wanted to change this such that Radar is deselected you would only have to click on the check box in front of Radar on the right side of the configuration preview. Then Radar would automatically be removed from the attribute "included features" and added to the attribute "excluded features". In the same way it is possible to make configuration decisions add instances or set values of parameterized features (also here editing works as described in previous section for the configuration dialog).

The left side of the configuration preview (still in the first mode of operation) works similar to allow editing the inclusion criterion of the selected product decision. However, since the

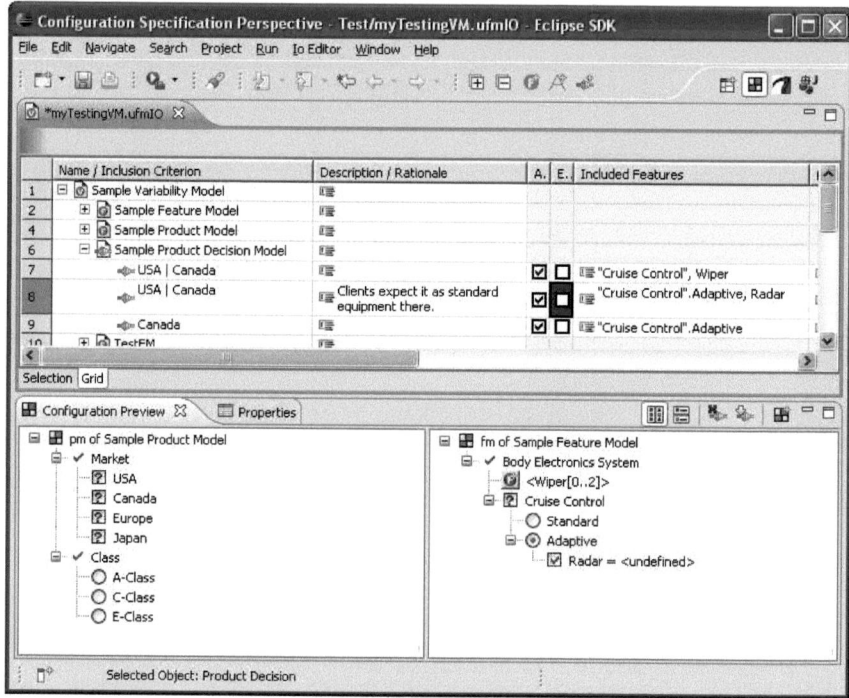

Figure 17.5: Support for editing configuration decisions.

17.4. Details on Selected Capabilities

inclusion criterion can be a complex logical expression, the current value cannot be shown on the left side of the configuration preview. For example, if the criterion would be `"(USA & A-Class) | (Canada & not E-Class)"` this could not be shown as a single configuration in the preview, because of the disjunction. Therefore the left side of the configuration preview is used not to show the current value of the inclusion criterion but only to *append* new constructs to this attribute. For example, consider we would want to extend the validity of the selected configuration decision in the example above by Japanese E-Class cars. Then we would click on `Japan` and `E-Class` on the left side of the configuration preview and then click the following button in the preview's toolbar:

This will then add the string `" | (Japan & E-Class)"` to the inclusion criterion of the currently selected configuration decision. Note that with this mechanism not all possible logical expressions can be created. Therefore it is sometimes needed to manually edit an inclusion criterion after editing it with the preview.

In contrast, the second mode of the configuration preview (when a complete configuration decision model instead of a single product decision is selected) is used to test the overall configuration specification in a configuration decision model. When the user changes the configuration on the left side of the preview, then the right side is updated automatically by applying the configuration specification captured in the decisions of the selected decision model. This means it is possible to "test drive" a configuration specification with this functionality. This mode is also in effect whenever several configuration decisions of the same configuration decision model are selected. The preview then works as described but only the selected decisions are taken into account.

17.4.4 Textual Variability Specification with VSL

All variability modeling information covered by the framework can be specified and edited textually. At first sight this merely provides an alternative form of variability specification equivalent to the data model and its XMI representation, without introducing additional capabilities. However, there are several important benefits to be drawn from this textual representation of variability information. This section briefly introduces the *variability specification language* (VSL) and then explains its additional benefits.

Figure 17.6 shows the VSL specification of the sample feature model already used in Figure 17.4. A single VSL file corresponds to the data model entity "VariabilityModel" and contains one or more feature models, configuration decision models, variable entities, feature and entity configurations or variability model folders to organize and package those elements. The example shows the specification of a feature model. As can be seen, the syntax was inspired by object-oriented programming languages such as Java. In addition, several optimizations were introduced to better fit the application area of variability specification, for example, all names such as those of features may contain special characters or white-space, which is simply achieved by enclosing them in quotation marks (e.g. `"Cruise Control"`). The hierarchy of the feature model is defined with the keyword `tree`. It is followed by a comma-separated list of root features. Each feature may be followed by a comma-separated list of child-features in brackets. Note how feature cardinality and parameterization can be defined

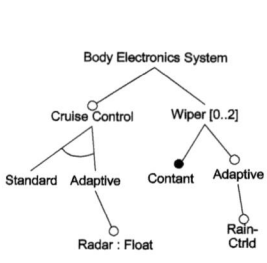

```
public featureModel SampleFM {
  tree
    "Body Electronics System" (
      "Cruise Control" (
        [1] (
          Standard,
          Adaptive ( Radar : Float )
        )
      ),
      Wiper[0..2] (
        Constant[1],
        Adaptive ( Rain-Ctrld )
      )
    );
  /* Let's set a feature's description. */
  feature Wiper.Adaptive {
    description = "Additional wiping mode \
                   with adaptive wiping speed.";
  }
}
```

Figure 17.6: A sample feature model specified in VSL.

within the hierarchy specification (e.g. `Constant[1]` and `Radar:Float`). Other properties of features, as well as other elements such as feature links, are specified below this hierarchy definition. This is shown exemplarily for feature `Adaptive`, for which the textual description is set. Since there are two features with that name, the feature's parent can be specified with a dot-notation in order to uniquely specify which feature is meant, in the example we chose the child of feature `Wiper`. Also note how feature groups are defined: as a cardinality without a name definition (e.g. below `Cruise Control`). Further details on VSL are beyond the scope of this thesis.

Among the obvious benefits of such a textual specification are:

- it is directly and immediately readable and editable, without relying on installing a viewer or editor

- ease of editing as compared to a tabular or graphical editor (depends on particular use case and taste)

- all parts of the specification are directly visible; nothing is concealed

- portability across platforms and tools

- stability

In the context of this thesis, however, three other benefits are of particular interest:

- version management and collaboration between persons or teams can be supported by applying standard tools (e.g. SVN [CSFP04])

- variability specifications can be partitioned and distributed across several text files by applying a simple import mechanism

17.4. Details on Selected Capabilities

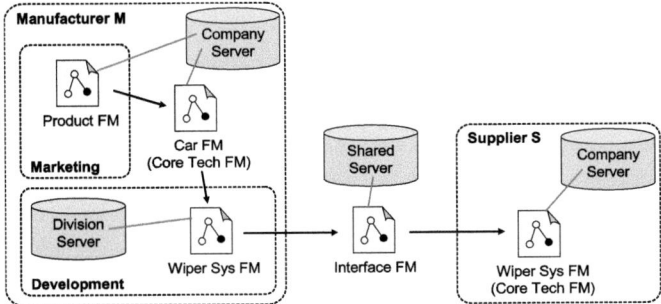

Figure 17.7: Example of a collaboration scenario between divisions and companies.

- collaboration between large units of a company or between companies can be achieved by combining the previous two benefits

Most standard version control tools are primarily targeted at software development projects and thus provide comprehensive support for plain text files. This way, it is possible to keep track of old versions of the variability specification in VSL files, compare versions, find out who performed certain changes or open branches. Furthermore, these tools allow to simultaneously work on the same file and provide support for later integrating the changes and resolving conflicts where necessary. This can also be done for VSL files without the need for additional concepts or tools.

Even more importantly, VSL files can easily be partitioned: it is possible to import one file into another on a plain textual level. This can be achieved, for example, with a standard C preprocessor. Thanks to such a partitioning, large specifications can be organized more easily and conflicts during collaboration can be minimized.

When combining version control and partitioning, even very complex scenarios of collaboration between large units of a company or between companies can be supported. This is illustrated in Figure 17.7. It shows a possible distribution of variability information for the situation in the following example.

Example 12. Car manufacturer M organizes its product line with a core technical feature model. The marketing division defines, in close cooperation with management, the options and packages available from a customer perspective in form of a separate feature model and a configuration link from that model to the core feature model. The development department responsible for the wiper system has a very consolidated requirements specification of a wiper which has been in use for a relatively long time and will be reused across model ranges and also for future models. Therefore, the variability inside this requirements specification is captured in a separate, local feature model together with a configuration link from the core feature model to this local feature model.

Supplier S was contracted for the wiper system. He does not develop the system from scratch but instead delivers an instance of his product line of wiper systems, which is tailored to the demands of several automotive manufacturers. Therefore, supplier S uses his own core technical feature model. Since this feature model contains a lot of information on the supplier's product strategy and also contains confidential information on innovative functionality which was exclusively licensed by another manufacturer—a competitor of manufacturer M—this core feature model must not be disclosed to M. This is solved by providing another feature model serving as a variability specification interface between M and S, again with appropriate configuration links. □

The simple, plain text-level import mechanism as assumed above has several drawbacks well known from older programming languages such as C. In particular, intricacies can arise regarding the location of imported files, the order of consecutive imports or optional imports. Therefore modern programming languages use import mechanisms which are part of the language and rely on a global name space spanning several source files, for example the Java language. The VSL may provide such an advanced import mechanism in future versions. For the purpose of the research demonstrator, however, the present mechanism is fully sufficient because it is not subject to any genuine limitations with respect to the above use cases.

Chapter 18

Prototypical Implementation of Multi-Level Requirements Artifacts

Multi-level feature models, i.e. the specific multi-level technique for managing feature models in a multi-level manner, was implemented as part of the variability management framework presented in the previous chapter. But, as stated in Part II, the multi-level approach can also be used to manage other types of artifacts than feature models. In that case, an appropriate multi-level technique is required for that artifact type, for example the one presented in Chapter 8 for requirements specifications in Telelogic DOORS, referred to as multi-level DOORS modules. In addition to the implementation of multi-level feature models, also this multi-level technique was prototypically implemented. This prototype was then applied in the N-Lighten case study (Section 19.2).

The reason for building on an existing commercial tool in this case was that this tool is already widely used at Daimler AG and in the automotive industry on the whole and it provides an extremely flexible extension mechanism in the form of the DOORS *Extension Language* (DXL), which actually constitutes a complete programming language.

A screen shot of DOORS running the multi-level prototype is shown in Figure 18.1. The upper window shows a reference module which is referred to by the module in the lower window. As can be seen in the upper window, the deviation permission attributes all go in one single column, i.e. a single DOORS custom attribute was created for them. The attribute lists the values of all deviation permission attributes that differ from the default value.

In the lower window in Figure 18.1, it can be seen that the feedback of the algorithm checking the conformance of the referring module is presented in another special column / attribute, called "Conformance". The conformance state for each object can be found here. Conformance violations are highlighted by a special background color.

In addition to the conformance-check algorithm, there is another function to resolve conformance violations as well as allowed deviations. This can be seen as a two-way synchronization algorithm with which changes on referring level or reference level can be propagated up or down, respectively. For example, when a referring module is created by an OEM for negotiation with a supplier, changes that arise from this interaction can be clearly identified and propagated to the reference level if they are to become valid in a broader context. The instructions for the synchronization algorithm, i.e. whether a certain deviation is to be propagated up or down, are given in another special column / attribute within the source module. In particular, the following propagation (or synchronization) actions are distinguished:

- restore attributes

174   Chapter 18. Prototypical Implementation of Multi-Level Requirements Artifacts

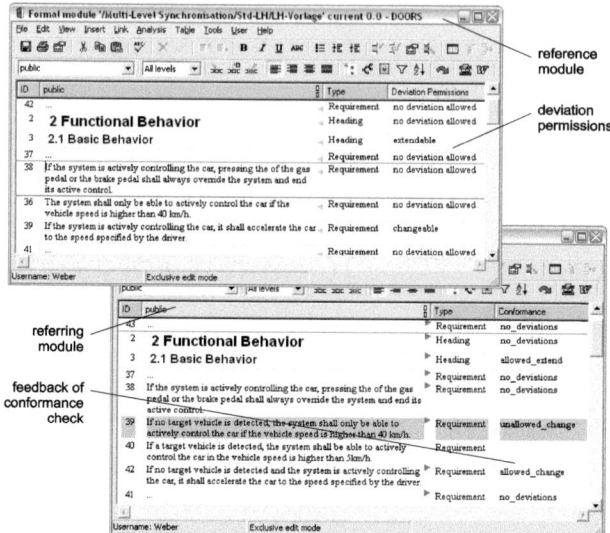

Figure 18.1: A prototypical implementation of multi-level DOORS modules.

- restore node (i.e. restore an object which was deleted)
- restore position
- restore order
- remove extensions
- restore reductions
- remove out-link extensions
- restore out-link reductions

As can be seen, for each of the forms of deviations identified for DOORS modules in Section 8.3 and for each of the deviation permission attributes summarized in the list on page 91 a corresponding propagation action is provided.

In multi-level feature models as implemented in the variability management framework from the previous chapter, the reference model link from a referring to a reference model and the reference feature links from referring features to their reference feature are part of the referring model. By contrast, in the DOORS prototype the links from referring to reference modules are kept in one or several separate DOORS modules solely dedicated to this purpose. This way, it is not necessary to add special objects to referring modules.

Some more details on the tool prototype for multi-level DOORS modules, including some considerations on usability, will be given below when the N-Lighten case study is presented.

Chapter 19
Case Studies

This chapter provides an overview of the case studies which served to evaluate and consolidate the concepts proposed in Parts II and III above.

19.1 The eSafety Case Study

19.1.1 Background, Content and Objectives

The ATESST "eSafety" case study mainly draws from experience of the project's industrial partners. It was reengineered from a previously existing case study provided by Siemens VDO, which consisted of an integration of several automotive subsystems and was available in the form of Matlab Simulink [SL08] models.

The study was focused on two main vehicle functions:

- ABS component (an anti blocking break system)

- EMS component (an engine management system)

The effort was divided into two main activities: (1) functional and architectural modeling was done in the EAST-ADL2 language with the Papyrus tool (only partly for the EMS function) and (2) an integration test on a hardware-in-the-loop platform was done with Intecrio/ASCET. These two aspects represent the two major parts of the case study, referred to as the architectural demonstrator and the RPU demonstrator respectively (RPU stands for Rapid Prototyping Unit).

Architectural Demonstrator

The architectural demonstrator was modeled using the tool Papyrus, provided by the French project partner CEA. This is a UML2 modeling tool with an emphasis on supporting extensions in the form of UML2 profiles [Web08]. However, this tool is only intended for basic architectural modeling with the EAST-ADL2 language; a range of additional functionalities specifically tailored to the EAST-ADL2 is provided by a number of associated Eclipse plugins:

- CVM Feature Editor:
  for variability specification both on the vehicle and artifact level.

- Variability Plugin:
  for generating configured instances of variable architectural EAST-ADL2 models.

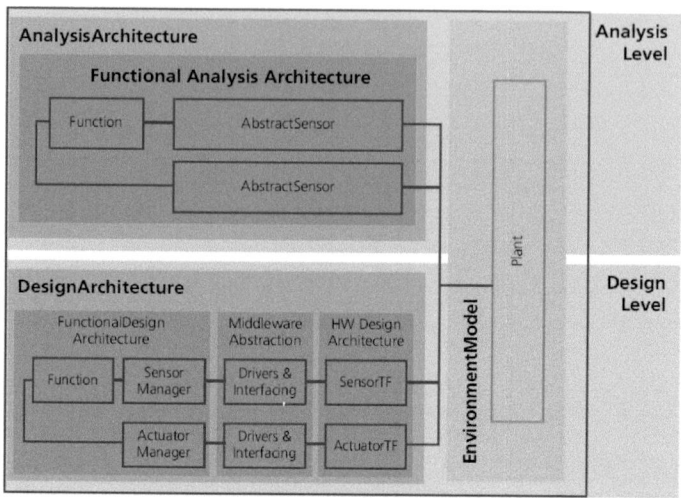

Figure 19.1: Overview of system organization according to EAST-ADL2.

- Hip-Hops Link:
  an interface for performing safety analysis with Hip-Hops tools.

- Simulink Import:
  import of Simulink structural model into Class diagram.

- Element Parsing:
  search and visualization functionality for EAST-ADL2 models.

These plugins are tightly coupled with Papyrus and together form an integrated development environment for automotive systems. Of course, this is not a perfected tool suite for immediate application in practice but rather a research prototype, which may, however, evolve into a practically applicable tool framework in the future.

The decomposition of the functional architecture follows the basic system organization insinuated by the EAST-ADL2 language: a vehicle feature model on the global vehicle level, an analysis architecture and a design architecture.

The vehicle feature model serves two main purposes: it defines the complete system's functions on a very abstract level and it specifies the product line's commonality and variability.

At the analysis level, the "AnalysisArchitecture" contains "ADLFunctions" that can be hierarchically composed and connected to each other. Entities called "FunctionalDevice" represent sensors and actuators with their interface software and electronics, and these are connected to the environment model. Figure 19.1 explains the entities involved and shows how they are related.

19.1. The eSafety Case Study

The design level contains a more detailed functional definition of the system. In contrast to the analysis architecture which is rather oriented toward the problem space, the design architecture reflects the eventual system decomposition on implementation level. "ADLFunctions" and "LocalDeviceManagers" represent application software in the functional design architecture. "ADLFunctions" in the Middleware Abstraction are used to capture middleware behavior affecting application functionality. The Hardware Design Architecture serves two purposes: sensors, actuators and I/O represent the application functions' interface to the environment; ECUs and busses represent the computation platform to which application functions are allocated. The objective here is to describe a representation of the vehicle hardware architecture from an abstract perspective, and to serve as an allocation target for functions. The hardware entities, in particular sensors and actuators, may also have a behavioral definition to allow end-to-end analysis of the functions.

To give an impression of the complexity and scope of the architectural demonstrator, its main packages are briefly introduced here:

- System: the top-level package, containing the root EAST-ADL2 entity "ADLSystemModel" as an entry point into the system.

- EnvironmentModel: description of the environment, containing the basic entity "VehicleEnvironment", and the different ADL elements to build the vehicle plant model. Interactions are depicted in composite structure diagrams.

- VehicleFeatureModel: the vehicle's functions on a global level (see above)

- AnalysisArchitecture: the analysis architecture as outlined above.

- DesignArchitecture: the design architecture as outlined above.

- ADLDependabilityModel: package for description of the error model of the demonstrator for the ABS function (for hardware and software element described at the Analysis Design level) with basic stereotype "ErrorBehavior". It defines the hazards and the definition of failure mode and propagation (of the ABS system).

- Datatypes: package describing the data types (Unit, ADLDesignDataType) of the ADLFlowPorts declared in the architectural models (ADLFunctionType). It includes 3 sub packages: Unit (for physical units), Abstract and Implementation (for description of the data types at analysis and design/implementation level respectively).

- IASystem: package for the AUTOSAR part containing the basic entity "AUTOSAR", with AUTOSAR software component descriptions, system topology descriptions, mapping etc.

The vehicle feature model is completely edited and managed with the framework implementation introduced in Chapter 17. On analysis and design level, this framework is used to edit and manage the local feature models of EAST-ADL2 software components, which are used to reveal and publish a component's internal variability.

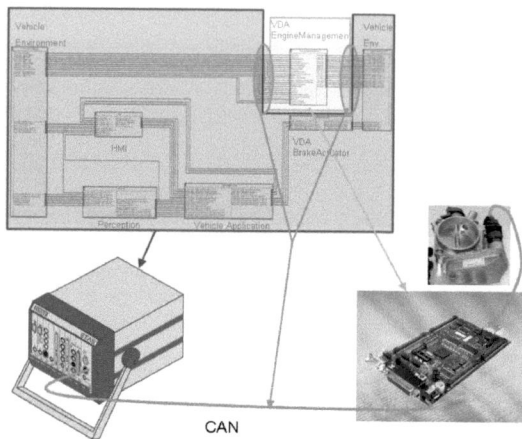

Figure 19.2: Virtual and physical representation of the RPU demonstrator.

RPU Demonstrator

The RPU demonstrator represents the functional integration test of the design architecture which was defined as part of the architectural demonstrator (cf. previous section). It consists of a virtual representation of the demonstrator, defined in a form appropriate for the ETAS Intecrio tool, and includes behavioral descriptions imported from other formats (MatLab/Simulink, ASCET). Then, this virtual representation was deployed on physical hardware in order to be actually executed, as defined in the physical representation (see Figure 19.2, the virtual representation is enclosed by blue and green borders).

The virtual representation of the RPU demonstrator is based on an ASCET model for the engine management system controlling the engine actuator. It includes also vehicle and driver models, part of the vehicle environment model (in Simulink).

In the context of this thesis, i.e. for evaluating the conceptions of subscoping and configuration links, only those parts of the eSafety case study were primarily profitable, that deal with functional modeling on the vehicle level or with variable architectural modeling and specification. In addition, due to harsh time constraints, variability on the implementation level was not examined in detail during the eSafety study. The RPU demonstrator was therefore of less significance during the preparation of this work and will therefore not be described in more detail here.

19.1.2 Lessons Learned

Several constructive observations emerged from the eSafety case study. In addition, the research work within the ATESST project—mainly the definition of the EAST-ADL2—also provided a fruitful source of inspiration. In particular, the requirement of integrating the

19.1. The eSafety Case Study

concepts of subscoping and configuration links as well as their prototypical implementation into a rigid, comprehensive methodology provided an excellent adaptability test, which was extremely helpful to consolidate both concepts and implementations. Therefore, this section does not only cover the practical case study but includes also the lessons learned from the conceptual work in the project.

1. **Meta-Model Refinement.** Several details of the information model for variability management as defined in Appendix A were refined during the discussions in the ATESST project. This regards terminology as well as the structuring of the meta-model. For example, there are several ways to realize a tree structure of optionally grouped entities: all entities might be contained in the root container (i.e. the feature model) and the parent/child-relationships as well as the groupings are realized by simple associations; or the entities might be hierarchically contained in their respective parent entities and the entities for grouping form a part of this containment hierarchy. Experience shows that all these "design choices" during meta-model definition are influenced by a multitude of conceptual and implementation related considerations and usually there is not the one correct solution but it is rather a question of balancing conflicting interests.

2. **Top-Level Propagation.** The case study showed that, when applying configuration links for the compositional variability use case (cf. Section 14.5), it is sometimes desirable or even indispensable to state at a very low hierarchical level that a certain variability, represented by one or more features, is directly propagated up to the top level, called *top-level propagation* in the following. According to the use case of compositional variability and the concept of configuration links, variability is usually propagated up in a step-by-step manner, one hierarchy level at a time, but sometimes it has to be propagated up to the top level in a single step. The key point here is that in the standard case the decision to propagate to the top level is distributed among all higher levels: on each level of hierarchy the propagation may be broken and the variability may be bound. In the case of an immediate top-level propagation however, the decision to make the variability appear on the top level is taken and fixed on the lower level where the variability occurred.

3. **Global Features.** Another important observation from the case study, also related to the use case of compositional variability, was that sometimes *global features* are required on the lower hierarchical levels. The difference to the standard case of features "locally" defined within the public feature models of lower level components is that such global features can be used in different subtrees of the system's composition hierarchy and will still eventually be configured identically.

   The concepts of top-level propagation and global features were not yet incorporated into the concept of configuration links and the corresponding tool prototype. This is an objective of the follow-up project of ATESST starting in mid 2008. The tricky part here is that these extensions may break, to some extent, the contract of information hiding which is key to component-oriented software design and which was extended to variability by establishing configuration hiding (cf. 14.3).

4. **Equivalences and Exclusive Folders.** Two other conceptions also emerged from the case study: equivalences and exclusive folders. These were already discussed in Section 15.1 and 15.2 respectively.

5. **Relations between Configuration Decisions.** The experience with the case study was also helpful in assessing the role and significance of relations between configuration decisions. A detailed account of this issue was given in Section 15.3.

6. **Dependency Propagation.** Another very intriguing idea that emerged from the case study is *dependency propagation*. The great importance and complexity of dependencies between an automotive system's variable aspects was described in Section 5.1 already. Such dependencies may arise on virtually all abstraction levels; for example, a certain dependency may represent a marketing decision, which will usually be defined on a high abstraction level, or it may represent a technical constraint, usually defined on a rather low level of abstraction. When structuring a product line infrastructure with configuration links according to the use cases from Chapter 14 these levels of abstraction and composition will be (partly) represented by their own feature models. A dependency occurring on a lower technical level will then be defined in that level's corresponding feature model. With configuration links—and the semantic relation they establish between their source and target feature models (cf. Figure 13.1 in Section 13.2.2)—it is now imaginable to propagate a dependency from the source to the target feature model, or vice versa. This way, for example, it would be possible to show the impact of a technical constraint in the marketing-oriented view of a feature model capturing customer variability. This idea of dependency propagation opens up a range of interesting research questions, which are expected to be examined in detail in the ATESST follow-up project starting in July 2008.

7. **Relevance of Flexible Parameter Assignments.** The experience from the case study suggests that flexible parameter assignments (Section 15.6) are not a truly critical asset of configuration links for application in practice. Of course, there will occur situations in which they are beneficial or even indispensable, but it will probably be possible to also model non-trivial applications of a substantial size without them. They seem to have a similar relevance as cloned features: often useful but truly indispensable only in relatively rare special cases (cf. Section 4.4.2).

In addition to these observations on a rather conceptual level, several more tool related findings resulted from the case study and the ATESST project on the whole. Two deserve particular mention here:

9. **Modularization.** In the ATESST project a modeling tool for the EAST-ADL2 was devised, called Papyrus UML [Web08]. The prototypical variability management framework presented in Chapter 17 then had to be tightly and seamlessly integrated into this modeling tool. This exercise proved to be an excellent opportunity to foster the modularity of the tool implementation as well as the underlying concepts. It is thus justified to say that the concepts and the tool prototype presented in this thesis are now defined such that they can be coupled quite straightforwardly with existing design methodologies in order to extend them with variability management.

10. **Configuration Decision Editing.** Finally, the ATESST project and eSafety case study proved valuable for experimenting with different editing functionality for facilitating the management of configuration decisions. As was pointed out before, configuration predefinition is inherently complex, no matter what concepts and means of expression

will be used for specification and modeling. Therefore an appropriate editing functionality is of particular importance here. The experience within the ATESST research effort lead to the tool interface and editing functionality sketched above in Section 17.4.3.

Overall, it can be said that prespecifying configuration with configuration links, as defined in Part III above, proved to be highly feasible and beneficial in principle. Of course, a relatively basic and abstract concept as that of configuration links requires extensive evaluation over a longer period of time and has to be tested in many diverse application areas before it is justified to claim its applicability in large-scale, industrial settings. In specialized application contexts of a manageable size, however, it may certainly prove viable. Furthermore, the experience from the eSafety case study and the ATESST project certainly justifies additional research on configuration links in order to further consolidate and extend the concept and tools.

19.2 The N-Lighten Case Study

A second case study, called the "N-Lighten case study", was intended for evaluating the basic idea of subscoping together with the supporting technical concepts as described in Part II. It was specifically focused on multi-level DOORS modules and could therefore make use of the corresponding prototype tool introduced above in Chapter 18. However, most observations will arguably be applicable to multi-level feature trees and other multi-level artifacts as well, especially those regarding the basic conception of subscoping.

19.2.1 Background, Content and Objectives

The N-Lighten case study was conducted at Carmeq GmbH in 2007 and was based on several authentic technical specifications for up-to-date vehicle models from Volkswagen [BW07]. A functionality of the body electronics system, the lights and illumination function group, was chosen as the subject of investigation, hence the name of the case study. The involved specifications contained between 1.300 and 3.500 requirements, which represents a sufficient scale to evaluate the concepts under realistic conditions.

As a starting point of the survey, three existing technical specifications were used. These were available as three DOORS modules: one for the lights and illumination functionality of the new Lupo model, one for the same functionality of the new Golf model, and a third which originally served as the template of the other two, i.e. from which the other two modules were once derived by way of copy and paste. In the following, these three DOORS modules will be referred to as Lupo module, Golf module and base module respectively.

This initial setting matches exactly the intention of subscoping and the multi-level concept: the overall product line, comprising Lupo *and* Golf cars, is split up in two sublines, namely Lupo and Golf, and each subline is enhanced independently from the other; the multi-level management now allows to track and strategically coordinate the commonalities and differences between these two sublines without having to introduce a rigid product line organization. As was described in Chapter 6 as one of the core intentions of subscoping, the variability *between* Lupo and Golf does no longer appear as variation points within the Lupo and Golf specifications, which substantially reduces complexity of the specifications.

In order to set up a multi-level hierarchy with these three specifications, an auxiliary synchronization module (as described in Chapter 18) had to be created, which provided

Table 19.1: Statistics for the Lupo and Golf specifications.

	Base	DOORS Modules			
		Lupo		Golf	
Objects, thereof ...	1,908	1,351		3,501	
- without reference object		590	43.7%	1,714	49.0%
- with reference object		761	56.3%	1,787	51.0%
Coverage		0.399	39.9%	0.937	93.7%
Innovation		0.437	43.7%	0.490	49.0%
Deviations:					
- Refinement		33	2.4%	107	3.1%
- Reduction		24	1.8%	18	0.5%
- Move		5	0.4%	36	1.0%
- Reorder		–		2	0.1%
- Textual Changes		220	16.3%	241	6.9%
- Merge		–		2	0.1%
- Split		65	4.8%	16	0.5%

the tool prototype with the necessary meta-information. This is very straightforward and mainly defines the hierarchy of reference and referring DOORS modules involved, in this case the base module as a single reference module and the Lupo and Golf modules as referring modules. Then, the reference links from the requirements in the Lupo and Golf modules to their corresponding reference requirements in the base module had to be established and defined in DOORS in a form suitable for the tool prototype. This was a more daunting task as will be discussed below. Together, these preparations then allowed for managing the two referring specifications according to the multi-level approach, for example to define deviation permissions in the base module, to reveal illegitimate deviations in the Lupo and Golf modules or to propagate novel additions from the Golf module, for example, to the base module.

The Lupo module contained 1.351 objects whereas the Golf module contained 3.501. This already shows the remarkable difference in system complexity between a low-end and a medium-class vehicle, not to mention luxury-class models. Table 19.1 presents some statistics of the case study that further characterizes the specification modules involved. Providing these figures would be one of the basic capabilities of a full-fledged multi-level tool. From such a statistic, several interesting facts become immediately obvious, which is already a first important benefit of the concept. For example, the number of non-referring objects, i.e. objects without a reference object, is an adequate measure for how much additional information was introduced in a subline, compared to the base module. The ratio of the number of referring objects in referring module to the total number of objects in the base module is a reasonable measure for how much information of the base module found its way into the referring module. The two measures introduced in Section 10.4, coverage and innovation, provide this information in a normalized form.

Another interesting fact to note about the two specifications is that the structuring of the original base module was conversely changed in the two subline specifications: in the Lupo module the hierarchy was flattened and in the Golf module it was deepened. This caused the conspicuous difference in the ratio of refinements to reductions in the two subline modules. From a case study perspective, this was an interesting additional test for the multi-level concept; in practice however, this will usually only occur in early phases of adopting the

19.2. The N-Lighten Case Study

concepts where the structure of the base module is still fairly unconsolidated.

19.2.2 Lessons Learned

Based on the results of this case study, it was possible to draw several interesting conclusions:

1. **Creating Reference Links.** As indicated above, one of the necessary activities for setting up the multi-level hierarchy proved to be a rather tedious task: the creation of reference links from the objects in the Lupo and Golf modules to their corresponding reference object in the base module. The most difficult part is to decide which object from the base module is the correct reference object for a certain lower-level object or if there is no such object at all. Except for the cases where an equal object is found in the reference module, this requires to take into consideration the detailed semantics of the two specifications. Given the large amount of 1.351 to 3.501 objects in the two lower level specifications, this difficulty is of high relevance.

   However, for several reasons this difficulty does not put into question the basic idea and concept of the multi-level approach:

   (a) The problem described here does only occur if a multi-level hierarchy is to be set up on the basis of preexisting legacy specifications. If the Lupo and Golf modules were initially created with the multi-level concept already in mind, then the reference links could have been established automatically when copying the base module, i.e. when creating a new subline.

   (b) But even in the case of legacy specifications, the problem can be alleviated by providing appropriate tool support. A tool could predefine the reference links based on an appropriate similarity measure and assist the user in reviewing and adapting them by way of an appropriate on-screen presentation. Designing such a *linking assistant* would not be trivial but relatively straightforward; experience from the model transformation field, where a similar issue exists [FV07], could be exploited. It is realistic that the linking problem could be reduced quite substantially that way.

   (c) However, even without such a linking assistant, the task of establishing the reference links is absolutely manageable, as the case study showed. And this was the case even though the person who defined the reference links, Martin Becker from Carmeq GmbH, did not know the content of the three specifications before starting to work on this case study. In many cases in practice however, the reference links will be established by engineers who already know the specifications very well, which will facilitate the task substantially.

   Therefore this difficulty does not actually represent a critical problem of the approach.

2. **Split and Merge.** The most important observation was that the splitting and merging of objects in a subline module is of great practical relevance. Since this finding leads to an important extension of the basic multi-level concept, it was already thoroughly discussed in Part II in Section 10.3.

3. **Overriding Deviation Permissions.** The intention of deviation permissions is to provide a means to allow or disallow certain forms of deviation on the reference level,

i.e. in the base module, which then equally applies to all referring modules, i.e. the Lupo and Golf modules. During the case study, this scenario has actually been approved as the standard case. However, an important special case showed up: sometimes a certain disallowed deviation has to be allowed as an exception for a single subline only. This might be necessary, for example, to realize a required stop-gap solution. With the basic multi-level concept this situation can be treated in two ways: either (a) the deviation permission in the base module is relaxed accordingly, but then the respective deviation is allowed in all sublines, which is not desirable or (b) the error message indicating the illegitimate deviation is simply ignored, which means that the fact that this particular error is not harmful has to be noted somewhere and always remembered, which is also an unsatisfying solution.

Therefore it would make sense to introduce a mechanism to override the deviation permissions of a certain object as defined in the base module within and for a single subline module only, e.g. only for the Lupo module.

4. **Changes Within a Subline Module.** The multi-level concept is useful to identify and manage changes in a subline module with respect to the base module. However, during the case study a similar question often occurred: what changes were introduced in a subline module with respect to an earlier version of this same subline module. After some consideration, this issue was deemed outside of the scope of the multi-level concept. It can and should be solved orthogonally to the multi-level concept, plainly on the level of a change management facility. While this observation did not lead to an extension of the multi-level approach, it still was beneficial for further clarifying the distinction between the multi-level approach and change management.

5. **Meta-Information and Process Support.** As was already briefly indicated in Part II above, it would be extremely useful to provide means to flexibly attach project- and company-specific meta-information to the entities of the multi-level approach[1]. In particular, certain processes of proposing, reviewing and accepting new deviations could be supported by introducing a specialized status attribute that shows for a certain deviation the current phase within this change process. In Section 1.4 it was already stated and justified that such organization and process related issues lie outside the scope of this thesis.

In addition to these rather conceptual observations, there are also several technical aspects to note:

6. **Comparison of OLE Objects.** In order uncover deviations in a subline module, it is of paramount importance to be able to compare two attribute values and, if they are unequal, to show what has been changed. DOORS provides a special functionality for editing attribute values which proved to be a daunting challenge in this regard: the value of a text attribute may contain OLE objects. OLE stands for "Object Linking and Embedding" and is the name of a distributed object system and protocol on the Microsoft Windows platform [Cha96], which provides a mechanism to embed editable objects of various types and origins within the document of a third-party tool. For example, an image drawn in Microsoft PowerPoint or a table created in Microsoft Excel can easily be included in the text of a textual attribute in DOORS.

---

[1]The same applies, by the way, to the entities related to configuration links.

19.2. The N-Lighten Case Study

The problem is that a DOORS DXL script cannot easily compare two attribute values for equality which contain such OLE objects, because that would require to compare the content of the OLE objects which in turn would require full support of the objects' internal format, for example the data format of an Excel sheet. Since OLE objects can have an arbitrary data format it is not possible to find a principle solution here, and even implementing a compare for only the most important types of OLE objects would be an enormous effort. Furthermore, OLE objects in DOORS are used extensively in practice and avoiding them is absolutely unrealistic.

Fortunately, a solution was found for at least comparing two OLE objects for exact equality. This is sufficient for checking whether any change occurred at all, but not for finding out, and presenting to the user, what was changed or whether the change was only superficial and should rather be ignored, e.g. a differing column width in a table. Given the fact that the OLE objects used in DOORS requirement specifications are usually not too complex—due to the imperative of requirement atomization [Poh07]—this partial solution proved sufficient for practical use. However, in full-fledged tool support it would be desirable to have a more sophisticated comparison mechanism for the most common types of OLE object, probably diagrams and tables imported from Microsoft Word or Excel.

7. **Miscellaneous Technical Intricacies of Doors.** In addition to OLE objects, a number of implementation specifics of DOORS caused difficulties during the case study. For example the precise technical realization of links in DOORS is associated with several intricacies. However, in contrast to the OLE object issue above, these technical complexities were completely unrelated to the fundamental idea of the multi-level approach and are therefore not discussed in further detail here.

In summary, the following general conclusions could be drawn regarding the feasibility of the overall multi-level approach:

8. **Forms of Deviation are Appropriate.** During the conceptual design of the multi-level approach, several different forms of deviation were identified and they had to be attached to the tree structure of DOORS objects as deviation permissions. A multitude of different distinctions and constructions would have been conceivable here; the aim was to find a solution which is as simple as possible and yet sufficiently differentiated to allow to formulate all distinctions required in practice.

The case study showed that the forms of deviation and how they cover changes of the hierarchical structure of the specification artifacts matches very well the deviations we came across in the three investigated authentic specifications. The only important exception is merging and splitting of objects, which was already highlighted as an issue above and discussed in detail as an advanced consideration in Section 10.3.

9. **Reference Links are Real-World Entities.** Semantically relating the objects of the subline modules to objects in the base module through reference links did not pose any substantial problems from a conceptual point of view. It might be a lot of work to initially define those links (as highlighted above), but for two particular objects it can usually be decided easily and definitely if one of the two should serve as the reference object of the other. This was the case even though the structure of the base module was

changed substantially in the subline modules; even if an object was put in a different section, it was still possible to clearly decide which reference object it should receive.

This suggests that a reference link is not an artificial concept only introduced to make the multi-level approach work, but instead it captures an actual conceptual relation between objects which naturally occurs in real-word use cases.

10. **Adequate Usability.** The usability of the tool prototype for multi-level DOORS modules proved to be quite reasonable. Even though it was not specifically designed for excellent usability, it was still quite convenient to perform the typical actions, such as spotting deviations, editing deviation permissions, finding out whether deviations are illegitimate, or propagating deviations up and down.

Considering these observations and the overall size of the investigated specifications, over three thousand objects in case of the Golf module, it is not implausible to expect that with a full-fledged tool solution the general multi-level approach will be actually feasible in practice.

Part V

Conclusion

Chapter 20
Summary and Outlook

20.1 Summary of Contributions

Certainly, subscoping and the multi-level approach together with configuration links and the associated concepts represent the major contributions of this thesis. However, several other noteworthy contributions are scattered across the text. To provide an overview and make them more accessible, a brief summary is provided here. Each is listed with a reference to the chapter or section where more information can be found. In addition, some of the author's publications are included for easy reference.

- Slightly modified definition of the term "product line" (Section 2.1),

- Differentiation between versions and variants (Section 2.6),

- Clear separation of artifact-level and product-line-level variability (Sections 3.1, 3.3–3.4, published in [MRW06]),

- Generic notion and purpose of variability modeling (Section 3.2),

- Identification, survey and detailed comparison of fundamental classes of variability modeling (Sections 3.3–3.5; published in [RTW07a]),

- Novel definition of the term "feature" highlighting the importance of a broad, abstract understanding of this concept (Section 4.3, published in [RW08, NSL08]) together with a detailed discussion and examples (Sections 4.3, 4.6),

- Discussion of the value and applicability of individual traditional feature modeling concepts in the automotive domain (Sections 4.4, 4.7),

- Novel feature modeling approach CVM, with formal definition (Section 4.5),

- Detailed discussion and classification of important characteristics of the automotive domain with respect to product line engineering (Section 5.1),

- Overall organizational scheme for highly complex (automotive) product lines (Section 5.2.2, published in [RW08, NSL08]),

- Basic notion of "unified feature modeling" and a list of requirements for unified feature modeling techniques (Section 5.3, published in [RTW07b]),

- Subscoping, multi-level feature models and multi-level requirements artifacts (Part II, published in [BBP+05, RW06, RW07]),
- Configuration Links (Part III, partly published in [RW05, RTW09]),
- Implementation of the CVM feature modeling technique, of configuration links and multi-level feature models as an Eclipse plugin ("CVM variability management framework", Chapter 17),
- Implementation of multi-level requirements artifacts as an extension to DOORS in the form of a DOORS DXL script (Chapter 18),
- eSafety case study (Section 19.1),
- N-Lighten case study (Section 19.2).

In addition to the publications given here, several of the above contributions were also presented in the deliverables of the European project ATESST [ATE08].

20.2 Outlook

The conceptions of subscoping and configuration links open up a wide range of application options and, as a consequence, a multitude of further research questions. For example, the multi-level technique might be augmented by an extension mechanism which allows to define additional types of deviations with corresponding deviation permissions, perhaps tailored to the specific nature of a certain artifact type or the specific needs in a concrete application context. Especially for string attributes many different special forms of deviation are conceivable (e.g. changes of a string attribute might be restricted to changing the substring "[]", if present, to some other character sequence; this way, a value within the reference model would become a template in which the characters "[]" serve as placeholders to be filled in within referring models). While the evaluation presented in Chapter 19 showed that the standard forms of deviation are entirely sufficient for non-trivial applications, such user-defined deviations might still prove useful.

Configuration links, on the other hand, also provide great potential for further research: many advanced analyses are conceivable that may assist the user while editing configuration decisions; the graphical visualization of the complex configuration mapping captured in a configuration decision model will certainly make for an intriguing and challenging research area; and the propagation of dependencies and constraints from a configuration link's source feature model to its target model(s), or vice versa, might be investigated, based on the formalization of configuration links provided above. The last issue is of particular practical relevance. Based on a product line infrastructure organized with configuration links, the constraint propagation would allow to directly detect how a low-level technical constraint on the variability (explicitly defined in a low-level, technically oriented feature model) becomes manifest in the high-level feature model used for end-customer configuration (in the form of a propagated, i.e. derived, constraint).

Another research topic, applicable to both multi-level artifacts and configuration links, would be to study ways to further support management activities as well as particular development and evolution processes by assigning relevant meta-information to the conceptual entities within multi-level artifacts or configuration decision models.

20.2. Outlook

In addition to aiming for such rather technical extensions, future research must certainly also further investigate the practical applicability of the proposed concepts. Before it is justifiable to say that multi-level artifacts and configuration links are truly applicable in mission-critical, industrial-size development projects, much more experience with the techniques has to be gained, the tool prototypes have to be refined, and the overall approach must be made more accessible, for example by providing end-user documentation and tutorials. Of course, this is particularly true for the vision of applying configuration links on a global scale for the entire organization of an automotive manufacturer's product line infrastructure (as outlined in Section 5.2.2). However, this is not surprising for a novel conception which lies on the spectrum from research to practice clearly on the research side.

In order to obtain an organizational context for working on these advanced issues, I took part in applying for a follow-up project to the ATESST European project [ATE08] and introduced many of the above research objectives in the project proposal. An entire work task of ATESST2 was designated to variability management. At time of writing, this follow-up project was accepted for funding by the European Commission as part of the 7th framework program and is scheduled to run from mid 2008 to mid 2010. This way, it is assured that the work on the approach can continue for the next two years.

Part VI

Appendices

Appendix A
An Information Model for Automotive Variability Management

Appendix A. An Information Model for Automotive Variability Management

A.1 Variability Models

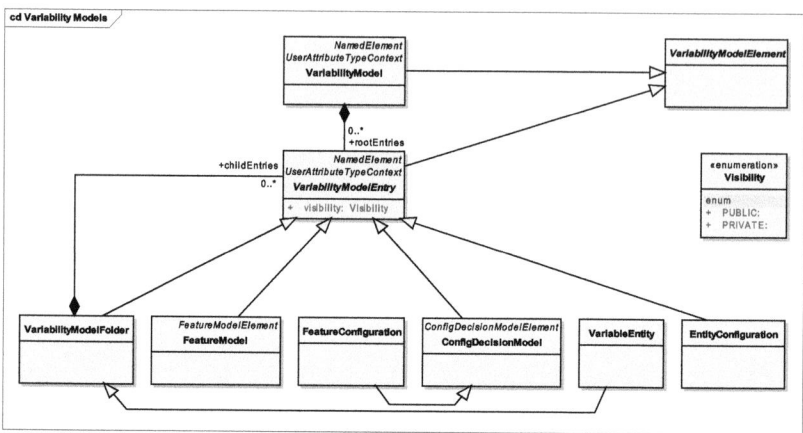

A.1.1 Class VariabilityModel

A variability model is the root container of all entities for variability specification. It is also the place where global user attributes can be defined (cf. Section A.7).

Attributes

name	*inherited from* `NamedElement`
description	*inherited from* `NamedElement`

Associations

rootEntries	The root variability model entries of this variabiliy model. This can be, for example, a feature model, a configuration decision model or a folder of variability model entries.

A.1.2 Class VariabilityModelElement

The abstract superclass of all non-trivial classes which are related to variability modeling, including `VariabilityModel` itself. These are the entities of primary concern during variability modeling and are usually those that will be visible in an editor. For example a `Feature` is a variability model element but `Cardinality` is not, because it is only a subordinate entity within a feature or feature group.

A.1.3 Class VariabilityModelEntry

All elements that can be directly contained in a variability model inherit from `Variability-ModelEntry`.

A.1. Variability Models

Attributes

visibility	The visibility of the entry within the containing variability model or variability model folder. Currently, only PUBLIC and PRIVATE are supported.

A.1.4 Class VariabilityModelFolder

A container for variability model entries. Except for visibility, this is used only for organizing variability model entires through packaging and has no further semantic impact.

Attributes

name	*inherited from* NamedElement
description	*inherited from* NamedElement
visibility	*inherited from* VariabilityModelEntry If a folder is defined PRIVATE then all contained variability model entires will be concealed; otherwise their overall visibility depends on the visibility defined for them.

Associations

childEntries	The variability model entries contained in this folder.

A.1.5 Enumeration Visibility

Visibility of an entity from outside its direct container. The precise meaning depends on the entity for which the visibility is defined.

Values

PUBLIC	This entity is disclosed. Concealment of contained entities depends on their visibility.
PRIVATE	This entity and all its contained entities are concealed.

A.2 Feature Models

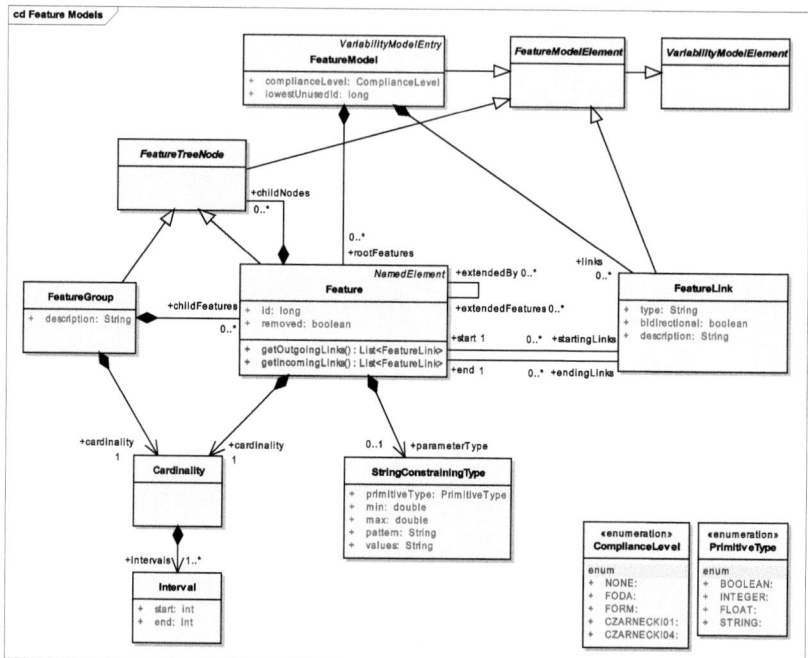

A.2.1 Class Cardinality

A non-empty set of intervals, i.e. a non-empty set of non-negative integers. The attribute end of the last and only the last interval in a cardinality may be set to -1. Such a cardinality is then called "unbounded".

Associations

| intervals | The intervals that make up this cardinality. At least a one interval must to be specified. |

A.2.2 Class Feature

A Feature is a characteristic or trait which may or may not be pertinent to a certain configuration of a variable entity. During configuration, a feature can be selected or deselected.

Attributes

| name | inherited from NamedElement |
| description | inherited from NamedElement |

A.2. Feature Models

id	A number greater than 0 which uniquely identifies the feature within the containing feature model or -1 to indicate that the feature does not have such a unique identifier. This ID is initialized within the class `CreateNewCommand` when a feature is created through an EMF EditingDomain. Note that it is legal for a feature to not have a valid unique id (represented by the value -1). See also: attribute `lowestUnusedId` in `FeatureModel`.
removed	see Section A.6

Associations

childNodes	The child nodes of this feature. A feature can have features and feature groups as children, therefore this association is of type `FeatureTreeNode`. Note that this only includes direct, non-inherited children. When retrieving a features children during configuration, then also inherited children have to be taken into account (see attribute `extendedFeatures`).
cardinality	The cardinality of the feature. It specifies how often this feature may be selected during configuration. Selecting a single feature more than once is called instantiating the feature. A feature with a cardinality of [1] is called a mandatory feature, one with [0..1] is called an optional feature and one with an unbounded cardinality or a maximum cardinality greater than 1 is called a cloned feature.
parameterType	If a type is defined, the feature is called a "parameterized feature". In that case, instead of only selecting or deselecting a feature, a value must be specified for this feature during configuration if and only if it is selected. In the case of a cloned feature, each instance is provided with its own value. The value of a parameterized feature is always a plain `String` value. The type defined by the `StringConstrainingType` is only used to restrict that string to certain values. Note the difference between such a parameter and an attribute (such as a feature's `name`): Attributes are assigned a value during feature modeling, parameters are defined during feature configuration.
extended-Features	If one or more features are defined as extended features, then feature inheritance takes place: the extending feature inherits all child nodes, i.e. child features and child feature groups, of the extended features. Only children are inherited. All other characteristics of a feature, e.g. its name, cardinality or parameterization, are not inherited and must be defined for each extending feature separately.
extendedBy	The reverse of `extendedFeatures`.

`startingLinks`	The feature links that are starting at this feature. Note that this does not include bidirectional links that are ending at this feature (cf. method `getOutgoingLinks()`).
`endingLinks`	The feature links that are ending at this feature. Note that this does not include bidirectional links that are starting at this feature (cf. method `getIncomingLinks()`).

Methods

`getOutgoing-Links()`	Convenience method. Returns all outgoing `FeatureLinks` for the receiving feature. An outgoing link in that sense is a link that either starts at this feature (i.e. it is one of the links in `startingLinks`) or is a bidirectional link that ends at this feature. This is necessary because bidirectional links only appear either as a starting link or as an ending link but they are at the same time incoming and outgoing. Together with method `getIncomingLinks()` this method allows client code to straightforwardly retrieve a feature's feature links. Usually, client code should always use these methods instead of the associations `startingLinks()` and `getEndingLinks()`.
`getIncoming-Links()`	Same as method `getOutgoingLinks()` but returns the incoming links.

A.2.3 Class FeatureGroup

A FeatureGroup aggregates two or more features and defines a constraint on how many of them can be selected during configuration. This constraint is expressed by the group's cardinality.

Attributes

`description`	Textual description of this feature group.

Associations

`childFeatures`	The child features of this FeatureGroup. A feature group may only contain features as children, not other feature groups.
`cardinality`	The cardinality of the feature group. This states how many child features of this group may be selected during configuration. Each single instance of cloned feature is counted equally as the selection of a non-cloned optional feature. A feature group with a cardinality of [1] is called a mandatory alternative (or simply alternative) group. One with a cardinality of [0..1] is called an optional alternative group.

A.2. Feature Models

A.2.4 Class FeatureLink

Feature links can be used to define certain semantic relations between features in a feature model. Such a relation may but need not result in a constraint on configuration of this feature model. Feature links are always 1:1 relations and can be directed or bidirectional. They are said to "start" at one feature and "end" at the same feature or, in most cases, at another one.

For technical reasons, also bidirectional feature links distinguish between the feature they are starting at and the one they are ending at. Therefore a second terminology is used: incoming and outgoing links. A feature link is always outgoing from the start feature and incoming at the end feature. In addition, a bidirectional link is said to be outgoing from the end feature and incoming at the start feature. The methods `getOutgoingLinks()` and `getIncomingLinks()` in class `Feature` are used to interpret feature links this way.

Attributes

`type`	The type of this feature link identified by a `String` value. The type determines the precise semantics of the relation. There are four pre-defined types (given a link that starts at feature A and ends at feature B): **exclude**: A and B can never be both selected in a single configuration (always bidirectional). **include**: if A is selected, then also B must be selected (unidirectional or bidirectional). **impede**: A and B can usually(!) not be selected in a single configuration, or: you can select A and B but you should have a good reason to do so (always bidirectional). **suggest**: if A is selected, then usually(!) also B must be selected, or: you can select A without B but you should have a good reason to do so (unidirectional or bidirectional). In addition, each project can decide to use additional link types by defining unique key-words for them. In cases where feature models are shared with third parties (other departments, companies, ...) a URL name scheme must be used to find globally unique names, e.g. as for packages in the Java programming language.
`bidirectional`	When set to true this feature link is bidirectional. This means that in addition to the semantic relation from the start to the end feature this feature link also represents a semantic relation from the end feature to the start feature.
`description`	Textual description for this feature link

Associations

`start`	The feature at which this feature link starts.
`end`	The feature at which this feature link ends.

A.2.5 Class FeatureModel

A feature model is a container for features and their related elements. It thus defines a configuration space and is usually edited with a certain variable entity in mind. However, this variable entity is not specified within the feature model. This association is defined in the opposite direction instead: from the model element called `VariableEntity` to a feature model that defines the entity's variability.

Attributes

name	*inherited from* `NamedElement`
description	*inherited from* `NamedElement`
complianceLevel	If set to some other value than NONE, this feature model has to comply to certain limitations that ensure compatibility with a certain feature modeling technique from literature or with the variability specification concepts of a certain tool.
lowestUnusedId	The lowest positive number that was not yet used as an `id` of a feature contained in this feature model. When a new feature is created, this value can be used as the feature's `id` as long as it is post-incremented. This is the default behavior of the add and create commands generated by the EMF EditingDomain provided with the implementation of this information model. The default value is 1.

Associations

rootFeatures	The root features of this feature model. Feature groups can only appear as children of features, therefore this association is of type `Feature` instead of `FeatureTreeNode`.
links	The feature links defined for features in this model. Note that unlike `rootFeatures` this association comprises all feature links in the model without considering the feature tree's containment hierarchy.

A.2.6 Class FeatureModelElement

The abstract superclass of all non-trivial classes which are related to feature modeling, including `FeatureModel` itself. These are the entities of primary concern during feature modeling and are usually those that will be visible in an editor. For example a `FeatureGroup` is a feature model element but `Cardinality` is not, because a cardinality is only a subordinate entity within a feature or feature group.

A.2.7 Class FeatureTreeNode

FeatureTreeNode is the abstract superclass of `FeatureGroup` and `Feature`. A feature tree node has no specific semantics. The subclasses will introduce semantics appropriate to the concept they represent.

A.2.8 Class Interval

An interval of non-negative integers.

A.2. Feature Models

Attributes

start	Non-negative integer representing the lower end of the interval. May be equal to `end`.
end	Non-negative integer representing the upper end of the interval or -1 to indicate an unbounded interval. May be equal to `start`.

A.2.9 Class StringConstrainingType

See Section A.7.1.

A.2.10 Class VariabilityModelElement

See Section A.1.2.

A.2.11 Enumeration ComplianceLevel

A compliance level states that a feature model has to comply to certain limitations that ensure compatibility with a certain feature modeling technique from literature or with the variability specification concepts of a certain tool. This is useful when interoperability with other methods and tools has to be ensured. At the moment, this concept is implemented only exemplarily for some selected techniques.

Values

NONE	No limitations apply. All supported concepts can be used without restrictions.
FODA	The feature model must be a valid FODA [KCH+90] feature model. In particular, feature cardinalities are restricted to [0..1] and [1], group cardinalities are restricted to [1] and feature parameterization and inheritance is forbidden.
FORM	The feature model must be a valid FORM [KKL+98] feature model.
...	Support for many more techniques and tools is conceivable. Details are beyond the scope of this thesis.

A.2.12 Enumeration PrimitiveType

See Section A.7.8.

A.3 Configuration Decision Models

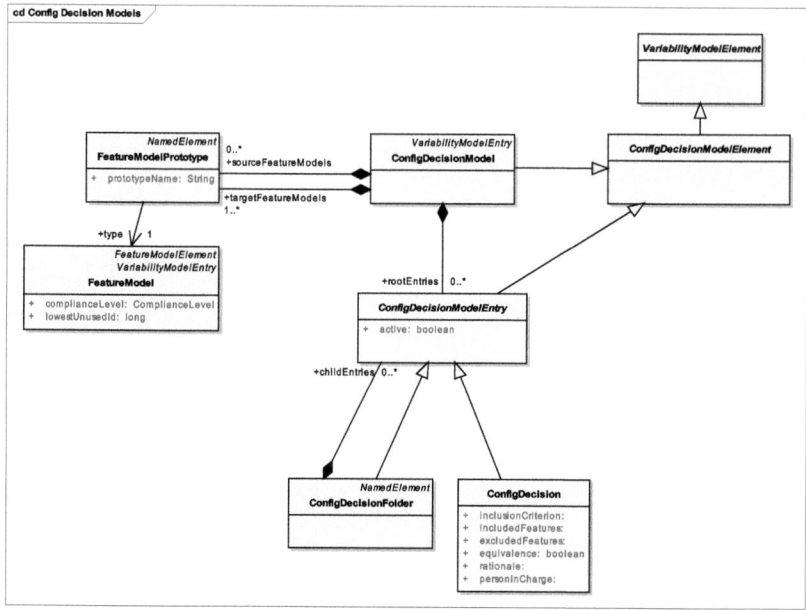

A.3.1 Class ConfigDecision

A configuration decision captures a single conceptual reflection on how to configure one or more target feature models depending on a certain configuration of one or more source feature models. Similar as for requirements in requirements engineering, atomicity is an important goal in defining configuration decisions. The conceptual reflection captured in a configuration decision is called configuration consideration.

Attributes

active	*inherited from* ConfigDecisionModelEntry
inclusion-Criterion	A logical expression that defines the configurations of the source feature model(s) for which this configuration decision is valid. The syntax of inclusion criteria is defined as part of the VSL language (Section 17.4.4).
included-Features	A comma-separated list of configuration steps which are to be applied to the target feature models whenever this configuration decision is valid. The default cardinality is [1], which means that for non-cloned features with only non-cloned predecessors the plain feature name is enough to achieve an *inclusion*. The syntax of configuration steps is defined as part of VSL.

A.3. Configuration Decision Models

excluded-Features	A comma-separated list of configuration steps which are to be applied to the target feature models whenever this configuration decision is valid. The default cardinality is [0], which means that for non-cloned features with only non-cloned predecessors the plain feature name is enough to achieve an *exclusion*. The syntax of configuration steps is defined as part of VSL.
equivalence	If set to true, then this configuration decision represents an equivalence (cf. Section 15.1).
rationale	An informal, textual description of the rationale behind the configuration consideration captured in this decision. This should provide enough information to decided in the future whether the configuration decision is still applicable or has to be removed.
personInCharge	The person or organizational unit which is responsible for the conceptual decision captured in this configuration decision and for maintenance. In cases where configuration decision models are shared with third parties (other departments, companies, ...) a URL name scheme must be used to find globally unique names, e.g. as for packages in the Java programming language.

A.3.2 Class ConfigDecisionFolder

An aggregate of configuration decisions. Except for the activation state, the hierarchy of configuration decision folders has absolutely no impact on the semantic of the contained configuration decisions. In other words, when configuration decision models are applied to target configurations, then the folders are ignored completely, except for activation.

Attributes

name	*inherited from* NamedElement
description	*inherited from* NamedElement
active	*inherited from* ConfigDecisionModelEntry If set to false, all contained sub-folders and configuration decisions are treated as inactive. Otherwise their activation state applies.

Associations

childEntries	The child entries of this folder. This can be other configuration decision folders ("sub-folders") or configuration decisions.

A.3.3 Class ConfigDecisionModel

A configuration decision model is a top-level container for configuration decisions. It defines the configuration of one or more target feature models in terms of a given configuration of zero(!) or more source feature models and thus defines a conceptual link from the source to the target models ("configuration link"). With this information, it is possible to derive configurations of the target feature models from given configurations of the source feature models.

Attributes

name	*inherited from* `NamedElement`
description	*inherited from* `NamedElement`

Associations

sourceFeature-Models	Zero or more feature models on which the configuration of the target feature model(s) may depend. The same feature model may be used several times, see section for `FeatureModelPrototype` below. In contrast to target feature models, no source feature models need to be defined for a configuration decision model. If none are supplied the model defines an invariable or "constant" configuration of the target feature model(s). The inclusion criteria of all configuration decisions must then be set to "true".
targetFeature-Models	One or more feature models for which this configuration decision model defines the configuration. The same feature model may be used several times, see section for `FeatureModelPrototype` below.
rootEntries	The root entries of this model.

A.3.4 Class ConfigDecisionModelElement

The abstract superclass of all non-trivial classes which are related to configuration decision modeling, including `ConfigurationDecisionModel` itself. These are the entities of primary concern during configuration modeling and are usually those that will be visible in an editor. For example a `ConfigDecision` is a configuration decision model element but `FeatureModelPrototype` is not, because it is only a subordinate entity within a configuration decision model.

A.3.5 Class ConfigDecisionModelEntry

This is the abstract superclass of `ConfigurationDecision` and `ConfigurationDecisionFolder`. It has no specific semantics. The subclasses will introduce semantics appropriate to the concept they represent.

Attributes

active	The activation state of the entry. When false, then the entry and all its contained entries, if any, will be ignored during application of the containing configuration decision model.

A.3.6 Class FeatureModel

See Section A.2.5.

A.3.7 Class FeatureModelPrototype

In order to define its source and target feature models, a configuration decision model does not refer to the class `FeatureModel` directly. Instead, a feature model prototype is used to define a feature model to be a source or target model. This is necessary because it may

A.3. Configuration Decision Models

be desirable to use a single feature model several times as a source model (or as a target model). For example, when having two wiper motors (front and rear) and a single feature model WiperMotorFM that defines the variability in both cases, then it may be necessary to provide a configuration decision model which maps the feature model of the complete wiper system to the feature models of the front and rear wipers, thus having WiperMotorFM twice as target feature model. In these cases the name of the prototype is used to distinguish between the two.

Attributes

name	*overrides* name *from* NamedElement
	The standard semantic of this attribute is slightly modified here: When prototypeName is set, then name is equal to that value, otherwise name is equal to the name of the feature model that is defined as this prototype's type.
description	*inherited from* NamedElement
prototypeName	An optional name for this feature model prototype that overrides the name of the feature model that is defined as this prototype's type.

Associations

type	The feature model that this prototype is a place-holder for.

A.3.8 Class VariabilityModelElement

See Section A.1.2.

A.4 Variable Entities

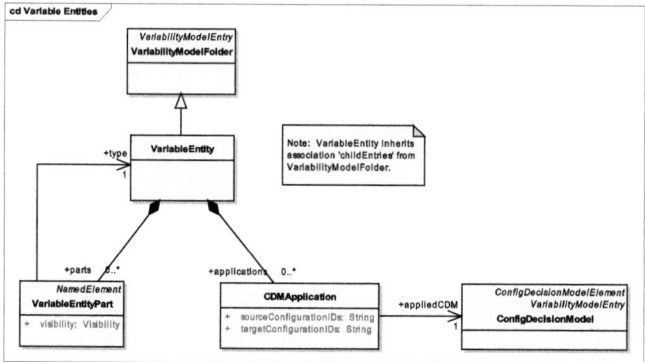

A.4.1 Class VariabilityModelFolder

See Section A.1.4.

A.4.2 Class VariableEntity

The model element "variable entity", or "entity" for short, represents some variable entity within the scope of the product line. This can be the final complete system to be developed, a sub-system or component of the complete system, a development artifact or a collection of sub-systems, components or development artifacts, such as all components developed by a certain supplier or all artifacts maintained by a certain department within the company.

Variable entities can be hierarchically structured by composition. Contained entities can be disclosed to higher-level or neighboring entities or they can be hidden. The same applies to other contents of variable entities such as contained feature configurations.

Variable entities define and publish their internal variability through one or more public feature configurations. Private feature configuration can be used to internally transform the public variability as needed, for example as input to locally used legacy components. `CDMApplications` are used to derive from the public feature configurations the private feature configurations as well as public feature configurations of contained entities.

From the perspective of the concept of configuration links, the main purpose of variable entities is to define and manage complex structures of feature configurations and configuration links between them and to effortlessly derive a complete tree of direct or indirect target configurations out of a few root source configurations.

In many respects, variable entities can be compared to classes in an object-oriented language such as Java.

Attributes

name	*inherited from* `NamedElement`
description	*inherited from* `NamedElement`

A.4. Variable Entities

Associations

`childEntries`	*inherited from* `VariabilityModelFolder` The child variability model entries of this variable entity. A variable entity is a container for such entries just as a variability model folder. For feature models, configuration decision models and similar model elements this containment has no sophisticated semantic and is simply used for packaging the definitions of these elements. This can be compared to static member classes in the Java programming language. For contained feature configurations however, there is the special semantic that the configuration defines the entity's internal variability. Such a contained feature configuration can therefore be compared to a member field in the Java language.
`parts`	The parts that make up this variable entity. These parts are again variable entities. They correspond to member fields of a class in Java. There is an important difference between putting an entity B inside an entity A as a child entry (see `childEntries`) and defining it as a part: in the first case the definition of B is put into A only for packaging but B will not be instantiated within A; therefore, in the first case, a configuration of A will not contain a configuration of B but in the second case it will. This is analogous to member classes in Java: putting a class definition B into class A does not mean that an instance of A will contain an instance of B; to achieve this a member field of type B has to be added to A, which corresponds to adding an entity part of type B to entity A.
`applications`	Defines a configuration dependency between zero or more source feature configurations and one or more target feature configurations. This means that whenever one of the source configurations changes, the target configurations need to be updated accordingly, as defined by the configuration decisions in the configuration decision model defined in the `CDMApplication`. This association is ordered.

A.4.3 Class VariableEntityPart

The purpose of this class is similar to that of `FeatureModelPrototype` as described above: it is often desirable to compose a higher-level variable entity A of two or more parts typed by the same contained variable entity B in order to make available several distinct configurations of B in A. The example with the front and rear wiper can correspondingly be applied to this situation.

The difference between adding one variable entity to another as a child entry or as a part was described in detail in the class description of `VariableEntity` above.

Attributes

`name`	*inherited from* `NamedElement`
`description`	*inherited from* `NamedElement`
`visibility`	The visibility of this part.

Associations

type	The variable entity that this part is a place-holder for. When an entity configuration of the container entity is created, a contained configuration of the entity specified here will be created.

A.4.4 Class CDMApplication

Defines a concrete configuration dependency between zero or more source feature configurations and one or more target feature configurations by way of a configuration decision model. A CDMApplication therefore states that a certain configuration decision model has to be applied to certain feature configurations in a variable entity. By applying configuration decision models that do not have source feature models, it is possible to initialize a variable entity's feature configurations.

The order in which the configuration decision models are applied is defined by the order of the association applications in VariableEntity.

Attributes

sourceConfigurationIDs	A comma-separated list of identifiers of feature configurations to which the configuration decision model is to be applied, relative to this CDMApplications containing entity. All feature configurations of the containing entity or any of its direct or indirect sub-entities (as defined by entity parts) can be referenced here, except they are not visible from the containing entity due to an intermediate entity of visibility PRIVATE along the path. The syntax of these identifiers is defined as part of the VSL language (Section 17.4.4).
targetConfigurationIDs	Same as above for target feature configurations.

Associations

appliedCDM	The configuration decision model to apply.

A.4.5 Class ConfigDecisionModel

See Section A.3.3.

A.5 Configurations

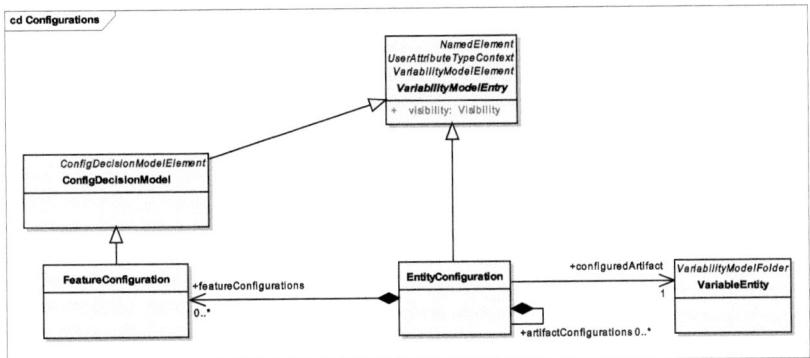

A.5.1 Class VariableEntity

See Section A.4.2.

A.5.2 Class EntityConfiguration

The configuration of a variable entity consists of a feature(!) configuration for each of the entity's contained feature configurations and an entity(!) configuration for each of the entity's parts. This way, a complex tree of interrelated feature configurations can be represented.

All feature configurations are contained, no matter if they were defined to be public or private. Entity configurations can be compared to objects, i.e. instances of classes, in object-oriented programming languages such as Java (with the configured entity being the instantiated class).

Attributes

name	*inherited from* `NamedElement`
description	*inherited from* `NamedElement`

Associations

`configuredArtifact`	The variable entity for which this provides a configuration.
`featureConfigurations`	The feature configurations.
`entityConfigurations`	The configurations of contained entites.

A.5.3 Class ConfigDecisionModel

See Section A.3.3.

A.5.4 Class FeatureConfiguration

The configuration of a feature model captures all configuration activities defined during configuration, such as narrowing a feature's cardinality, instantiating cloned features or setting the value of a parameterized feature. Partial configuration is supported.

As can be seen in the class diagram above, feature configurations are implemented as a special case of configuration decision models: a feature configuration is simply a configuration decision model without source feature models and with configuration decision which all have "true" as their inclusion criterion.

This allows for a very concise implementation of the algorithms for manipulating and applying configuration decision models and feature configurations. On the other hand, it is important to separate the two entities from a user perspective for usability reasons.

Attributes

name	*inherited from* `NamedElement`
description	*inherited from* `NamedElement`

Associations

sourceFeatureModels	*inherited from* `ConfigDecisionModel`
targetFeatureModels	*inherited from* `ConfigDecisionModel`
rootEntries	*inherited from* `ConfigDecisionModel`

Methods

isSelected	Returns true if and only if the specified feature is selected by this configuration when the configuration is interpreted as a full configuration. For a detailed discussion of selection and deselection and an explanation why this is necessary, see Section 13.4.
isDeselected	Returns true if and only if the specified feature is deselected by this configuration.

A.5.5 Class VariabilityModelEntry

See Section A.1.3.

A.6 Support for Multi-Level Feature Models

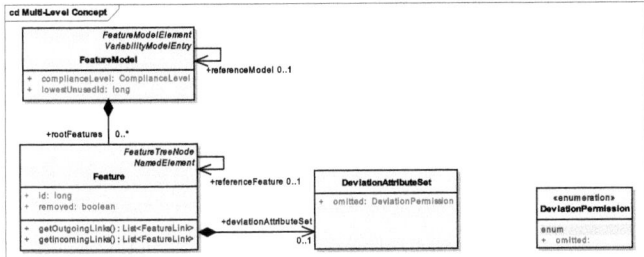

On the data model level, the multi-level level technique for feature models has two main constituents: feature models and features are augmented with reference links and deviation attributes are attached to features. The former is realized by additional attributes of features models and features and the latter is realized by a new class called DeviationAttributeSet which comprises all available deviation permissions.

A.6.1 Class DeviationAttributeSet

All available deviation permissions are realized as attributes in this class. An instance of this class may be attached to each feature in a reference feature model by way of the deviationAttributeSet association in class Feature. The detailed semantic of each deviation permission is not described here; it is the same as defined in Chapter 7 and summarized in the table in Appendix B.

Attributes

allowChangeName	
allowChangeDesc	
allowChangeParam	
allowChangeCard	
allowRemoval	
allowMove	
allowRefinement	
allowReduction	
allowReordering	
allowRegrouping	

A.6.2 Class Feature (Contd.)

See Section A.2.2.

Attributes

	...
removed	If this is set to true, the feature is to be treated as deleted. This attribute is necessary to be able to explicitly mark deleted a reference feature on the subline level.

Associations

	...	
reference-Feature	The template feature for this feature. Must be contained in the reference feature model.
deviation-AttributeSet	The deviation permissions. Only applicable to features in a reference model. If this is undefined for a reference feature, the default value applies for all deviation permissions.

A.6.3 Class FeatureModel (Contd.)

See Section A.2.5.

Associations

	...	
referenceModel	The template feature model for this feature model. By setting this association, the multi-level management of this feature model is initiated.

A.6.4 Enumeration DeviationPermission

The legal values for deviation permissions.

Values

YES	This is the default value which is in effect when a new instance of DeviationAttributeSet is created or if the association deviation-AttributeSet is undefined for a reference feature.
APPEND	
SUBSET	
SUBTREE	
NO	

A.7 User Attributes

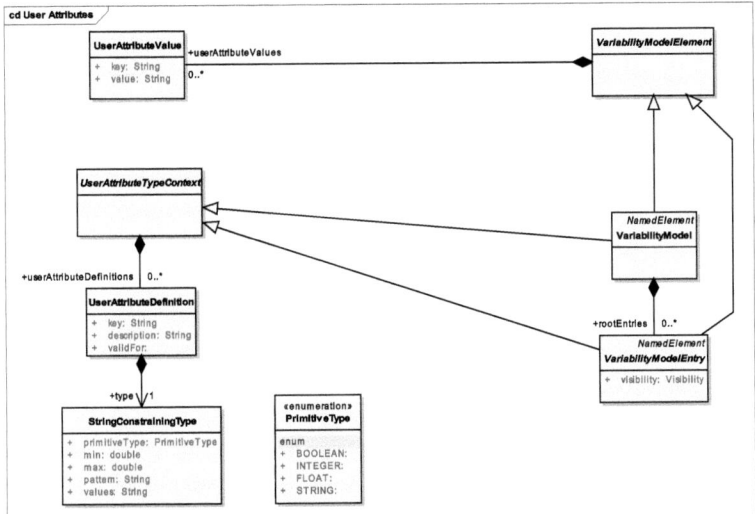

This section covers user attributes which are intended to provide a mechanism for augmenting a variability model and most of its elements with customized meta-information.

The mechanism was optimized for flexibility and simplicity. Therefore, the actual implementation type of the attribute values always remains String. The type defined by the class StringConstrainingType only restricts the allowed values of this string, as the name of the class suggests. This type concept is also used for feature parameters.

A.7.1 Class StringConstrainingType

This class introduces a very simple type system based on plain string values. The type defined by this class serves to restrict the legal values of a certain string property. It is used to restrict the values of parameterized features (see Section A.2.2) and user defined attributes (see Section A.7.2).

Attributes

primitiveType	The primitive type. BOOLEAN: The string value constrained by this class must be either "true" or "false" (case ignored). INTEGER: The string value must be a valid string representation of a signed integer. For unsigned integers set attribute min to 0. FLOAT: The string value must be a valid string representation of a signed float. For unsigned floats set attribute min to 0. STRING: The string value is not at all restricted except as defined by attributes pattern and values.

min	If this attribute is set *and* the primitive type is INTEGER or FLOAT, then the constrained string value must be a valid string representation of a number greater than or equal to the specified value.
max	If this attribute is set *and* the primitive type is INTEGER or FLOAT, then the constrained string value must be a valid string representation of a number less than or equal to the specified value.
pattern	If this attribute is set *and* the primitive type is STRING, then the value must be a string that matches the specified regular expression, e.g. "*.gif".
values	A comma-separated list of allowed string values. If this attribute is set, then the string value constrained by this class must be equal to one of the specified, comma-separated values. White-space is ignored in the comma-separated list of allowed values but not in the string constrained by this class. For example, if this attribute is set to "NEW, IN_REVIEW, ACCEPTED, REJECTED", the values "NEW" or "IN_REVEIW" would be valid, but " IN_REVIEW" would be invalid.

A.7.2   Class UserAttributeDefinition

This class defines a user attribute, i.e. it states that all variability model elements of a certain type are to be attached with an attribute identified by key. For example, it can be specified that all features and configuration decisions should be amended with an attribute "Status".

Attributes

key	A unique identifier for the user attribute. Whenever interoperability with third parties is required a URL naming scheme should be used.
description	Textual description of the attribute.
validFor	Specifies the element types for which this user attribute is defined. All non-abstract classes that inherit from VariabilityModelElement can be specified, e.g. Feature or FeatureGroup.

Associations

type	The string constraining type that specifies the legal values for this attribute.

A.7.3   Class UserAttributeDefinitionContext

An abstract class from which all classes inherit, that are able to introduce new user attributes, i.e. that can contain UserAttributeDefinitions.

Associations

userAttribute-Types	The UserAttributeDefinitions newly defined for this element and all its contained elements. For example, if an attribute definition which is valid for features is attached to a VariabilityModelFolder, then all features of all feature models in this folder will get the newly defined attribute.

A.7. User Attributes

A.7.4 Class UserAttributeValue

This class represents a specific value for a certain user attribute. User attributes are simple key/value pairs which can be attached to all variability model elements. User attribute definitions can be used to state what attributes should be attached to elements of certain types and what the allowed values are.

Attributes

key	The unique identifier of the attribute for which this `UserAttribute-Value` provides a value for.
value	The value. This is always of type string, but the allowed string values can be restricted by attribute definitions.

A.7.5 Class VariabilityModel

See Section A.1.1.

A.7.6 Class VariabilityModelElement (Contd.)

Support for user attributes added here. Main class description is given in Section A.1.2.

Associations

	...
userAttributeValues	The attribute values which are attached to this variability model element. **Important:** It is technically possible and legal to attach any key/value pair, even if this is in conflict with the attribute definitions of a containing attribute definition context. All implementations of this information model must expect such attribute definition violations. The reason for this is that the attribute definitions and the types they define for the attributes are only meant as a guideline for working with user attributes on the modeling level, not as an implementation level type system.

A.7.7 Class VariabilityModelEntry

See Section A.1.3.

A.7.8 Enumeration PrimitiveType

A primitive type.

Values

BOOLEAN	
INTEGER	
FLOAT	
STRING	

Appendix B
Constraints in Multi-Level Feature Models

The table on the next page summarizes the deviations found in multi-level feature models together with the corresponding deviation permission attributes. Many deviations also apply to other types of artifacts, as was discussed in detail for requirements specifications in form of DOORS modules in Chapter 8. In addition, this summary may serve as a user reference for the two implementations of the multi-level concept introduced in Chapter 18 (with minor, implementation-related discrepancies in both cases).

Table B.1: Summary of possible forms of deviation and the attributes allowing or disallowing them.

Form of Deviation	Permission Attribute	Values	Constraint
different name	allowChangeName	NO	$f.name = f_{ref}.name$
		APPEND	$\exists s \in \mathbf{String} : f.name = f_{ref}.name + s$
		YES	true
difference in other basic attribute, such as a feature's description	allowChange...	as above	...
difference in feature attributation	allowChangeAttrib	NO	$Type(f) = Type(f_{ref})$
		YES	true
different cardinality	allowChangeCard (in Feature and Group)	NO	$Card(f) = Card(f_{ref})$
		SUBSET	$Card(f) \subseteq Card(f_{ref})$
		YES	true
no referring feature for a reference feature (**Removal**)	allowRemoval (in Feature)	NO	$\exists f' \in F : RefF(f') = f_{ref} \wedge \neg f'.removed$
		YES	true
no reference feature for a referring feature (**Addition**)	-	always allowed	true
different parent, including $parent = null$ (**Move**)	allowMove	NO	$RefF(parentOf(f)) = parentOf(f_{ref})$
		SUBTREE	$RefF(parentOf(f)) = parentOf(f_{ref}) \vee (parentOf(f_{ref}), RefF(parentOf(f))) \in Predecessor$
		YES	true
referring feature f has a child without a corresponding reference feature among children of f_{ref} (**Refinement**)	allowRefinement	NO	$\forall f' \in childrenOf(f) : RefF(f') \in childrenOf(f_{ref})$
		YES	true
reference feature f_{ref} has a child without a corresponding referring feature among the children of f (**Reduction**)	allowReduction	NO	$\forall f'_{ref} \in childrenOf(f_{ref}) : \exists f' \in childrenOf(f) : RefF(f') = f'_{ref}$
		SUBTREE	$\forall f'_{ref} \in childrenOf(f_{ref}) : \exists f' \in childrenOf(f) : f'_{ref} = RefF(f') \vee (f'_{ref}, RefF(f')) \in Predecessor$
		YES	true
order of children of f is different (**Reordering**)	allowReordering	NO	$\forall f', f'' \in childrenOf(f), f_R', f_R'' \in childrenOf(f_{ref}) : (f_R' = RefF(f') \wedge f_R'' = RefF(f'')) \rightarrow (f' < f'' \Leftrightarrow f_R' < f_R'')$
		YES	true
difference in the grouping of the children of f_{ref} and f (**Regrouping**)	allowRegrouping (in Group)	NO	$\exists g \in childGroupsOf(f) : g \leadsto g_{ref} \wedge$
		WIDEN	$(\forall f' \in g' \exists f_R' \in g_{ref} : RefF(f') = f_R')$
		YES	$\exists g' \in childGroupsOf(f) : g \leadsto g_{ref}$
			true
no corresponding link l in referring model for link l_R in reference model (**Link Removal**)	allowRemoval (in Link)	NO	$\exists l \in F.links : l.src = l_R.src \wedge l.dest = l_R.dest \wedge l.type = l_R.type$
		YES	true

Bibliography

[ABB+02] Colin Atkinson, Joachim Bayer, Christian Bunse, Erik Kamsties, Oliver Laitenberger, Roland Laqua, Dirk Muthig, Barbara Paech, Jürgen Wüst, and Jörg Zettel. *Component-based Product Line Engineering with UML*. Component Software Series. Addison-Wesley, 2002.

[AC04] Michal Antkiewicz and Krzysztof Czarnecki. FeaturePlugin: Feature modeling plug-in for Eclipse. In *Proceedings of the 2004 OOPSLA Workshop on Eclipse Technology eXchange (ETX 2004)*, pages 67–72. ACM Press, 2004.

[ADA04] Allgemeiner Deutscher Automobilclub e.V. (ADAC). *Pannenstatistik 2003*, 2004.

[AMS06] Timo Asikainen, Tomi Männistö, and Timo Soininen. A unified conceptual foundadtion for feature modelling. In *10th International Software Product Line Conference (SPLC 2006)*, pages 31–40, 2006.

[AP03] Andrew W. Appel and Jens Palsberg. *Modern Compiler Implementation in Java*. Cambridge University Press, 2 edition, 2003.

[AS02] Adam and Schäfer. Handbuch der Produktdokumentation. Internal technical report, DaimlerChrysler AG, Sindelfingen, September 2002. In German.

[ATE08] ATESST Project Web-Site, 2008. www.atesst.org.

[Aue04] Georg Auer. Mercedes ditches glitches with electronics—defects, complexity doom 600 features. *Automotive News*, May 2004.

[AUT08] AUTOSAR Consortium Web-Site, 2008. www.autosar.org.

[Bat05a] Don Batory. Feature models, grammars, and propositional formulas. Technical Report TR-05-14, University of Texas at Austin, March 2005.

[Bat05b] Don S. Batory. Feature models, grammars, and propositional formulas. In *9th International Software Product Line Conference (SPLC 2005)*, 2005.

[BBP+05] Margot Bittner, Ali Botorabi, Alexander Poth, Mark-Oliver Reiser, and Matthias Weber. Managing variability and reuse of features and requirements for large and complex organizational structures. In *Proceedings of the 13th IEEE International Requirements Engineering Conference (RE 2005)*, pages 469–470, 2005.

[Bed02] Thomas Bednasch. Konzept zur Implementierung eines konfigurierbaren Metamodells für die Merkmalsmodellierung. Diplomarbeit, Fachbereich Informatik und Mikrosystemtechnik, Fachhochschule Kaiserslautern, 2002. In German.

[BFG+01] Jan Bosch, G. Florijn, D. Greefhorst, J. Kuusela, H. Obbink, and K. Pohl. Variability issues in software product lines. In *Proceedings of the 4th International Workshop on Product Family Engineering (PFE-4)*, volume 2290 of *Lecture Notes in Computer Science (LNCS)*, pages 13–21. Springer, October 2001.

[BGdPL+03] Felix Bachmann, Michael Goedicke, Julio Cesar Sampaio do Prado Leite, Robert L. Nord, Klaus Pohl, Balasubramaniam Ramesh, and Alexander Vilbig. A meta-model for representing variability in product family development. In *Proceedings of the 5th International Workshop on Software Product-Family Engineering (PFE 2003)*, volume LNCS 3014, pages 66–80. Springer, 2003.

[BKPS04] Günter Böckle, Peter Knauber, Klaus Pohl, and Klaus Schmid. *Software Produktlinien*. dpunkt Verlag, 2004.

[BLP05] Stan Bühne, Kim Lauenroth, and Klaus Pohl. Modelling requirements variability across product lines. In *Proceedings of the 13th IEEE International Requirements Engineering Conference (RE 2005)*, pages 41–50, 2005.

[BLPW04] Stan Bühne, Kim Lauenroth, Klaus Pohl, and Matthias Weber. Modeling features for multi-criteria product-lines in automotive industry. In *Proceedings of the Workshop on Software Engineering for Automotive Systems (SEAS)*. ICSE 2004, 2004.

[Bos00] Jan Bosch. *Design and Use of Software Architectures – Adopting and Evolving a Product-line Approach*. Addison-Wesley, 2000.

[Bos05] J. Bosch. Software product families in Nokia. In *9th International Software Product Lines Conference (SPLC 2005)*, volume 3714 of *LNCS*, pages 2–6, 2005. Keynote.

[Bro86] Frederick P. Brooks. No silver bullet. In *Information Processing 1986, the Proceedings of the IFIP Tenth World Computing Conference*, pages 1069–76, 1986.

[BSME03] Frank Budinsky, David Steinberg, Ed Merks, and Raymond Ellersick. *Eclipse Modeling Framework*. Addison Wesley, 2003.

[BvdBK98] M. Broy, M. van der Beeck, and I. Krüger. Softbed: Problemanalyse für ein großverbundprojekt "systemtechnik automobil – software für eingebettete systeme". Technical report, Technische Universität München, Mar 1998.

[BW07] Martin Becker and Matthias Weber. Das Multi-Level Konzept zur strategischen Wiederverwendung von Entwicklungsartefakten. Internal presentation slides, Carmeq GmbH, September 2007.

Bibliography

[CAD03] Ivica Crnkovic, Ulf Asklund, and Annita Persson Dahlqvist. *Product Data Management and Software Configuration Management.* Artech House Publishers, 2003.

[CE00] Krzysztof Czarnecki and Ulrich Eisenecker. *Generative Programming.* Addison-Wesley, 2000.

[Cha96] David Chappell. *Understanding ActiveX and OLE.* Strategic Technology Series. Microsoft Press, August 1996.

[CHE05a] Krzysztof Czarnecki, Simon Helsen, and Ulrich Eisenecker. Formalizing cardinality-based feature models and their specialization. *Software Process: Improvement and Practices*, 10(1):7–29, 2005.

[CHE05b] Krzysztof Czarnecki, Simon Helsen, and Ulrich Eisenecker. Staged configuration through specialization and multi-level configuration of feature models. *Software Process: Improvement and Practices*, 10(2):143–169, 2005.

[CK05] Krzysztof Czarnecki and Chang Hwan Peter Kim. Cardinality-based feature modeling and constraints: A progress report. In *Proceedings of the OOPSLA'05 Workshop on Software Factories*, oct 2005.

[CKK06] Krzysztof Czarnecki, Chang Hwan Peter Kim, and Karl Trygve Kalleberg. Feature models are views on ontologies. In *Proceedings of the 10th International Software Product Line Conference (SPLC 2006)*, pages 41–51, 2006.

[CN02] Paul Clements and Linda Northrop. *Software Product Lines: Practices and Patterns.* Addison-Wesley, 2002.

[CSFP04] Ben Collins-Sussman, Brian W. Fitzpatrick, and C. Michael Pilato. *Version Control with Subversion.* O'Reilly, 2004.

[CUE02] Thomas Czarnecki, Krzysztof Bednasch, Peter Unger, and Ulrich Eisenecker. Generative programming for embedded software: An industrial experience report. In *Proceedings of the ACM Conference on Generative Programming and Component Engineering (GPCE'02)*, volume 2487 of *Lecture Notes in Computer Science (LNCS)*, pages 156–172. Springer, 2002.

[Cza04] Krzysztof Czarnecki. Overview of generative software development. In J.-P. Bantre, editor, *Unconventional Programming Paradigms (UPP)*, number 3566 in LNCS, pages 313–328. Springer, 2004.

[DAG08] Daimler AG Web-Site, 2008. www.daimler.de.

[Dav89] Alan M. Davis. *Software Requirements — Analysis and Specification.* Prentice Hall, December 1989.

[DFHH06] Jörg Donandt, Johannes Fasolt, Matthias Hoffmann, and Frank Houdek. Ergebnisüberblick der Arbeitspakete "RE für Innenraum BR204" und "Integrierte Funktionsbibliothek für Systeme" — Funktionsbibliothek. Internal report, DaimlerChrysler AG, 2006. In German.

[EAS08]   EAST-EEA Project Web-Site, 2008. www.east-eea.org.

[Ecl08]   Eclipse Foundation Web-Site, 2008. www.eclipse.org.

[EKLM97]   J. Eisenmann, M. Köhn, Ph. Lanchs, and A. Müller. Entwurf und Implementierung von Fahrzeugsteuerungsfunktionen auf Basis der TITUS-Client/Server-Architektur. *VDI Berichte*, 1374:399–425, 1997.

[FAZ04]   Auf elektronische Spielereien verzichten — Innovationssymposion von DaimlerChrysler. Frankfurter Allgemeine Zeitung, 18. Mai, 2004.

[Fed97]   Federal Republic of Germany. V-Model 97, Lifecycle process model — Developing standard for IT systems of the Federal Republic of Germany. General Directive No. 250, June 1997. Available at www.v-modell.iabg.de.

[Fed04]   Federal Republic of Germany. V-Model XT, Developing standard, 2004. Available at www.v-modell-xt.de.

[FV07]   Marcos Didonet Del Fabro and Patrick Valduriez. Semi-automatic model integration using matching transformations and weaving models. In *Proceedings of the 22nd Annual ACM Symposium on Applied Computing (SAC-2007) — Model Transformation Track*, pages 963–970, Seoul, Korea, March 2007.

[GFd98]   Martin Griss, John Favaro, and Massimo d'Alessandro. Integrating feature modeling with the RSEB. In *Proceedings of the 5th International Conference on Software Reuse*, pages 76–85, 1998.

[GHJV95]   Erich Gamma, Richard Helm, Ralph Johnson, and John M. Vlissides. *Design Patterns — Elements of Reusable Object-Oriented Software*. Addison-Wesley, Reading, 1995.

[Gom04]   Hassan Gomaa. *Designing Software Product Lines with UML*. Addison-Wesley, 2004.

[Gri03]   Klaus Grimm. Software technology in an automotive company – major challenges. In *Proceedings of the 25th International Conference on Software Engineering (ICSE 2003)*, pages 498–503. Association for Computing and Machinery & IEEE Computer Society, 2003.

[Gri05]   Klaus Grimm. Anforderungen an das software-engineering aus sicht der automobilindustrie. In *Simulations- und Testmethoden für Software in Fahrzeugsystemen (Proceedings der Jahrestagung der ASIM/GI-Fachgruppe 4.5.5)*, Berlin, 2005.

[GS04]   Jack Greenfield and Keith Short. *Software Factories — Assembling Applications with Patterns, Models, Frameworks, and Tools*. Wiley Publishing, September 2004.

[GY05]   Jonathan L. Gross and Jay Yellen. *Graph Theory and Its Applications*. Chapman and Hall, 2005.

Bibliography

[Hal73] Patrick A. V. Hall. Equivalence between AND / OR graphs and context-free grammars. *Communications of the ACM*, 16(7):444–445, 1973.

[Hei04] Harald Heinecke. AUTomotive Open System ARchitecture — An industry-wide initiative to manage the complexity of emerging automotive E/E architectures. In *Convergence 2004, International Congress on Transportation Electronics*, Detroit, 2004.

[Her07] Herstellerinitiative Software (HIS). *Requirements Interchange Format (RIF) – Specification*, May 2007. Version 1.1a.

[HH05] Reinhard Höhn and Stephan Höppner. *Das V-Modell XT*. Springer, 2005.

[HIS08] Herstellerinitiative Softwaretechnik, 2008. www.automotive-his.de.

[HSVM00] Andreas Hein, Michael Schlick, and Renato Vinga-Martins. Applying feature models in industrial settings. In *Proceedings of the 1st International Conference on Software Product Lines (SPLC 2000)*, volume 576 of *International Series in Engineering and Computer Science*, pages 47–70. Springer, 2000.

[Jav08] JavaCC Project Web Site, 2008. javacc.dev.java.net.

[Kay79] Martin Kay. Functional grammar. In *Proceedings of the 5th Annual Meeting of the Berkeley Linguistics Society*, Berkeley, CA, 1979. Berkely Linguistics Society.

[KB82] Ron M. Kaplan and Joan Bresnan. *Lexical-Functional Grammar: A Formal System for Grammatical Representation*, pages 173–281. MIT Press, Cambridge, MA, 1982.

[KCH+90] Kyo C. Kang, Sholom G. Cohen, James A. Hess, William E. Novak, and A. Spencer Peterson. Feature-oriented domain analysis (foda) – feasibility study. Technical Report CMU/SEI-90-TR-21, Software Engineering Institute (SEI), Carnegie Mellon University, 1990.

[KK06] Martin Kreuzer and Stefan Kühling. *Logik für Informatiker*. Pearson Education, 2006.

[KKL+98] Kyo C. Kang, Sajoong Kim, Jaejoon Lee, Kijoo Kim, Euiseob Shin, and Moonhang Huh. Form: A feature-oriented reuse method with domain-specific reference architectures. *Annals of Software Engineering*, 5:143–168, 1998.

[KLD02] Kyo C. Kang, Jaejoon Lee, and Patrick Donohoe. Feature-oriented product line engineering. *IEEE Software*, 19:58–65, 2002.

[Kru06] Charles W. Krueger. New methods in software product line development. In *Proceedings of the 10th International Software Product Line Conference (SPLC 2006)*, pages 95–102, 2006.

[KS04] E. Knippel and A. Schulz. Lessons learned from implementing configuration management within electrical/electronic development of an automotive OEM. In *Proceedings of the 14th International Symposium of the International Council on Systems Engineering (INCOSE 04)*, Toulouse, June 2004.

[LR04]   Neil Loughran and Awais Rashid. Framed aspects: Supporting variability and configurability for aop. In *Proceedings of the 8th International Conference on Software Reuse (ICSR-8)*, Madrid, Spain, 2004.

[Mau02]   Guido Maune. *Möglichkeiten des Komplexitätsmanagements für Automobilhersteller auf Basis IT-gestützter durchgängiger Systeme*. Doctoral thesis, Fachbereich Wirtschaftswissenschaften, Universität Paderborn, February 2002. In German.

[MJA+04]   Dirk Muthig, Isabel John, Michalis Anastasopoulos, Thomas Forster, Jrg Drr, and Klaus Schmid. Gophone – a software product line in the mobile phone domain. IESE-Report 025.04/E, Fraunhofer IESE, Mar 2004.

[MO04]   Mira Mezini and Klaus Ostermann. Variability management with feature-oriented programming and aspects. In *Proceedings of the 12th ACM SIGSOFT International Symposium on Foundations of Software Engineering (FSE-12)*, pages 127–136, Newport Beach, CA, USA, 2004.

[MRW06]   Katharina Mehner, Mark-Oliver Reiser, and Matthias Weber. Applying aspect-orientation techniques in automotive software product-line engineering. In *International Workshop on Automotive Requirements Engineering 2006 (AuRE 06)*, Mineeapolis / St. Paul, USA, 2006.

[Nei08]   Lukas Neitsch. Multi-Level Modellsynchronisation für die Entwicklung komplexer Produktfamilien software-intensiver Systeme. Master thesis, Hasso Plattner Institut, Universität Potsdam, February 2008. In German.

[NSL08]   Nicolas Navet and Francoise Simonot-Lion, editors. *Automotive Embedded Systems Handbook*. CRC Press Inc., December 2008.

[Obj06]   Object Management Group (OMG). *Meta Object Facility (MOF) – Core Specification, Version 2.0*, 2006. OMG Document `formal/06-01-01`.

[Par76]   David Lorge Parnas. On the design and development of program families. *IEEE Transactions on Software Engineering*, SE-2(1):1–9, Mar 1976.

[PBvdL05]   Klaus Pohl, Günter Böckle, and Frank van der Linden. *Software Product Line Engineering: Foundations, Principles and Techniques*. Springer, Heidelberg, 2005.

[Poh07]   Klaus Pohl. *Requirements Engineering — Grundlagen, Prinzipien, Techniken*. Dpunkt Verlag, 2007.

[PS03]   Sriram Pemmaraju and Steven Skiena. *Computational Discrete Mathematics: Combinatorics and Graph Theory with Mathematica*. Cambridge University Press, 2003.

[PS08]   Pure-Systems GmbH Web-Site, 2008. `www.pure-systems.com`.

[RBSP02]   Matthias Riebisch, Kai Böllert, Detlef Streitferdt, and Ilka Philippow. Extending feature diagrams with UML multiplicities. In *Proceedings of the 6th Conference on Integrated Design & Process Technology (IDPT 2002)*, 2002.

Bibliography

[RH04] Gunter Reichart and Michael Haneberg. Key drivers for a future system architecture in vehicles. In *SAE Convergence 2004. Vehicle Electronics to Digital Mobility*, Detroit, MI, October 18–20 2004. SAE 2004-21-0025.

[RS77] D. T. Ross and K. E. Schoman. Structured analysis for requirements definition. *IEEE Transactions on Software Engineering*, 3(1):6–15, 1977.

[RT04] Ernst Richter and Roland Trauter. Modellierung von Embedded Software Produktlinien-Architekturen — Eine Strukturierte Arbeitsanleitung. Internal technical report, DaimlerChrysler AG, Sindelfingen, June 2004. In German.

[RTW07a] Mark-Oliver Reiser, Ramin Tavakoli, and Matthias Weber. Manifoldness of variability modeling — considering the potential for further integration. In *Proceedings of the 2nd IFIP TC 2 Central and East European Conference on Software Engineering Techniques (CEE-SET 2007)*, volume 5082 of *Lecture Notes in Computer Science (LNCS)*, pages 291–303. Springer, 2007.

[RTW07b] Mark-Oliver Reiser, Ramin Tavakoli, and Matthias Weber. Unified feature modeling as a basis for managing complex system families. In *Proceedings of the 1st International Workshop on Variability Modeling of Software-Intensive Systems (VAMOS), Lero Technical Report 2007-01*, pages 79–86. University of Limerick, Ireland, January 2007.

[RTW09] Mark-Oliver Reiser, Ramin Tavakoli, and Matthias Weber. Compositional variability. In *Processings of the 42nd Hawaii International Conference on System Sciences (HICSS-42)*. IEEE Computer Society Press, 2009. to appear.

[RW05] Mark-Oliver Reiser and Matthias Weber. Using product sets to define complex product decisions. In *Proceedings of the 9th International Software Product Line Conference (SPLC 2005)*, volume 3714 of *Lecture Notes in Computer Science (LNCS)*, pages 21–32, 2005.

[RW06] Mark-Oliver Reiser and Matthias Weber. Managing highly complex product families with multi-level feature trees. In *Proceedings of the 14th IEEE International Requirements Engineering Conference (RE 2006)*, pages 146–155. IEEE Computer Society, 2006.

[RW07] Mark-Oliver Reiser and Matthias Weber. Multi-level feature trees – a pragmatic approach to managing highly complex product families. *Requirements Engineering*, 12(2):57–75, Apr 2007.

[RW08] Mark-Oliver Reiser and Matthias Weber. Product lines in automotive electronics. In Nicolas Navet and Francoise Simonot-Lion, editors, *Automotive Embedded Systems Handbook*, chapter 7. CRC Press Inc., December 2008.

[Say84] Manfred Saynisch. *Konfigurationsmanagement – Entwurfssteuerung, Dokumentation, Änderungswesen*. Verlag TÜV Rheinland, 1984.

[Sch02] Klaus Schmid. A comprehensive product line scoping approach and its validation. In *Proceedings of the 24th International Conference on Software Engineering (ICSE 2002)*, pages 593–603. ACM Press, 2002.

[SDNB04] Marco Sinnema, Sybren Deelstra, Jos Nijhuis, and Jan Bosch. COVAMOF: A framework for modeling variability in software product families. In *Proceedings of the 3rd International Conference on Software Product Lines (SPLC 2004)*, volume 3154 of *Lecture Notes in Computer Science*, pages 197–213. Springer, 2004.

[Sha00] David C. Sharp. Component-based product line development of avionics software. In *Proceedings of the 1st Conference on Software Product Lines (SPLC 2000)*, volume 576 of *International Series in Engineering and Computer Science*, pages 353–370. Springer, 2000.

[SHS+05] Th. Scharnhorst, H. Heinecke, K.-P. Schnelle, H. Fennel, J. Bortolazzi, L. Lundh, P. Heitkmper, J. Leflour, J.-L. Mat, and K. Nishikawa. AUTOSAR — challenges and achievements 2005. *VDI Berichte*, 1907:395–408, 2005.

[SHTB06] Pierre-Yves Schobbens, Patrick Heymans, Jean-Christophe Trigaux, and Yves Bontemps. Feature diagrams: A survey and a formal semantics. In *Proceedings of the 14th IEEE International Requirements Engineering Conference (RE 2006)*, pages 136–145. IEEE Computer Society, 2006.

[SHTB07] Pierre-Yves Schobbens, Patrick Heymans, Jean-Christophe Trigaux, and Yves Bontemps. Generic semantics of feature diagrams. *Computer Networks*, 51(2):456–479, 2007.

[SL08] Simulink tool suite. The MathWorks, 2008. www.mathworks.com/products/simulink/.

[Smo88] Gert Smolka. A feature logic with subsorts. *LILOG-Report*, 33, 1988.

[Som04] Ian Sommerville. *Software Engineering*. International Computer Science Series. Addison-Wesley Longman, 7th edition, 2004.

[Ste07] Angelika Steger. *Diskrete Strukturen 1 – Kombinatorik, Graphentheorie, Algebra*. Springer, 2007.

[SZ06] Jörg Schäuffele and Thomas Zurawka. *Automotive Software Engineering: Grundlagen, Prozesse, Methoden und Werkzeuge effizient einsetzen*. Vieweg, 3rd edition, 2006.

[Szy02] Clemens Szyperski. *Component Software: Beyond Object-Oriented Programming*. Addison-Wesley Professional, Boston, 2nd edition, 2002.

[Tav06] Ramin Tavakoli. *Requirements Engineering für Software-Produktlinien eingebetteter, technischer Systeme*. Dissertation, Universität Ulm, Fakultät für Informatik — Abteilung Programmiermethodik und Compilerbau, June 2006.

[TGTG05] Patrick Tessier, Sébastien Gérard, François Terrier, and Jean-Marc Geib. Using variation propagation for model-driven management of a system family. In *Proceedings of the 9th International Software Product Line Conference (SPLC 2005)*, volume LNCS 3714, pages 222–233. Springer, 2005.

Bibliography

[TH03] Jeffrey M. Thompson and Mats Per Erik Heimdahl. Structuring product family requirements for n-dimensional and hierarchical product lines. *Requirements Engineering*, 8(1):42–54, 2003.

[TIT96] TITUS Projet-Team. *TITUS — Technisches Handbuch*. DaimlerChrysler AG, 1996. Internal user manual.

[TR07] Ramin Tavakoli and Mark-Oliver Reiser. Reusing requirements: The need for extended variability models. In *Proceedings of the IPM International Symposium on Fundamentals of Software Engineering (FSEN 07), Tehran, April 17-19, 2007*, 2007.

[VAM+98] Alessandro Dionisi Vici, Nicola Argentieri, Azza Mansour, Massimo d'Alessandro, and John Favaro. Fodacom: An experience with domain analysis in the italian telecom industry. In *Proceedings of the 5th International Conference on Software Reuse (ICSR 05)*, pages 166–175, 1998.

[Ves06] Jennifer Vesperman. *Essential CVS*. O'Reilly, 2006.

[vGBS01] Jilles van Gurp, Jan Bosch, and Mikael Svahnberg. On the notion of variability in software product lines. In *Proceedings of the Working IEEE/IFIP Conference on Software Architecture (WICSA 2001)*, 2001.

[vL01] Axel van Lamsweerde. Goal-oriented requirements engineering: A guided tour. In *Proceedings of the 5th IEEE International Symposium on Requirements Engineering (RE 01)*, pages 249–263, Toronto, August 2001.

[vO00] Rob van Ommering. Beyond product families: Building a product population? In *Proceedings of the 3rd International Workshop on Software Architectures for Product Families (SAPF-3)*, LNCS 1951, pages 187–198, 2000.

[vO04] Rob van Ommering. *Building Product Populations with Software Components*. PhD thesis, University of Groningen, 2004.

[vOvdLKM00] Rob van Ommering, Frank van der Linden, Jeff Kramer, and Jeff Magee. The koala component model for consumer electronics software. *IEEE Computer*, 3:78–85, 2000.

[WDT76] Thomas R. Wilcox, Alan M. Davis, and Michael H. Tindall. The design and implementation of a table driven, interactive diagnostic programming system. *Communications of the ACM*, 19(11):609–616, 1976.

[Web08] Papyrus UML Web Site, 2008. www.papyrus-uml.org.

[Wij00] J.G. Wijnstra. Component frameworks for a medical imaging product family. In *Proceedings of the 3rd International Workshop on Software Architectures for Product Families (IW-SAPF-3)*, volume 1951 of *Lecture Notes in Computer Science (LNCS)*, pages 4–18. Springer, 2000.

[Win07] Martin Winterkorn. Interview mit Martin Winterkorn, dem Vorstandsvorsitzenden der Volkswagen AG. Süddeutsche Zeitung vom 9. Februar, 2007. In German.

[WL99] David M. Weiss and Chi Tau Robert Lai. *Software Product-Line Engineering: A Family-Based Software Development Process.* Addison-Wesley, 1999.

[WRW+04] Matthias Weber, Mark-Oliver Reiser, Thomas Wierczoch, Ulrich Freund, Orazio Gurrieri, Jochen Küster, Henrik Lönn, and Jörn Migge. An architecture description language for developing automotive ECU-software. In *14th Annual International Symposium of the International Council on Systems Engineering (INCOSE 04), June 20-24, 2004, Toulouse, France*, 2004.

[WW02] Matthias Weber and Joachim Weisbrod. Requirements engineering in automotive development – experiences and challenges. In *Proceedings of the 10th IEEE International Requirements Engineering Conference (RE 2002)*, pages 331–340. IEEE Computer Society, 2002.

[XF08] XFeature Feature Editor Web-Site, 2008. www.pnp-software.com/XFeature/home.html.

Index

advice (in aspect-oriented development), 24
alternative features, 40
application of a configuration link, 123, 131
artifact, 21
artifact dimension, 23
artifact line, 61, 144
aspect, 24
aspect weaving, 25
attribute (in DOORS), 89
attribute (of a feature), 42
attributed feature, 42

binding of variability, 18
binding time, 18
branch (in version control), 105
branch (in version management), 19

cardinality based feature modeling, 40
checkout (in version control), 105
child feature, 39
child group (of a feature), 49
cloned feature, 41
commit (in version control), 105
commonality / variability modeling, 23
compliance constraint, 65
compositional variability, 145
concept (in feature modeling), 39
configuration activities (set of ~), 127
configuration consideration, 115
configuration decision, 116, 121
configuration hiding, 62, 144
configuration link, 111, 122, 131
configured feature identifier, 125
conformance, 86
conformance state, 86
contradiction (in a configuration specification), 134
core variability model, 59
corresponding group, 83

coverage (of referring artifacts), 103
CVM, 44

database (in DOORS), 89
decision graph, 27
decision table, 27
decision tree, 27
dependency propagation, 180
derived configuration, 123, 131
deviation, 79
deviation permission attribute, 84
disjoint sublines, 70
domain engineering, 15
DXL (DOORS Extension Language), 173

equivalence, 148
event (configuration decision ~), 152
excluded features (set of ~), 122
exclusive folder, 149

feature, 37
feature attribute, 42
feature configuration, 120
feature diagram, 165
feature group, 41, 48
feature link, 40
feature logics, 37
feature model (advanced), 49
feature model (basic), 46
feature model prototype, 141
feature modeling, 27
feature parameter, 43
folder (for configuration decisions), 149
full configuration, 129

global feature, 179
grouped feature, 48

included features (set of ~), 122
inclusion criterion, 117

innovation (of referring artifacts), 103
instance specification, 124
invalid configuration, 121

join points (in aspect-oriented development), 24

link (between features), 40
link (in DOORS), 89
local amendment, 71
local innovation (in a subline), 71

mandatory feature, 39
merge (as a multi-level deviation), 101, 183
module (in DOORS), 89
multi-level approach, 71
multi-level artifact hierarchy, 73, 101
multi-level artifact tree, 73
multi-level feature tree, 78
multi-level hierarchy, 73, 101
multi-level product line management, 71
multi-level technique, 72
multi-level tree, 73

narrowing (of a feature group), 82

object (in DOORS), 89
optional feature, 40

parameter (of a feature), 43
parameterized feature, 43, 47
parent feature, 39
parent feature (of a feature group), 49
partial configuration, 129
point cut (in aspect-oriented development), 24
preconfiguration, 111
prioritization (of configuration decisions), 150
product, 15
product (of a product line), 14
product engineering, 15
product instance, 14, 15
product model, 113
product population, 15
product set, 117
product subline, 70
product superline, 70

product-line infrastructure, 14, 15
proper product subline, 70
provided variability, 144

range (of a configuration decision), 122, 131
reduction, 81
reference artifact, 72
reference feature, 77
reference feature model, 75, 77
reference module, 90
referring feature, 77
referring feature model, 75, 77
referring module, 90
refinement, 80
regrouping, 81
relation (between configuration decisions), 149
repository (in version control), 105
required variability, 144
runtime variability, 18

selection criterion, 112
software family, 15
software product line, 13, 15
source (of a configuration link), 122
split (as a multi-level deviation), 102, 183
staged configuration, 157
steps (set of configuration $\sim$), 131
stop-gap solution (in a subline), 71
subline, 70
subscoping, 74
system product line, 15

target (of a configuration link), 122
top-level propagation, 179

unified feature modeling, 63

valid configuration, 121
variability, 16, 17
variability dimension, 23
variability modeling, 23
variability specification language, 169
variant, 16
variation point, 17
version, 18
VSL, 169

widening (of a feature group), 82

Die VDM Verlagsservicegesellschaft sucht für wissenschaftliche Verlage abgeschlossene und herausragende

Dissertationen, Habilitationen, Diplomarbeiten, Master Theses, Magisterarbeiten usw.

für die kostenlose Publikation als Fachbuch.

Sie verfügen über eine Arbeit, die hohen inhaltlichen und formalen Ansprüchen genügt, und haben Interesse an einer honorarvergüteten Publikation?

Dann senden Sie bitte erste Informationen über sich und Ihre Arbeit per Email an *info@vdm-vsg.de*.

Sie erhalten kurzfristig unser Feedback!

VDM Verlagsservicegesellschaft mbH
Dudweiler Landstr. 99   Telefon +49 681 3720 174
D - 66123 Saarbrücken   Fax   +49 681 3720 1749
www.vdm-vsg.de

Die VDM Verlagsservicegesellschaft mbH vertritt

Printed by Books on Demand GmbH, Norderstedt / Germany